Little Laureates 2008

Poems From London & The Home Counties

Edited by Donna Samworth

YoungWriters
First published in Great Britain in 2008 by:
Young Writers
Remus House
Coltsfoot Drive
Peterborough
PE2 9JX
Telephone: 01733 890066
Website: www.youngwriters.co.uk

SB ISBN 978-1 84431 685 4

Foreword

Young Writers was established in 1991 and has been passionately devoted to the promotion of reading and writing in children and young adults ever since. The quest continues today. Young Writers remains as committed to the nurturing of poetic and literary talent as ever.

This year's Young Writers competition has proven as vibrant and dynamic as ever and we are delighted to present a showcase of the best poetry from across the UK and in some cases overseas. Each poem has been selected from a wealth of *Little Laureates 2008* entries before ultimately being published in this, our seventeenth primary school poetry series.

Once again, we have been supremely impressed by the overall quality of the entries we have received. The imagination, energy and creativity which has gone into each young writer's entry made choosing the poems a challenging and often difficult but ultimately hugely rewarding task - the general high standard of the work submitted ensured this opportunity to bring their poetry to a larger appreciative audience.

We sincerely hope you are pleased with this final collection and that you will enjoy *Little Laureates 2008 Poems From London & The Home Counties* for many years to come.

Contents

The Poems

Pretty Girl

Pretty girl, who is to blame?
Frightened girl, they don't know her name.
Saddened girl, who cries at night.
Distant girl, who's out of sight.
Psycho girl, who doesn't exist.
Fairy tale girl, without a name.
Silent girl, who's filled with shame.
Faking girl, with plastic smiles.
Freakish girl, from a thousand miles.
Emotionless girl, can't feel much pain.
Darkened girl, who brings the rain.
Crying girl, tears start to flood.
Psychotic girl, who drains her blood.
Hated girl, whom no one loves.
Cruel girl, that's jealous of people.
Friendly girl, who's everyone's friend.
Lovely girl, that everyone loves.

Ladan Hersi

We're Going To The Pool

We're going to the pool,
To try and stay cool,
So what we need to do
Is know how to swim.
Pick a twin and dip in.

Play volleyball,
Make a big mall.
Go in the mall man, yeah!
Kicking the ball,
Jumping in the mall.
Win the game, oh yeah!

We're going to the pool,
To try and stay cool,
So what we need to do
Is know how to swim.
Pick a twin and dip in, yeah.

Fore Obatusin (8)

The Concrete Jungle

As I walked past the tower,
Strangers walked past
With blank faces.
There was so much in sight,
I ran with my fear,
Without giving up the fight.
I could not hear,
But didn't stop me,
Running away from my fears.
The end of humanity,
Judgement Day.
I was supposed to feel safe,
Bit I didn't.
So I kept running,
Trying to escape.
I ran from my fears,
Until a black figure appeared
And then,
The lights went out.

Thanathat Fahey (11)
Andrew Ewing Primary School, Hounslow

The Wolf

The wolf growls
Like an echo in the cold white mountains.
Its claws as fierce as a yellow lion.
Its ears flap in the cold air.
Its eye is orange and like a black dot.

Warsan Hashi (7)
Andrew Ewing Primary School, Hounslow

What Is The Moon?

The moon is a silver-white ball
Hanging in the sky.

The moon comes out at night
When the sun sets.

Staring at the moon,
Turning you beautiful.

Many days we long to see
The full moon.

But when we stare at it too long
It hypnotises us.

Now night is closing in,
Getting darker,
With diamonds in the sky.

The moon is shining,
Showing your path of life.

Leoné Wan (10)
Andrew Ewing Primary School, Hounslow

The Golden Wolf

The golden wolf
Sits on the highest, greenest hill,
Lifts his golden head up and howls
In front of the big, round moon.

The tumbling moon and the great golden wolf
Reflect in the cold, deep, blue river.

Abbie Erodotou (7)
Andrew Ewing Primary School, Hounslow

No Family Worries

My family is my shield,
Protecting me through good and bad.
My family is my comfort,
Helping me through my fear.
My family is my funny face,
Cheering me up when sad.
My family is my shoulder to cry on,
Comforting my fears.
My family is my candle,
Helping me through the troublesome night.
My family is my bandage,
Helping to soothe my wounds.
My family is a pair of magic contacts,
To help me with my sight.

My family is . . .
Forever!

Simrit Kaur Ghatore (10)
Andrew Ewing Primary School, Hounslow

Clouds

Oh, the clouds, the graceful clouds
Are like candyfloss drifting across the sky
Like a blowing, gentle bird
And as the moon comes out
The clouds go floating away.

Walid Akouche & Ibrahim Abdi (7)
Andrew Ewing Primary School, Hounslow

Leopard

A leopard has really long legs
So it can run as fast as a
Blue jet aeroplane.
Leopards have medium ears
Like a lion's, so they can hear properly.
They lie on the branch like a flat bird.

Isaac Dhadli (7)
Andrew Ewing Primary School, Hounslow

What Is Colour Like?

Red is the like the sweet smell of cherry
Green is like the leaves on a tree, swaying in the breeze
Gold is like shiny lights, shining in the night
White is like fluffy clouds, puffy in the sky
Silver is like shiny metal, glowing in the moonlight
Blue is like the wavy sea
Purples is like yummy grapes, sweet and ripe.

Reshmi Patel (9)
Aylward First & Middle School, Stanmore

What Is Colour Like?

Green is a CO_2 free world
Blue is like a healthy person
Gold is like pride
White is like nothing
Purple is like rain
Silver is like winning
Yellow is like heat
Orange is like sand
Black is like disappointment
Brown is like losing
Grey is like cutting down the woodland.

Alec Feldman (8)
Aylward First & Middle School, Stanmore

What Is Colour Like?

Red is the beautiful scent of sweet spring roses
Green is the sweet mellow grass of summer
Blue is the cloudless sunny sky
Gold is like the hot yellow sunshine
White is like the feeling of peace
Purple is like the angry sound of thunder
Silver is like the glistening riches of Arabia
Yellow is like the sweet taste of melted butter
Orange is like the calm, peaceful, swimming goldfish
Black is like the deep murky shadows
Brown is like hard delicious chocolate
Grey is like the dark, cloudy, winter sky.

James Chapman (8)
Aylward First & Middle School, Stanmore

What Is Colour Like?

Red is like the hot, burning fire
Green is like the lovely, green grass
Blue is like the big, round world
Gold is like a shiny, expensive metal
White is like a big, smoky cloud
Purple is like a dirty colour
Silver is like a mighty, shiny shield
Yellow is like a bright, big sun
Orange is like a scary, stripy tiger
Black is like a dark, scary cave
Brown is like a spiky, sharp wig
Grey is like a dark, grey raincloud.

Ahmad Naeem (8)
Aylward First & Middle School, Stanmore

The Flower

As watery tears fall from the sky
Onto my bud to give me life
As water, like blood, drips through my stem
I still shed tears, I have not yet blossomed

The mist of the sky flies past
The eye of the sky, the sun, then opens up wide
It helps me form my beautiful self
The excitement in me forms as well

As I open up to the daylight
I feel happiness in the sky
I have opened up now and feel happy as well

What's that noise I hear? A loud, roaring sound
I thought it was like a tiger
I saw a big machine coming towards me
It came and shaved me down
I have shattered
So has my life.

Sugra Rashid (10)
Aylward First & Middle School, Stanmore

What Is Colour Like?

Red is like a fresh juicy apple
Green is like the fresh grass
Blue is like the clear sky
Gold is like the shiny sun
White is like the fluffy clouds
Purple is like the thundery sky
Silver is like shiny metal
Yellow is like the shining sun
Orange is like a burning hot fire
Black is like the night sky
Brown is like a rough tree trunk
Grey is like a stormy rain cloud.

Kritin Kapur (8)
Aylward First & Middle School, Stanmore

What Is Colour Like?

Red is warm, like a hot fire
Orange is like autumn leaves falling from the trees
Yellow is like the shining sun
Green is like grass, fresh and soft
Purple is like an angry thunderstorm
White is like soft tissues
Black is like the dark sky at night
Silver is like a shiny and clear coin
Gold is like shimmering stars.

Shivani Patel (9)
Aylward First & Middle School, Stanmore

Monday's Child

Monday's child rolled down the lane
Tuesday's child has a big brain
Wednesday's child climbed up a tree
Thursday's child loves to eat cheese
Friday's child has just turned forty
Saturday's child is so, so naughty
But the one that is born on the seventh day
Likes to do nothing but play, play, play!

Jaimin Bhanderi (9)
Aylward First & Middle School, Stanmore

What Is Colour Like?

Red is a bright, bright rose
Blue is like a parrot's feather, flying in the sky
Gold is like a shining trophy
White is like the frosty snow
Green is like the fresh cut grass
Purple is like a flower, swinging in a bay
Yellow is like the shining sun
Orange is a big brave lion.

Sarah Serrao (8)
Aylward First & Middle School, Stanmore

Mirror

I am simple but effective,
When I see you your features immediately come into me,
I can only tell the truth,
But I cannot be responsible.

I mean a lot to you, my girl,
You're my little golden pearl,
I feel sympathy
When your life is a misery.

Day in, day out, I see the same features
Of the same old creatures.
I will have to nag,
Are you a mahogany-weathered punch bag?

I am there when you are happy,
I am there when you are sad,
I will always keep a memory
Of the little girl I had.

Alisha Varsani (11)
Aylward First & Middle School, Stanmore

Nobody Loves Me

There was time, not so long ago
I was the most favourite thing in her life you know
She would not leave the house without me near
She would not sleep without me here
I used to stop her crying when she fell
I used to be the one her secrets she would tell

But now for some reason, I know not why
I am stuck on a shelf, way up high
I think I am next to someone I recognise
Who has the same sad look in his eyes
I heard her mum say one day
'Where is that lovely teddy with which you used to play?'

Jenna Dixon (10)
Aylward First & Middle School, Stanmore

Rapunzel

The beautiful girl, Rapunzel,
Who lived in a tower so high,
Could only sit spinning with her thread,
Watching the days go by.

A witch, who was old,
Went down to the house,
'I claim your daughter
as you stole the food for my grouse.'

Now that Rapunzel had grown,
She was locked in the tower, alone.
She had long, fair hair
And a voice that was rare.

As she sang,
As the church bells rang,
A prince heard her voice and cried,
'Rapunzel, Rapunzel, let down your hair.'

When the knight had finished his climb,
The witch thought it was time
For him to say goodbye,
Even though he did not know why.

The witch, who had a plan,
Pretended to be the man,
And cried,
'Rapunzel, Rapunzel, let down your hair.'

When the witch got to the top,
The girl got such a shock.
When the prince came back, that was that,
He fell to the thorns like a rock.

The prince, who searched for years,
Found his princess by the call of her tears.

Danielle Swift (12)
Aylward First & Middle School, Stanmore

Mirror

I bring reflection and truth
I am trusted but sometimes bring sadness
When disliked I am in pieces, heartbroken
When I am tearful no one cares
Forgets the past, renews the future
I look exactly like the people who look at me
I wipe the tears of beauty
I cannot change the way others look
Light and sparkle I watch forever

Joy of sight, poor in mind
The thieves I see threaten me not to tell
I am frozen in a position
In the night I am frozen with darkness, alone
I bring no lies, but am still hated
When shattered I am still alive
But no one notices
Forgotten forever, but not really gone.

Adeola Alade (11)
Aylward First & Middle School, Stanmore

My Grandmother

My grandmother is the best,
She is always happy and caring.
Her spirit is always joyous and sharing,
Her wonderful love is never sparing.
Her courage always gives others a message,
Displaying every virtue.
Her spirit; an energy never-ending.
We visit her every weekend,
The memories fill every day.
Grandma is no longer with us in body,
But her spirit is in our hearts and here to stay.

Hannah O'Donnell (11)
Aylward First & Middle School, Stanmore

White Dress Of Purity

Lonely,
Needs a lover,
Sir Lancelot, the hero, arrives,
Camelot,
The curse is here,
The mirror cracks from side to side,
Her white dress of purity,
Fails to shield her from the curse.
The Lady of Shalott dies amongst the reeds,
She floats down to Camelot,
Her singing in the mist dies,
No one hears her mournful song again.
The curse has stolen her soul.

Samuel Walton (11)
Aylward First & Middle School, Stanmore

Mirror

I am scared and afraid of this horror mansion,
Whatever I see swiftly passes me by,
Before I can reflect, it's gone,
Till I see the opposite wall.
It is black, with spiders,
I've looked at it every day.
I want to escape from this horror house,
I cannot take it any longer.
I cannot reflect the truth,
If there is no one to reflect to.

Anjali Sonigra (11)
Aylward First & Middle School, Stanmore

The City

A city, so chatty and very loud,
Buses come speeding through the crowds,
Cars on the bridges look up at the clouds,
During the day vast buildings feel so proud . . .

The sea is still running
And the wheels are still spinning
While the church bells are ringing,
The sky is still twinkling.

Everyone is looking at the sky,
Far away planes are so very high,
Heavens are where all the birds can fly,
But down in the city jungle
Is where the fast life goes by . . .

A city, so chatty and very loud,
Buses come speeding through the crowds,
Cars on the bridges look up at the clouds,
During the day vast buildings feel so proud . . .

Whitney Ferguson (10)
Aylward First & Middle School, Stanmore

The Lady Of Shalott

The Lady of Shalott is wearing a long white robe.
White symbolises the purity of her heart.
She is sitting in a dark, old boat,
In her damp, dark, waterless grave.
There are three candles, only one is alight,
Black chains in her hand,
Slowly slipping away her life.

Ryan Shirley (12)
Aylward First & Middle School, Stanmore

Dreaded Love

Her boat had her name which was the Lady of Shalott
And she was sitting on her beautiful tapestry.
She wore her pearl necklace as she was sitting sadly.
She knew that her life was fading away.
She loosened the chain,
as she slowly floated down the dreadful river.
She wore a white dress, which showed she was sad like snow.
Nothing kept her from going down to her love, Sir Lancelot.
It was a cold, misty day.
As she floated down the river her candles went out.
The cold wind blew her black hair back as she died.

Guleed Hashi (11)
Aylward First & Middle School, Stanmore

Mirror

I am a mirror, always looking, never blinking,
I look in an everlasting stare,
I tell the truth, no lies,
The people who look into my eyes,
Do not realise they are being watched . . .

When people are angry they try shattering me,
Breaking me into a million pieces,
I look sadly into their eyes,
Into their eyes of darkness . . .

I am now in a fancy hotel,
Men in smart looking suits shuffle their ties
And women in beautiful dresses brush their hair,
As I watch them from my gloomy lair . . .

I am a mirror, always looking, never blinking,
I look in an everlasting stare,
I tell the truth, no lies,
The people who look into my eyes,
Do not realise they are being watched . . .

Danny Williams (10)
Aylward First & Middle School, Stanmore

Mirror

I am silver and honest, I hate no one.
If I see something, it splurges into me.
I am like a hungry animal that swallows everything.
I am like God, I can see everything.
I am normally staring at the opposite wall,
But sometimes it disappears.

Suddenly a big boy walks up to a fearing little boy,
I see him saying these exact words to the little boy,
'If you do not become a bully Jack, I will never stop bullying you.'
One hour later, tears were dripping out of my eyes,
As I see the little boy bullying another kid.
Then a teacher walks up,
This is the most furious and strict teacher in the school.
Jack is shivering, the teacher is speaking,
So loud my glass almost shatters.
Then the teacher calls Jack's mum.

I am silver and honest, I hate no one.
If I see something, it splurges into me.
I am like a hungry animal that swallows everything.
I am like God, I can see everything.
I am normally staring at the opposite wall,
But sometimes it disappears.

Christian Labiran (11)
Aylward First & Middle School, Stanmore

The Writer Of This Poem Is . . .

(Based on 'The Writer of this Poem' by Roger McGough)

As cute as a ginger kitten.
As clever as a rocket scientist.
As pretty as the best mum in the world (mine).
As rich as a pop star who has a mansion in Spain.
As tall as a football player.
As famous as a movie star.
As crazy as a monkey.

Ellen Davis (9)
Aylward First & Middle School, Stanmore

The Lady Of Shalott

Locked up in a tower,
Helpless, with no power,
Weaving tapestry,
Grieving silently,
Singing in her spare time,
For she has done no crime,
Her white dress says it all.

She is as pure as her call to be free,
The curse, her weakness,
The mirror, her strength,
She cannot look down to Camelot,
She cannot make amends.

Sir Lancelot comes as a knight
Doing what is right.
Singing 'Tirra Lirra,' by the river,
A melody which he hears,
She cannot bear it and out of the window she looks.
The mirror cracks, the water lilies bloom,
She sees her love, the web flies wide,
'The curse has come upon me,' weeps the Lady of Shalott.

As she sits she engraves her name,
She sails down to Camelot,
Her eyes become glassy,
The door to her soul closes,
The reeds slowly die as she lays down in the boat.
Surrounded by people, one is Sir Lancelot,
He does not know why she dies,
But, 'It is for love,' she cries.

Disha Patel (12)
Aylward First & Middle School, Stanmore

The Lady Of Shalott

Her facial expressions as she edges to death
Distressed and distraught as she takes her last breath
She struggles as she unties her chain
She sadly succeeds, although in great pain

As she leans back and lets the chain go
Her pure white sleeve and dress in water they flow
Down the stream the boat floats to Camelot
The calm river that flows through Shalott
The magpies fly in twos, bringing joy to Shalott
One flies away, it will bring sorrow in a knot

People are baffled as they cannot hear a voice
She is always locked up so it cannot be her choice
Community is worrying, 'Where is the Lady?'
They scatter about as if she were a baby.

As the boat floats down, as silent as a church mouse
Watching as she dies, sitting beside her, a sweet grouse
The village waits patiently
They all run about in despair, ungracefully
She is made to be as important as a king
A boy runs to the crowd, good news he does not bring

He says, 'Quick, quick, dead in a boat the Lady lies'
As they reach the bank their tears cannot stay
In the boat lies the lady, there's nothing they can do
The sorrow flows through the town like flu.

Lewis Gray (11)
Aylward First & Middle School, Stanmore

The Lady Of Shalott

The Lady of Shalott is in a large, black boat
She has stitched up a beautiful tapestry
There are three candles but only one is still alight
She is terrified, facing the green and black river
The sad trees are surrounding her like a pack of wolves
She is sad as her life is coming to an end
She is dressed in white, but far from Heaven
She is holding a rusty, silver chain
When the sunlight dies, the moon will arrive and she will die
As the candles die she will die as darkness comes
A damsel in distress, but her knight can't save her.

Craig James Headech (12)
Aylward First & Middle School, Stanmore

The Lady Of Shalott

She, the Lady of Shalott,
Has just loosened a chain,
She is now floating down the river.
Looking disconsolate, upset and miserable.
She knows she is going to die.
The sky is dark and gloomy,
The wind is howling and the rain is falling.
There are three candles, two of which are blown out.
When the light is dim,
A pale shaft of light,
The fragile candle will burn,
She will die.
The ruined reeds are dying,
As is she.
She has woven her last stitch,
This was her life's work.
Around the prow is written her name,
People will know who she is.
Her pure white gown floats beautifully on the streaming river,
This symbolises her purity.

Riddhi Thakrar (11)
Aylward First & Middle School, Stanmore

Life In The Mirror

I can be wood, I can be silver
I chew in the truth
I spit out the lie
Others come, others go
But them they always shiver

I may be alive
I may be dead

I am in the rivers
I am in the hallway
But each morning I see the young girl
She looks and then she quivers
Her tears drop
Softly, like feathers
The youth has gone
The old age has come
Now the girl is wrinkly
But the moon is still twinkling!

Simran Chahil (10)
Aylward First & Middle School, Stanmore

The Writer Of This Poem Is . . .

(Based on 'The Writer of this Poem' by Roger McGough)

As smooth as spun silk.
As wily as a scientist with a secret experiment in their head.
As kind as the warm sun.
As fresh as a sweet-smelling daisy.
As greedy as a fat, heavy pig.
As charming as a beautiful princess.
As adorable as a cute baby sister.
As beautiful as a rainbowfish.
As cute as a waddling penguin.
As pretty as a tropical beach.
As rich as a millionaire - so there!

Bhavisha Pandya (8)
Aylward First & Middle School, Stanmore

The Writer Of This Poem Is . . .

(Based on 'The Writer of this Poem' by Roger McGough)

As skilful as Ronaldinho
As sneaky as a thieving monkey
As devilish as a zombie master
As funny as Bart and his family
As brave as the strongest Hulk you can be
As flexible as a gymnast
As crazy as a talking gorilla
As fat as Ronaldinho's big teeth
As clever as me.

Qaiz Noormohamed (8)
Aylward First & Middle School, Stanmore

The Writer Of This Poem Is . . .

(Based on 'The Writer of this Poem' by Roger McGough)

As tall as the great Karl Lee
As thin as a ruler
As wily as a snake
As lazy as a fat cat
As mad as an angry chimpanzee
As brave as a charging knight
As busy as a shopper in the sales
As rich as a football player in the Premier League.

Jay Gezer (8)
Aylward First & Middle School, Stanmore

The Writer Of This Poem Is . . .

(Based on 'The Writer of this Poem' by Roger McGough)

As sneaky as a monkey stealing food.
As busy as a buzzing foolish bee.
As clever as a teacher's brain.
As rich as the Queen.
As beautiful as Sleeping Beauty.
As kind as Khayr, who cheers me up.

Parisha Sonigra (8)
Aylward First & Middle School, Stanmore

The Writer Of This Poem Is . . .

(Based on 'The Writer of this Poem' by Roger McGough)

As cute as a puppy
As pretty as a purple, silky rose
As clever as a big dolphin
As thin as a giraffe's long neck
As kind as a pretty dog
As funny as a monkey running in the forest
As fast as a motorbike
As flexible as a gymnast doing the crab
As rich as a pop star that is on a poster
As lovely as a cute robin
As delightful as a surprise present.

Jemina Gajparia (9)
Aylward First & Middle School, Stanmore

The Writer Of This Poem Is . . .

(Based on 'The Writer of this Poem' by Roger McGough)

As moany as Moaning Myrtle
Fussy as a pink calculator working
As nice as a pretty princess
As cunning as a black-hearted robber
As beautiful as a rose
As funny as a clown
As sure as a tick
As difficult as finding an X
As vast as a giant
As clear as a window
As light as a pea.

Iman El Kady (8)
Aylward First & Middle School, Stanmore

Our World

Before -
Once Earth was a happy face
Full of forests
Full of goodness
He took in deep breaths
They were full of oxygen
Nobody took Earth for granted
Everyone loved him

Now -
Now the Earth is an angry face
Full of factories
Full of badness
He takes in deep breaths
They are filled with fumes and gases
Everyone takes Earth for granted
Everyone forgets about him
Now he is dying
Withering away to nothing . . .

Rhiannon Esther O'Keefe (11)
Caversham Primary School, Caversham

Things Around Us

Smooth waves,
Cool breeze.
Green grass,
Tall trees.

Summer sun,
Winter moon,
Spring morning,
Autumn noon.

Things around us,
That we can see,
Here for sharing,
With you and me.

John Livesey (10)
Caversham Primary School, Caversham

Autumn

Leaves, golden like crunchy honey toast,
Crackling, scrunching, munching.
Rotten as a witch's hand,
Twirling down to the ground.

Toadstools, caramel-brown like a deer's coat,
Floating, thumping, swaying.
Silky as a baby's skin,
Dancing in the breeze.

Acorns, smooth like pebbles from the sea,
Tumbling, dropping, plopping.
Shiny as the gleaming eye of an eagle,
Whirling down to Earth.

Jessica Stone (8)
Caversham Primary School, Caversham

Autumn

Leaves, brown like chocolate melting in your mouth,
Scrunching, scattering, soaring,
Crumbly as dust in the places where nobody goes,
Floating from the trees.

Conkers, plonky like hailstones falling on the wall,
Lumpy, bumpy, clonky,
Smooth as silk glinting from their tree,
Dropping from the sky.

Mushrooms, poisonous like a witch's sniggering laugh,
Swaying, breaking, squishing,
Delicate as a spider's web,
Warning others away.

Stephanie Glendinning (8)
Caversham Primary School, Caversham

Senses

Touch, hear, smell, taste and sight
These are each of my senses
They work all day, all night
And as soon as I wake up,
Their work commences.
Through my hands I touch
I touch what is to be touched
Maybe the touch of cold ice
So cold it makes my heartbeat rushed.

Through my ears I hear
I hear what is to be heard
Maybe the tweeting and chirping
Of a beautiful little bird.

Through my nostrils I smell
I smell what is to be smelt
Maybe the smell of a delicious meal
That on a dinner table will soon be dealt.

Through my tongue I taste
I taste what is to be tasted
Maybe the taste of glorious chips
That nobody would ever have wasted.

Through my eyes I see
I see what is to be seen
Maybe the sight of a glorious sunset
That is where I would have liked to have been.

William Underwood (10)
Caversham Primary School, Caversham

My Musical Body

Tap, tap, tap, goes the beat of my heart,
Pumping blood from start to start.
A message to my brain goes *thump, thump, thump,*
My feet are walking, *clump, clump, clump.*

Toes all wriggle, my hands all sway,
Enjoying the excellent musical play.
My ears hear, my tongue tastes,
With my hands I can paint my face.

I'm dancing and prancing, having fun,
I could do it all day long.
My voice sings high and low,
I can tap the beat with my big left toe.

Inside my lungs, they work all day,
Letting me breathe, doing fun and play.
You could call me a one man band,
Playing guitar with an elastic band.

Fingers snap, feet tap, tap to the rhythm
Of my heart, *clap, clap, clap.*
When I'm asleep I still work, tapping all day,
At work and play.

I'll never stop, until that day,
I hope it never comes;
Meanwhile I'll go and play.

Fingers snap, feet tap, tap,
To the rhythm of my heart,
Clap, clap, clap.

Tap, clap, snap, thump, clump,
I have a musical body,
Even when I jump.

Alice Horncastle (10)
Caversham Primary School, Caversham

The Voyage Of Life

The melancholic surge,
Pumping and thumping,
Of an everlasting mission,
Of microscopic
Sensitivity.
The rhythm and beat,
Gushing life around us,
The stream races,
Pulsing, exploring.
Ever wondered when? How?
Who? Where? Or what?
About the world
The shaken dream
Bringing reality.
The emotion, shaking
As the nerves surrender
Defeating the waves of
The voyage.
Helping eyes to watch,
Ears to hear
And nose to smell . . .

The organs.

Olivia Horncastle (10)
Caversham Primary School, Caversham

Jenny Lemming

Jenny Lemming is sort of normal, I guess,
But of all the lemmings at the zoo
She stood out from all the rest.
But never did I stop to think,
She snuck out at night,
That was definitely way, way, way,
Way over the brink.

The thing is that, that was true,
It's real I'm telling you.
At 12 o'clock, she'd slip through the bars,
Grab a Coke, take a bath.
If by chance she drank a coffee, she'd get hyper,
She might even open the cage of a very venomous viper!

When she was found out,
We had to send her away,
Unfortunately, she's probably not still out there to this day.
For lemmings are known to commit suicide,
She ran off a cliff and I think she died
But just maybe,
Just maybe,
Maybe she survived.

Tom Childs (10)
Caversham Primary School, Caversham

Autumn

Leaves, fiery red like a burning bonfire,
Twirling, floating, wrinkling,
Crusty as stale bread,
Rustling in the wind.

Conkers, smooth like a new leather jacket,
Dropping, plopping, rolling,
Quite hard, like a hockey ball,
Clicking when dropped.

Frost steaming like a good hot bath,
Freezing, misting, nipping,
As chilly as your numb toes when Jack Frost nips at them,
Shivering all day long.

Elizabeth Livesey (8)
Caversham Primary School, Caversham

Autumn

Leaves, amber, like a lion's mane,
Swirling, floating, falling silently to the ground.
Crisp as a loaf of freshly made bread,
Dancing along the ground.

Conkers, smooth as a shell washed upon the shore,
Plonking, bonking, donking.
As round as a pearl from under the sea,
Plummeting to the floor.

Frost, white like the ice in the Snow Queen's palace,
Glimmering, shimmering, shining.
As cold as a giant's heart,
Melting on the ground.

Millie Vibert (8)
Caversham Primary School, Caversham

Anger

Anger is like the fire burning on the Devil's fist.
It looks like the bubbling lava from the core of the Earth.
It looks like a burning body in mounts of Hell.
It sounds like a screeching sound of violins performed at the opera.
It tastes like dark brown bread and rotten eggs.
It feels like a burning heart attack happening right before your eyes.
Anger reminds me of all the bad things that have happened,
In school and out.

Dominic Parkhurst (11)
Caversham Primary School, Caversham

Space

Space is a never-ending dark sky,
A gigantic black desert.
Millions of stars
And thousands of planets.

Billy Helm (9)
Dulwich Hamlet Junior School, Southwark

The Computers

The computer blinks on and smiles at me.
Starts off excited and then calms down.
It cleverly answers the questions I give it.
While the mouse scuttles about the table.
The computer yawns before it goes to bed.
It blinks, turns off as quickly as you can say cows.

Hamish White (10)
Dulwich Hamlet Junior School, Southwark

Fear

Fear dawns on you when you least expect him.
He is sly and is everywhere.
He is in clowns, roller coasters and many more.
He walks up to you and wrenches your guts.
He is invisible and can fly.
Fear is flies covering the dump
And when you enter, creeping up and landing upon you.
You hope that luck will find you,
But he will not come.
Fear is bats, swooping everywhere,
Like the night sky being ripped and torn,
Raining down on people.

Sliding,
Falling,
Creeping,
Clawing,
Attacking . . .

Fear!

Oliver Kvam (9)
Dulwich Hamlet Junior School, Southwark

The Sea

The sea is like a world of its own,
From its taste of salt,
It's home to a mystery.
With dangerous sharks and killer whales
And dolphins swimming free.

With corals of wonder and fish all shapes,
It's heaven beyond belief,
But . . .
When the wind howls, it's a dangerous place,
For you and for me.

Elliot Humbles (10)
Dulwich Hamlet Junior School, Southwark

The Computer

I turn on the computer,
Suddenly there is a buzz, like a blender.

It yawns, a person waking up,
The fan talking so much
The hard disk tells it off.

The screen stares at me,
A one-eyed Cyclops,
Stretching its arms out,
It whirrs busily.

The mouse scutters about,
Looking for icons to eat.

I change my mind
And decide to put it to bed.

It starts to relax and sighs gently.
All is quiet.

William Davis (9)
Dulwich Hamlet Junior School, Southwark

Sunset

The shining sun tiptoes behind the dark, green hills
as night-time falls.
A golden ball, drifting across a red, deserted football pitch.
A shining disco ball, coloured in orange.
A shiny marble, rolling across the glowing sky.

Silently,
Gracefully,
It sets.

Isabel Azzopardi (9)
Dulwich Hamlet Junior School, Southwark

Homework

There are loads of reasons
Why we shouldn't do our homework.

My mum took me to the shop
I bought some sweets to eat
I told the shopkeeper to do my work
Then I stepped on his feet.

At home, an alien came
He shot the book with his gun
I looked at him
And said that was fun.

Mithursha Kesavan (9)
Glebe First & Middle School, Harrow

Bee, Dog And Cat

A dog and a cat went to sea
And saw a bee littering up the sea.
Although they could see
They just let it be.
The bee went buzzing
Round the apple tree.
The tree fell on the bee
And the bee fell into the sea
And the dog and the cat could see.

Billy Rowe (9)
Glebe First & Middle School, Harrow

Do Something Better

We've got to be eco-friendly,
Not Mr Earth bendy,
We've got to try harder
And the Earth will be fine.

We've got to care for the Earth,
God's the one who gave it birth,
We've got to try harder
And the Earth will be fine.

We can always recycle,
With our unicycles,
We've got to try harder
And the Earth will be fine.

We can also reduce
And also re-use,
We've got to try harder
And the Earth will be fine.

So remember these messages
In your everyday life,
They might come in handy
At any time!

Megha Zavar (8)
Glebe First & Middle School, Harrow

My Life

My name is Abyan,
I am ten years old.
I was born in a hospital,
Called Queensbury Bold.

I live in a flat,
But have lived in several houses
And in each one
There were a few mouses.

One of my friends is Klaudia,
But she left,
I know she's my friend
But not exactly the best.

I love my school,
It is the best.
There's police outside it,
It has something to do with theft.

I hope you like my poem,
I hope you like it good,
If you listen to it properly,
It makes you think you should.

Abyan Mahamud (10)
Glebe First & Middle School, Harrow

I Am An Eco-Warrior

I am an eco-warrior,
Oh yes I am.
I never drop litter
And I never drop cigarettes.

I am an eco-warrior,
I love to be one.
In fact you can be a warrior too
And it is fun.

I am an eco-warrior,
I listen to the council,
Whatever they say, I hear,
Keep the environment clear!

I am an eco-warrior,
I am telling the truth,
That using cars too much
Does not keep the environment clean.

I am an eco-warrior,
Oh yes I am,
I never drop litter
And I always remember the three Rs.

Keep the planet clean!
Keep the environment clean!

Rules:
Stop using cars.
Don't throw litter.
Stop smoking.
Listen to the council.

Remember the three Rs
Reuse, reduce, recycle!

Amulya Dixit (8)
Glebe First & Middle School, Harrow

Forever Friends

My name is Ekta
My friends are what I care about

She is my friend
If she's gone I will fall apart
She is my family
Everything for me

All the times we argue and fight
I know deep inside that it isn't right
I then feel bad and a lot of pain
It feels like I've fallen from the sky like the rain

Make new friends
But keep the old
One is silver the other gold!

Like me and my friend
We are friends forever.

Ekta Vaghela (9)
Glebe First & Middle School, Harrow

The Animal Of Destruction

A storm is an animal ready to pounce
Ready to leap out and roar
It will jump out when you are not looking
And then it will come out for more

The world will shake as a storm runs round
Cities will get stamped and drowned
The work of the animal of destruction
Can make whole towns never get found.

Anna Davitt (10)
Gorse Ride Junior School, Wokingham

The Christmas Pudding

You'll need a wheelbarrow to mix this in.
You'll need a pin.
You need a shoe.
You really need part of a loo.

You will definitely need a footballer,
That will make it taller.
You need some smelly socks
And some heavy and hard locks.

You need one hundred wiggly worms,
Spit in the wheelbarrow for some germs.
You need your lovely daughter
And lots of muddy water.

Then leave it in the sun,
It will weigh a tonne.
That would be fun,
Putting it in the sun.

Leah Sims (10)
Gorse Ride Junior School, Wokingham

Pirates

P irates, sailing the stormy sea,
I know one day they'll come for me,
R iding down the darkened streets,
A sking where Pirate Jack Sparrow sleeps.
T reasure hidden by my bed,
E ight gold coins beside my head,
S oon they will come for me!

Alex McClarron (8)
Gorse Ride Junior School, Wokingham

Back In The Playground

I dreamed I was back in the playground, only nine years old.
I dreamed I was back in the playground, only nine years old.
I was scared to death of the playground, dreading going out.

It was gloomy and surrounded by tall pine trees.
It was gloomy and surrounded by tall dead trees.
And it had a special name, the killing ground.

Got a mum and dad, but there's now way I can get them now.
Oh no, here comes the ruler of the killing ground.

You got picked on for:
Being too tall or too small,
Fat or skinny,
Actually no darn reason at all.
I got picked on for most of these things.

But it is not too late,
I can still tell an adult.
Now I've told an adult, I'm no longer dreading going outside.
I don't stand alone, I have many friends.
The bullies' days are at their end.

The playground is sunny and cheery,
It's no longer a scary place.
I dreamed I was back in the playground, only nine years old.
Yes, I dreamed I was back in the playground, only nine years old.

There was no worse place than the killing ground for me,
But now I know it's the place I like to be!

Kerys Meredew (10)
Gorse Ride Junior School, Wokingham

Death

I'm rowing into nowhere,
The river's murky and dark,
Where can I be?
I'm lost, when I get home, if I do,
Dad will cook me into a stew!

I can hear the growls of water around me,
I can hear the waterfall splashing,
I'm nearly there, to the death stone,
I've heard the screams falling before,
Now it's my turn.

I'm falling down, unconscious,
In my head I hear cries from the water,
Grasping me at death's end,
Am I dead after that journey?

A man is staring at me,
He reaches out,
His hand goes in, comes out,
I run through thick trees,
Getting scratches everywhere,
I try to get back to my house,
The door is locked.

I run with tears of joy,
My family don't stir, just sitting there weeping.
I scream and shout, but they just sit there blankly,
It's then I realise, after all that journey,
I'm dead!

Sophie McClarron (10)
Gorse Ride Junior School, Wokingham

The Dancing Snowflakes

The snowflakes danced around,
In the air and then fell to the ground.
They tried to walk for a little longer,
But melted because they had to be stronger!

The snowflakes waved goodbye,
Because they knew they had to fall from the sky,
They twinkle like Christmas tinsel,
Oh, they look so pretty with their patterned crinkle!

The snowflakes had nowhere to go,
What to do they didn't know,
They fly when they spread their wings,
Oh, aren't they such beautiful things?

Georgia Denham (10)
Gorse Ride Junior School, Wokingham

The Monster River

The river rushes past me,
As fast as can be,
I don't know what to do,
Can you help me please?

I'm starting to hear,
The water, all clear,
It's silent
Except for the splashes.

I'm coming to the waterfall,
More sound, more splashes and all.
I'm really scared I might fall
Onto the sharpest stone of all.

I've just gone past that dreaded place,
It really gave me a worried face.
I can go home now to my own place
And I will no longer have a horrified face!

Jessica Alam (10)
Gorse Ride Junior School, Wokingham

It Wasn't My Fault

(I'm not the brightest Collie in the world)

I am a Border Collie,
My name is Coco Flynn.
I look cute from the outside
But mischievous within.

I didn't really mean to
Knock over Katy's game of Jenga,
Or chew up Jenna's favourite toy;
A penguin called Small Penga.

I have got no idea why
I'm blamed for everything.
How could it have been my fault?
I was *fed* that wedding ring!

I was absolutely bursting,
I had to go to the loo!
So what if I went in Samuel's bed?
I really needed a poo!

I was feeling really sick,
I was being forced to spew,
It wasn't really my fault
That I went in Robert's shoe!

And what about when Josh came round?
I can't help it that my smell lingers!
And it wasn't my fault that I ate
One of Anne's tasty looking fish fingers.

I obviously didn't know
I'd chewed the TV cable,
Or eaten half the Sunday roast
That was cooling on the table.

What's wrong with Clara when she takes a nap?
All I did was bark.
I cannot help but wake her up,
I did want a walk in the park.

I cannot help that Mum's the judge and
The children are the jury.
I basically don't understand
Why they are filled with fury.

I even get shouted at,
If I begin to moult.
So now you've read my excuses
You'll see . . .
It's not my fault!

Alice Flynn (9)
Gorse Ride Junior School, Wokingham

My Cat

My cat is almost nine years old,
To me she's like 90 stacks of gold.

Her teeth are sharp
And her eyes glint when dark.

When I put down my cup
Her ears prick up.

She's got padded feet,
She looks so neat.

Her whiskers are long
And are growing strong.
She sleeps on my bed
And sometimes my Ted.

Her nose is wet,
She's the best cat you can get.

I love her purr,
When I stroke her fur.
She's always with me,
She makes me feel full of glee!

That's my cat!

Charlotte Butler Johnson (9)
Gorse Ride Junior School, Wokingham

At The Vet's

The Dalmatian had an operation,
The furry, ginger cat from next door
Sat on the rat, under the mat.
A grey, bouncy rabbit had the habit of scratching herself.

A thin snake had a tummy ache,
A tall horse had a piece of gorse stuck to him,
The baby pig had a gigantic wig,
The sheep had lost Little Bo Peep.

And the vet got upset!

Stephanie Gaddum (9)
Gorse Ride Junior School, Wokingham

God

I'm your soul,
I'm your heart,
I'm your dreams that keep you smart.

I'm the sky,
I'm the night,
I'm the sun and the light.

I'm the trees,
I'm the grass,
I'm the flowers that always last.

I'm the fish,
I'm the waves,
I'm the rocks in the caves.

I'm the life that keeps it together,
I'm the world that lasts forever.
I'm the universe,
I'm space,
I'm you,
I'm *God.*

Chloe Moore (11)
Gorse Ride Junior School, Wokingham

The Remarkable Cake

It's Christmas - the time we gather to make
A truly remarkable, once a year cake.
The recipe's written in letters of gold
By a family, that's terribly old.

The rule of this cake is it has to be made
In a wheelbarrow, (stirred with shovel or spade).
At Christmas, the season of love and goodwill,
Other time of year it might make you feel ill.

You must nail it together or stick it with glue,
Then hammer it flat with the hell of your shoe.
You must stretch it out thin; you must tie it in knots,
Then get out your paintbox and paint it with spots.

What a taste! What a flavour! It's certain to please,
It's rather like ice cream with pickles and cheese.
In June it would taste like spaghetti and mud,
While the taste in September would curdle your blood!

Oh what a cake! It looks simply delicious,
Now get out the carving knife, get out the dishes.
Be careful, be careful! This cake might explode
And blow up the kitchen and part of the road!

Oh dear! It exploded! I thought it might,
It's not very often we get it right.
Let's comfort the baby, revive Uncle Dan
And we'll start over again as soon as we can.

For Christmas - that lovely day - comes and goes,
For sooner than ever we dare to suppose,
Once more we gather together to make
That truly remarkable, one a year cake.

Sophie Anne Bessell & Michelle Taylor (11)
Gorse Ride Junior School, Wokingham

A Day In The Classroom

She sleeps peacefully in the darkness
Closing her tired eyes
Not a sound all around her
Dreaming what lies ahead

She suddenly awakes to the sound of the teacher
Yawning slow and loud
She gradually opens her weary eyes
Waiting for all the children

She laughs and smiles as her friends join her
Ready for the long day ahead
The children sit on her white sparkly teeth
And she quickly eats her yummy food!

The day comes to an end as the caretaker comes in
The room sparkles and brightens up
She gets ready to rest her eyes
And go to sleep!

Becky Ward-Webb (11)
Gorse Ride Junior School, Wokingham

The Sea And The Cliff

The sea woke up with a grin
And reached out with his white, white hands.
He said to the cliff,'Move, O great white thing.'
'Not a chance,' said the cliff of the Isle of Man.

The sea pushed and pushed
But the cliff who was stronger than the sea
Would not give in to he.

The sea gave up and walked away
And found another game to play!

Emily Carter (10)
Gorse Ride Junior School, Wokingham

My Aunty

She's always mollycoddling me
And pampering me,
When she starts she never stops.

All I remember, when I was a baby
Was a red-cheeked, plump old lady.
Smothered in strong perfume and bright red lipstick,
Getting in the way of the exciting view from my blue pram.

She always pinches my cheeks
And buys me lots of presents.
I dread the day when she arrives
At the door, with her great big bag
And giant hat hanging from her belt.
She is here to babysit me!

Parisha Majeethia (11)
Holland House School, Edgware

First Day At School

My first day at school is terrible
My blazer is too big
My shoes are too tight and
Nothing seems right!

My mum said, 'The first day at school
Is the best of all.'
I thought that as well!
But now I can tell my mum was wrong
To me, it was the worst day of all.

Evelyna Hadass (10)
Holland House School, Edgware

Christmas

Christmas happens during winter
Though it hardly snows
However, if you go out in the cold
The wind tickles your nose.

Christmas dinner is delicious
Especially the mince pies
The meal usually finishes
With many sighs!

On Christmas morning
The presents are there
They all get opened at once
Leaving the tree completely bare!

Viraj Alimchandani (11)
Holland House School, Edgware

Friends

It is a normal, dull school day
When I walk up the street alone
And hear the ding-dong of a bell
School has started, I've got to go.

But, it is different today,
I can see friends waving to me.
They are all bunched up, laughing and chatting.
A smile is put on my gloomy face!

I run up to them, put out my hand,
What has happened? They are not there.
Is it an illusion
Or is it all a dream?

Riya Patel (10)
Holland House School, Edgware

Imagination

I like imagination! It can be found
On any piece of floor or ground.
Can you imagine a unicorn on a cloud
Or a mouse talking very loud?
Would it be easier to visualise
A rabbit eating all your pies?
For me, I just let anything go,
Like a man with only one big toe.
Just think of what it would be like
To have your own flying bike.
The world's full of possibilities,
Like a set of magical keys,
Which opens the door to your imagination,
Like a shop which sells a pink Dalmatian!

Paige Linden (11)
Holland House School, Edgware

My Hamster

My hamster is so small and cute,
She loves to run a mile
And when she looks up at me
She has a great big smile.

When my hamster finishes her meal,
She goes straight on her running wheel.
If I let her loose on the floor,
She tries to escape out of the door!

Michael Elia (11)
Holland House School, Edgware

When I Started School

At the age of four I started school,
My blazer was big, I felt like a fool.
But I held my head high and I took my seat,
I admit I was nervous, numb to my feet.

I raised my head slowly to look around the class,
Since when had the room filled up so fast?
Everywhere I looked, there were girls and boys,
Together with shelves of books and toys.

My mum had left, I was alone,
I wanted to scream, cry and moan.
But no, I won't - I'm not a baby anymore,
I am big, I am smart, I am now aged four!

Molly Grossman (10)
Holland House School, Edgware

My Hamster

He has a small and furry tummy
And he loves to play with his mummy.
He sometimes looks like he's a flying jet,
I'm not sure where he's trying to get!

Most of the time he's sleeping,
Nobody knows what he's dreaming.
He is a curious little spark
Who likes to keep you in the dark!

Harshil Joshi (10)
Holland House School, Edgware

Seasons

When spring is alive
Trees rejoice with all their might
By bursting into bridal blooms
Of sugar-pink and snow-white.

Trees love to bask
In the fiery summer sun,
Their spreading green leaves
Provide shade for everyone.

As autumn creeps up,
It's time for trick or treat!
The trees prepare rustling costumes
Of gold, russet and beet.

Winter finally crawls along,
I wonder what the trees will wear.
But I am in for shock -
They are completely bare!

Monica Anson-Tsang (11)
Holland House School, Edgware

Bonfire Night

In the night-time darkness,
In the night-time
Did you spot a Catherine wheel
Raining showers of gold?
Did you watch a rocket
Go zoom into the sky?
And hear a bonfire crackle
As the sparks lit up the guy?
In the night-time darkness,
In the night-time cold,
Did you clutch a sparkler
As it scattered stars of gold?

Kowsiya Kugarajah (7)
Oldfield Primary School, Greenford

Yellow

Yellow is a ripe mango,
Waiting to be shed,
Yellow is the golden light,
Shining on the world.

Yellow is a bright colour,
Growing to be big.
Yellow is a small thing,
Trying to glow.

Yellow is a colour
Ready to be worn.
Yellow is curved,
Patience to be peeled.

Yellow is everything
But just waiting!

Rama Jha (8)
Oldfield Primary School, Greenford

Monster

Monsters are cruel and unkind.
Monsters are hard to find.
Monsters are big and scary.

Monsters are big and hairy.
Monsters have big hands and feet.
Monsters might run down the street.

Monsters are green and never seen.
Don't look behind, there may be one there!

Jemma Fowler (8)
Oldfield Primary School, Greenford

Julius Caesar

Julius Caesar he was bad
And he was extremely mad.
After killing Brutus he was glad,
But Julius' wife was very sad.

Caesar wore his boots of red,
But he only ended up dead.
If he had listened to what his wife said,
He could have spent the day in bed.

On March 15th, the day arrived,
This was when Julius Caesar died.
He wanted to live, he really tried,
But he just did not survive.

Kim White (8)
Parsons Down Junior School, Thatcham

Julius Caesar

Julius Caesar he was bad
And he was extremely mad.
After killing Brutus he was glad,
But Julius' wife was very sad.

Caesar liked to be the boss,
This always made his wife so cross.
She said, 'March 15th, you will be offed,
Stabbed, beaten, squished and squashed.'

Her dream same true, chased with a knife,
'I wish I'd listened to my wife!'
Indeed he had some trouble and strife,
This was the end of Caesar's life.

Abbie Walker (9)
Parsons Down Junior School, Thatcham

Julius Caesar

Julius Caesar he was bad
And he was extremely mad.
After killing Brutus he was glad,
But Julius' wife was very sad.

Julius Caesar felt quite ill,
Brutus drew his dagger getting ready to kill.
His wife said 'Stay very, very still.'
Then his wife had to pay a big bill.

Julius Caesar's wife had a dream,
That she could be crowned queen.
His wife's hopes that she had seen
Will not come true, because she was too mean.

Dominic Adams (8)
Parsons Down Junior School, Thatcham

The Moon

The moon is a white dinghy,
Sailing on the black sea.

The moon is a worm,
Withering beneath,
Gently feeling the darkness.

Crawling to the gates of Heaven,
To stare down on you.

Matthew Hawkes (10)
Parsons Down Junior School, Thatcham

Love Is . . .

My dad's cooking, which I love so much.
My brother's artwork, that I can't touch.
My mum's cakes, which make me smile.
My cat letting me stroke him -
Which hasn't happened for a while.
My best friends playing with me
And my teacher saying how clever I can be.

Megan Burnett (9)
Parsons Down Junior School, Thatcham

Love Is . . .

A snow-white swan on a lake,
My sweet smelling birthday cake,
The relief I felt when Pantalaimon came back,
My cat when she sneaks food out of the rubbish sack,
The soft crunch when you step on snow,
My sister who never seems to grow.

Love is . . . never-ending.

Cansu Türkoğlu (10)
Parsons Down Junior School, Thatcham

Love Is . . .

Love is a jewel that you can't resist,
Love is a bracelet around your wrist,
Love is a cuddle that is so fine,
Love is my mum with a glass of wine,
Love is fine and delicate,
Love is in you and love is in me.

Josie Pearce (10)
Parsons Down Junior School, Thatcham

Happiness

Happiness is yellow, like the sun blazing brightly.
Happiness sounds like children laughing loudly.
Happiness is ice cream slipping down your throat.
Happiness smells like chocolate melting in my mouth.
Happiness looks like a flower just in bloom.
Happiness feels like the sand under my feet.
It reminds me of finding my best friend.

Megan Davis (9)
Parsons Down Junior School, Thatcham

The Moon

The moon is the warrior of space,
It lights up like its burning sister
And spies on you during the night.
He leads an army of stars to shine,
As everything is silent around the moon.
The moon falls asleep, not woken until darkness.

Joseph Baron (10)
Parsons Down Junior School, Thatcham

Love

Love is ruby-red.
It tastes of melting chocolate.
It sounds like a bird tweeting.
It looks like a great big heart.
It smells like roses.
It feels like laughter.

Aaron Parsons (10)
Parsons Down Junior School, Thatcham

Love

Love is a ruby-red rose,
It glows in the dark,
It is yellow sunshine,
It is a star blazing in the night sky.
It tastes like a sugar, sweet on a hot sunny day,
It feels like a soft cushion.
It smells like a rose,
It sounds like bells.
Love is the best feeling of all!

Megan Mackenzie (9)
Parsons Down Junior School, Thatcham

Beauty

Beauty is pink,
It tastes like strawberry ice cream.
It sounds like the click of straighteners in the morning.
It looks like a rose, full of bloom.
It smells like honey fresh from a hive.
It feels nice and tingly down your spine.

Lily Meechan (9)
Parsons Down Junior School, Thatcham

Anger

Anger is a mean, swirling hole of red and black,
It is red and dark.
It tastes like a bitter, rotten, burning lemon.
It smells like a ball of smoke rolling up my nose and it won't stop.
It is evil and twisted.
It reminds me of being locked in my room forever.
It sounds like an out-of-tune drummer.
It feels ice-cold.
Anger is the worst feeling of all.
I'm warning you, don't go near it.

James Beechey (9)
Parsons Down Junior School, Thatcham

Love

Love is red,
It tastes like strawberries,
It sounds like a welcome at the end of the day,
It looks like flowers dancing,
It smells like roses,
It feels like a blanket,
But sometimes it leaves you and your heart fades away.

Aaliyah Lewis (10)
Parsons Down Junior School, Thatcham

Anger

Anger is red,
It tastes like blood,
It sounds like cymbals,
It looks like fighting in my head,
It smells like smoke from a burnt burger,
It feels like fire on my back,
It's not in us all the time.

James Clyde (9)
Parsons Down Junior School, Thatcham

Fun

Fun is red,
It tastes like strawberry milkshake,
It sounds like the quiet rustling of the wind,
It looks like sunflowers dancing in the sun,
It feels like a smooth blanket,
It smells like popcorn popping in the air,
It's in my heart as it carries on.

Gabriel Hopes (10)
Parsons Down Junior School, Thatcham

Fear

Fear is black and blue,
It tastes like vomit,
It sounds like the scream of the Grim Reaper.

It looks like ghosts,
It smells like wolves,
It feels like a scare
And sometimes it happens too much.

Sian Beardmore (9)
Parsons Down Junior School, Thatcham

Beauty

Beauty is pink,
It tastes like grapes, freshly picked,
It sounds like the blow from a hairdryer,
It looks like petals falling from the sky,
It smells like a bowl full of honey,
It feels like softness from a feather,
You see it every day.

Freya Mills (9)
Parsons Down Junior School, Thatcham

Cheerfulness

Cheerfulness is pale pink
It tastes like a strawberry smoothie
It sounds like the laughing and clapping of children
It looks like a smile on my face
It smells like a freshly made cake
It feels like a rush of wind
It is with me from day to day.

Sarah Hutt (10)
Parsons Down Junior School, Thatcham

Love

Love is red
It tastes like cherries
It sounds like the tweeting in the morning breeze
It looks like a heart in your hands
It smells like freshly baked cakes
Without it life couldn't go on.

Shannon Wood (10)
Parsons Down Junior School, Thatcham

Sadness

Sadness is blue, like the sky
It sounds like my little sister screaming
It tastes like lemonade
It smells like wine
It looks like a graceful bird
It feels like soft fur
It reminds me of when I cut myself.

Gemma Ackrill (9)
Parsons Down Junior School, Thatcham

Love Poem

Love is pink, like hearts in the sunlight,
It sounds like hearts beating madly,
It tastes like strawberries being licked,
It smells like dazzling roses, swaying in a field,
It's soft like melted chocolate,
It feels like a fluffy, cuddly cushion, being hugged,
It reminds me of great weddings.

Aiden Gale (10)
Parsons Down Junior School, Thatcham

Love

Love is pink like sweet roses,
It sounds like hearts beating madly!
It smells like sweet honey,
Love looks like tasty strawberries.
It is fluffy cat fur!
Love reminds me of a chocolate fountain,
Trickling slowly.

Jade May (10)
Parsons Down Junior School, Thatcham

Sadness

Sadness is blue like deep salty sea.
It tastes like bitter beer.
It smells like London's rubbish bins.
It looks like grey mist.
It feels like rain falling from the clouds.
It sounds like someone weeping.
It reminds me of being lonely in the playground.

Tom Cane (10)
Parsons Down Junior School, Thatcham

Happiness

Happiness is yellow like the sun blazing.
Happiness sounds like children laughing happily.
Happiness is ice cream slipping softly down my throat.
Happiness smells like hot chocolate melting.
Happiness looks like a flower in full bloom.
Happiness feels like a treat being given to me.
Happiness reminds me of a family playing together,
On the beach.

Lucy Birtwistle (10)
Parsons Down Junior School, Thatcham

Eruption

Long ago, far away, there lived a town next to a huge volcano.
It was a normal day, until a man dropped his money,
To buy a jar of honey.
The man then picked up his money,
But suddenly there was a rumble and a tumble,
The man started shouting, 'The ground, the ground, it's shaking!'
'You're mad,' a woman said who was baking.
Bang!
An explosion from the volcano.
Panic!
Everybody ran to the boats
Without their coats.
People left behind,
Because some people were not kind.
Sadness at leaving others behind,
People crying,
People dying.
The town was wrecked
And so were all the people.

Amy Cottingham (10)
Parsons Down Junior School, Thatcham

Mrs Winsor

(Based on the poem by Brian Moses.)

Mrs Winsor knows all about cars,
Or so she said, but that was many years before
She became a Head.
Recently she bought a Mercedes,
As she thought they were designed for ladies,
Now she ought to sell it as per school ethics,
By buying a bike and going kinetic.

Kelly-Marie Looker (10)
Parsons Down Junior School, Thatcham

The Four Seasons

There is happiness in seeing the beautiful spring
come to a bloom.
The bees and the butterflies
come to visit the garden,
The sweetness of the flowers brings honey to
make a more beautiful life.

There is gladness in seeing the sun shine
on the surface of the Earth,
Even darkness thinks it's beautiful,
God's creation plays till the sun sets.

There is joy in seeing the leaves falling
in the autumn season,
They come in colours that the fairies adore,
Let autumn come every year for us to enjoy
these wonderful sights.

There is coldness in seeing the snow fall on the icy earth,
Let us follow the glistening trail of winter every year
So freedom can dawn in our minds.

Charlotte Lloyd-Butler (8)
Parsons Down Junior School, Thatcham

Sadness

Sadness is my heart burning,
It is a hole of grey and blue.
All I see is a black sea,
It is whispering in the foggy mist.
Quietly ripping my soul apart in the darkness.
I wish I'd never felt this way,
For I know what had made me feel this way,
When people tease me about my grandad,
It makes me feel this way.

Megan Smith (8)
Parsons Down Junior School, Thatcham

The Ugly Duckling

Once in a nest,
Hatched the very best,
Delightful little ducklings with feathers of gold.

They were very fine,
But they used to whine,
Because of their brother
Who seemed like another
And who had scruffy feathers of grey.

The delightful little ducklings were not all they seemed,
They used to tease the ugly duckling,
They used to laugh and shout and scream.

This made the grey, kind-hearted duckling very, very sad,
Now you see, the delightful ducklings were very, very bad!

He was so ugly,
Everyone would tease
And wherever he went
He never felt at ease.

The summer grew nearer
And things were a mess,
The duckling was so unhappy
He decided to leave the nest.

The summer passed by,
He was lonesome and shy,
Because of his shape and his tattered grey feathers,
His life was destroyed
And his life was in tethers.

As the seasons passed,
The duckling asked whether he would ever be happy again,
He went to sleep, not remembering his feet,
That were under the water,
Which turned to ice.

The duckling woke up
To find that he was stuck,
His feet were not able to move.

A farmer came,
He broke the ice
And didn't think twice
About taking the little duck home.

The duckling wasn't used to being inside
And people's strokes and pokes,
He did not like it at all!

In the dead of night,
When there wasn't a light,
The duckling crept out
And flew to a lake to hide.

When he woke up
He saw some swans,
So gracious and so elegant!
He had to speak to them, even if they mocked him.

He started to move,
But stopped in hesitation
And he looked at his reflection.

He saw brilliant white feathers that were extremely fine,
The radiant white looked so divine!
He gracefully moved towards the swans
And they greeted him as one of their own.

The children came, all ran and played,
The new swan they saw,
They gasped in awe,
As he swam round the lake,
He knew he felt perfect and accepted at last.

Kamila Sinoplu (11), Charlotte Lloyd-Butler & Amy Cottingham (10)
Parsons Down Junior School, Thatcham

Julius Caesar

Julius Caesar, he was bad
And he was extremely mad.
After killing Brutus he was glad,
But Julius' wife was very sad.

On March 15th he felt quite ill,
His wife warned him to sit quite still,
He went to the Senate and listened until
Brutus drew his dagger to kill.

Julius had a dream,
The crown and boots the Roman people had seen,
His wife's hopes of being a queen,
Were dashed, because Brutus was mean.

Courtney Parsons & Bryony Marsh (8)
Parsons Down Junior School, Thatcham

The Moon

The moon is a smiling little man,
Anticipating Christmas Eve.
With a twinkle in his eye,
Singing the stars a lullaby.

He's singing merrily,
To keep the stars shining bright.
Blazing more than ever,
To guide Santa through the night.

Grinning from ear to ear,
To greet Santa
As he does every year.

Megan McConkey (10)
Parsons Down Junior School, Thatcham

Mrs Winsor's Secret

(Based on the poem by Brian Moses.)

Mrs Winsor was a circus queen,
Or so she said,
But that was probably just a dream,
Before she became a Head.
The children were all speechless,
As she summoned a rabbit out of a tureen,
She really was a circus queen!
Some head teachers just aren't what they seem!

Kamila Sinoplu (11)
Parsons Down Junior School, Thatcham

Mrs Winsor, The Football Coach

(Based on the poem by Brian Moses)

Mrs Winsor was a football coach,
Or so she said,
She trained at Man United
Before becoming a Head.
But she couldn't stand the rain,
In her heels it was a pain.
Mrs Winsor was a football coach,
Or so she said.

Jake Welford (11)
Parsons Down Junior School, Thatcham

Reading

R eading is so much fun.
E xciting stories about dinosaurs.
A fabulous story about Africa
D racula stories and vampires jumping from every page.
I like reading so many books, especially about swimming.
N ever stop reading, find out interesting facts.
G o on, read a gigantic book today!

Thomas Sloan (7)
St Edmund's Catholic Primary School, Whitton

Reading

R is for reading, reading a book.
E is for enjoying, enjoying a good book.
A is for adventure and creepy tales.
D is for dangerous and devilish characters on every page.
I is for invigorating characters, filling my mind.
N is for new, learning something you never knew before.
G is for gigantic, large and small books, all equally as fun.

Lauren Gilbert (7)
St Edmund's Catholic Primary School, Whitton

Reading

R adiant princesses fill my head.
E very night before I go to bed.
A ction books are sort of cool.
D oubling books are good for school.
I always like to read a good book.
N ever say you won't have a look.
G o on, reading is fun, you never know what might happen!

Danielle De Leon (8)
St Edmund's Catholic Primary School, Whitton

Reading

R eading is simple, just pick up a book.
E very evening the characters are still until the page is turned.
A dventures filling every page.
D aring characters and fascinating pictures.
I nteresting information.
N obody disturb me, please!
G o on and read, read, read!

Amelia Kirk (7)
St Edmund's Catholic Primary School, Whitton

Reading

R eading is fun and exciting!
E very day and night it fills me with enjoyment.
A mazing colours, fantastic information to fill your hearts, it's divine.
D ragons prowl and princesses dance across each page.
I am not sure how they draw fantastic pictures by Quentin Blake.
N ight, night, put your books away, you can read them the
very next day.
G o on, read a story, because if you don't life will be very boring.

Lucy Elliman (8)
St Edmund's Catholic Primary School, Whitton

Reading

R eading is my favourite thing.
E very evening I read my book.
A n amazing story fills each chapter.
D id you know I loved reading, from the first time I opened a book.
I can't wait to find out what happens.
N obody had read my book.
G on on then, I will let you borrow it!

Keira Moore (8)
St Edmund's Catholic Primary School, Whitton

Reading

R eading is great!
E very time I have spare, I read.
A nd if you want to, have a go.
D ads love to read interesting books.
I only wish my little sister could read and join in the fun.
N early everyone knows I love to read.
G reat books make great minds!

Oscar Crowe (7)
St Edmund's Catholic Primary School, Whitton

My Three Books

I have a good book,
About this horrid crook.
He steals everything
And always loves to sing.
He does a ridiculous dance,
But has never been to France.

And that's the end of my first book.

I have a second book,
About an ugly cook.
He cooks delicious food,
But always in a sullen mood.
He has a flabby belly
And is really smelly.

And that's the end of my second book.

I have a third book,
About a man who shook.
He has a ridiculous face
And has a broken lace.
He has huge feet.
And loves to eat meat.

And that's the end of my third book.

Shaun Pursooramen (10)
St Edmund's Catholic Primary School, Whitton

Reading

R eading is fun!
E very day is a great day to read something new.
A mazing things fill up the page.
D azzling characters.
I magination running wild.
N othing stops me from reading.
G iant books and small books are good fun!

Edward Morgan (7)
St Edmund's Catholic Primary School, Whitton

Happiness

My happiness is like a circle, never-ending.
The colour blue is happiness' colour.
My happiness is an acquiescent dog.
My happiness is like an immortal, never to die.
My happiness tastes like a luscious bar of dark chocolate.
My happiness takes the form of a shiny sapphire.
Happiness reminds me of birds tweeting cheerfully.
How lucky I am to have such happiness.

Alex Moreland (9)
St Edmund's Catholic Primary School, Whitton

Anger

Anger is as red as blood from a bat.
Anger tastes like malicious contagion from a black widow spider.
Anger sounds like a grey wolf's lament at the full moon.
Anger smells like a potion from a witch and her distressing cat.
Anger is like a sabre-toothed tiger, ready to hunt.
That's my anger.
Anger feels like wanting to destroy many things.
Anger is like millions of tigers sprinting and destroying many things.
Anger feels like perfidious apples.

Jack Bartrip (9)
St Edmund's Catholic Primary School, Whitton

Frustration

Frustration looks like the darkest alleyway of the darkest town.
Frustration tastes like rotten Brussel's sprouts.
Frustration sounds like the cries of injured children.
Frustration smells like the blood pouring out of an innocent girl.
Frustration's animal is a lion, teasing you and calling you a bug.
Frustration feels like 500 volts of lightning
Going straight through your mind.

Martin Conway (9)
St Edmund's Catholic Primary School, Whitton

Love Is . . .

Love is as magenta as friendship.
Love tastes like a Saturday ice cream sundae.
Love sounds like a soft and smooth drumming sound, like my heart.
Love smells like a field, growing bright flowers on a summer night.
Love is a cute brown puppy.

Renee Brenya (9)
St Edmund's Catholic Primary School, Whitton

Betrayal

Betrayal is as dark and deserted as Hell.
Betrayal is like the everlasting thunder on Jupiter.
Betrayal is like antagonism at its most terrible.
Betrayal is as sour as toxic water.
Betrayal is like being tormented by a sniper rifle.
Betrayal is like a scorpion continuing itself in a ring of fire.
Betrayal is as deadly as a ferocious tiger's bite.

Ciaran Tomlin (9)
St Edmund's Catholic Primary School, Whitton

Anger

Anger looks like a volcano erupting over land.
Fury tastes like a rotten egg, all bronze and jet-black.
Temper sounds like ear-piercing thunder on a winter's night.
Outrage smells like blood, freshly pouring out of your heart.
Anger is a lion, bellowing and rumbling in the jungle.
Anger shouts out 'Death,' straight at you, like a tiger roaring
in the night.

David Diaper (9)
St Edmund's Catholic Primary School, Whitton

Happiness

Happiness is bright yolk like a shimmering sun.
Happiness looks like the softest beach on a summer day.
Happiness tastes like scrumptious white chocolate, melting
in my mouth.
Happiness sounds like the joyful, jolly children, playing hide-and-seek
between lush bushes.
Happiness smells like fresh blooming bluebells.
Happiness is an amusing cute puppy, making people happy.
Happiness feels like me hugging my tender-hearted, loving mum.
Happiness reminds me of my family going on holiday.
Happiness is my favourite emotion.

Sarah Bainbridge (9)
St Edmund's Catholic Primary School, Whitton

Anger

Anger looks like a dumpster with a stench of death.
Anger tastes like a bowl of salt that's ten days old.
Anger sounds like The Scream,
terrorising people with its deadly voice.
Anger feels like toxic waste, burning you with its evil sting.
Anger is as aggressive as a polar bear with its mighty claws.

Harry Frampton (8)
St Edmund's Catholic Primary School, Whitton

Anger

Anger smells like blood from an injured bird.
Anger looks like charcoal burning.
Anger is like a man chopping a worm.
Anger looks like darkness outside.

Christy Walsh (8)
St Edmund's Catholic Primary School, Whitton

Hurt

Hurt is a black and mad feeling, like a black emerald dragon,
destroying towns.
Hurt looks like your best friend in serious pain.
Hurt tastes like dirty water coming from your crying eyes.
Hurt sounds like great, powerful people in unbelievable pain.
Hurt smells like ruby-red blood dripping from an enormous, painful cut.
Hurt is a dead, playful pig, who just got killed to be eaten.
Hurt is lots of sharp thorn bushes, that will make a lot of invisible cuts.
All these things come from your heart as strong as God!

Jack Saville (9)
St Edmund's Catholic Primary School, Whitton

Sadness

Sadness is a horrible scorpion creeping up my shivering spine.
Sadness smells like rotten eggs left in a drain.
Sadness is an unlucky man howling in pain.
Sadness tastes like mouldy cheese 20 years over its expiry date.
Sadness looks like a minute spider with evil little eyes.
Sadness is evil, cruel and extremely unkind.
Sadness, sadness, I hate sadness.
I definitely do, do you?

Matthew Bainbridge (9)
St Edmund's Catholic Primary School, Whitton

Happiness

Happiness looks like wonderful scarlet roses.
Cheerfulness tastes like sweet and refreshing oranges.
Delight sounds like children gambolling amazingly,
as happily as a baby.
It smells like luscious cakes coming out of a boiling hot oven.
It feels like my magnificent mum's cold hand touching my soft skin.
If I had to choose an animal to describe happiness
It would be a beautiful, pretty and colourful butterfly.

Maya Smith (9)
St Edmund's Catholic Primary School, Whitton

Happiness

Happiness is like stroking the smooth fur of a sleeping kitten
Happiness is like blooming flowers in the greenest grass
Happiness is like tasting the freshest fruit on the tree
Happiness is like smelling the fresh air when it's just been raining
Happiness is like a circle, as it never ends.

Kimono McDonald D'Souza (8)
St Edmund's Catholic Primary School, Whitton

Happiness

Happiness is a baby's first smile and a rainbow with a pot of gold
at the bottom
It tastes as beautiful as a chocolate cake
Twice the size of a building, with magenta icing on top
Ecstasy is a yellow colour, with emeralds on its delicate petals
It's a multicoloured peach with the sun sparkling on the
ancient seabed.
Joy is the loveliest thing on Earth!

Emmanuel Fayomi (9)
St Edmund's Catholic Primary School, Whitton

Happiness

Happiness looks like the blessed animals playing.
Happiness tastes like scrumptious sweeties.
Happiness sounds like the lovely songs of the singing birds.
Happiness smells like the scented rose from the pretty fairy's garden.
Happiness is the nice people not hurting any peaceful animals
And the animals are all safe!

Jemma John (8)
St Edmund's Catholic Primary School, Whitton

Anger

Anger is as scorching red as lava in an immense volcano.
Anger tastes like a mouldy, rotten apple.
Anger sounds like the loudest roar of a lion on a winter's night.
Anger smells like the blood of a green zombie in the darkest,
deepest cave.
Anger is like a viper, venomous snake.
That's what my anger feels like.
Anger feels like I really want to explode.
Anger is like a vicious lion in the jungle, rushing to gobble me up.
Anger feels like I am in a scorching African desert.
Anger feels like my frustrated mum, sending me to outer space.
That's what my anger feels like.

Beth Clarke (8)
St Edmund's Catholic Primary School, Whitton

Jealousy

Jealousy is as auburn as a rotten apple that has fallen from a lofty tree.
Jealousy sounds like an enormous, iniquitous owl, calling
an ancient lady.
Jealousy tastes like burnt sausages that are pitch-black.
Jealousy smells like plain, green grass.
Jealousy is as cold as ice in an ice rink.

Amelia Wapshott (8)
St Edmund's Catholic Primary School, Whitton

Love

Love looks like a shiny, special ruby.
Love tastes like a piece of cherry cake.
Love smells like bright red and yellow tulips.
Love sounds like a bluebird singing a song.

Rachel Clark (9)
St Edmund's Catholic Primary School, Whitton

One Spring Morning

One spring morning,
the birds came out to play,
singing their own little tune
with the children, 'Hip hip hooray.'

One spring morning,
the baby buds came out,
daffodils shone so brightly
and the fox cubs ran about.

One spring morning,
blossom was pink and bold,
flowers bloomed out like sun rays
and shone in the sun so gold.

One spring morning,
the spring breeze brushed my ear,
freshly hit my tanned cheek,
howling and whistling I can hear.

One spring morning,
shy lambs started walking,
with farmers laying back
on this spring morning.

One spring night,
spring closed its door,
birds started sleeping,
all that's left is a dreaming snore . . .

Kerrica Ammilyn Kendall (10)
St Edmund's Catholic Primary School, Whitton

Happiness

My happiness is the universe.
My happiness is as blue as Chelsea city.
My happiness is as fast as a rapid dog.
My happiness tastes like an enormous pizza.
My happiness smells like a phenomenal jam roly-poly.

Thomas Formby (8)
St Edmund's Catholic Primary School, Whitton

Spring At Its Highest

The springtime rain drizzles down
And the king fox wears his crown,
All the colourful flowers smile in the sun,
The spiders' webs gleam, finished and spun.

The springtime breeze shivers past
And the deep blue lake stands wide and vast,
The springtime blossom begins to burst
And all are ready to see the world first.

The weather starts to become mild
And everything starts to go wild,
All the animals have a free lifestyle,
So everyone starts to go freestyle.

The icy dew lays quiet and still
And the rabbits sit on the green hill,
The young birds begin to start to fly
And up and away, deep into the sky.

Goodbye spring, as it draws to an end
And the cold air starts to ascend
And all the stars will start to appear
And all nature is suddenly clear.

Finbar Downing (10)
St Edmund's Catholic Primary School, Whitton

Spring

Spring sounds like Mozart's best piece of music.
Spring tastes like sweet strawberries dipped in chocolate.
Spring smells like frying bacon.
Spring feels like a soft velvet quilt.
Spring looks like a sunny beach with children having fun.

Joe Manorajah (10)
St Edmund's Catholic Primary School, Whitton

My Favourite Season

Spring is a season of life
Everything is new
Everything is refreshed
Everything is beautiful

The welcoming sun beckons
The daffodils towards
Him and he soothes them
With his warmth and radiance

Agile birds cover the sky
In a colourful blanket
As they return to the north
Filling the atmosphere with chirrups

As I step into the morning dew
I realise the delicate beauty
Of Mother Nature, her hands
Bringing life to all

Spring is a season of beauty
The fruits of all creation
In the palm of Mother Nature's hands
And me witnessing this is a blessing.

Ali D-Nayeri (11)
St Edmund's Catholic Primary School, Whitton

Spring

The sun shines on the dewed grass, making it glisten,
The chicks hop out from their eggs,
The flowers blossom and grow,
The lambs stumble and fall,
The rabbits jump for joy,
For it is spring!

Anna Blake (11)
St Edmund's Catholic Primary School, Whitton

My Spring Dragon

If I were a painter
I'd paint a dragon
A dragon with all the colours of spring
One made from the Earth itself

I'd paint the eyes as red as sunset,
The head as bright green as the leaves of a young holly tree,
The ears as blue as the sparkling sea on a spring morning,
Its teeth made of glittering razor pebbles, sharpened to perfection.

I'd paint wings of pure green grass, shimmering through the air,
Its underbelly made of daffodils, yellow as the sun,
The scales would be as white as a cloud, the whitest ever.
The legs would be made of the nicest indigo I could find.

Its tail is violet, violet as lavender,
The spikes are black, black as my hair in the summer glare,
Finally the fire, red-hot fire,
It will be made of every colour of spring, endless
Oh, how I love the colours of spring.

William Kirk (10)
St Edmund's Catholic Primary School, Whitton

Springtime

Lambs are born,
Rabbits too,
The sun always shines
And skies are blue.

Flowers bloom,
In yellow and red,
The sun beats down brightly,
Warming the back of my head.

This poem's about spring,
All things nice,
Hate is banned
And war and strife.

Molly Ellis (10)
St Edmund's Catholic Primary School, Whitton

The Wonders Of Spring

Spring is the time of year
When birds chirp and make everybody cheer,
Flowers jump to say, 'Hello,'
But when winter comes, it's time to go.

Spring is the time of year
When flowers sway in the wind,
While the golden sun sends its rays
And gives everybody praise.

Spring is the time of year
When people walk for hours,
Even when there are rain showers,
But it helps the gleaming flowers.

Spring is a time of year
When dark bluebells
Stand under the sky,
Waiting for people to stop and stare.

I'm looking back now on the springs I've had,
Such a wonderful season it is.

Sian Linnane (10)
St Edmund's Catholic Primary School, Whitton

Anger

Anger is the colour red
Anger is a volcano erupting
Anger is a burning curry
Steaming down your throat
Anger is when lightning and thunder fight
Anger is a dragon, breathing his fiery breath.

Joseph Jackson (11)
St Edmund's Catholic Primary School, Whitton

Springtime Is Here

Flowers glow as much as the sun,
Animals awake from hibernation.
Trees start to grow new leaves,
Springtime is here.

Snow starts to disappear,
Green, green plants start to grow,
The world just got warmer,
Springtime is here.
Rain clouds start to fade away,
All the creatures come out to play,
The sun starts to cover the land,
Springtime is here.

Birds start to sing so loudly,
Butterflies fly through the air,
Fields go from white to green,
Springtime is here.

Bees start to make honey,
Squirrels start to collect acorns,
Flowers shine for all to see,
Springtime is here.

Connor Hageman (11)
St Edmund's Catholic Primary School, Whitton

Anger

Anger is like a dark soaked tomato.
Anger tastes like bright, gory, dangerous lifeblood.
Anger is a land of people screaming.
Anger smells like a dragon's breath.
The sight of anger is a dark and shady alleyway.

Emma Roberts (8)
St Edmund's Catholic Primary School, Whitton

What Is Spring . . . ?

As I step into the season spring,
I think of all the joy it will bring,
Children playing, laughing, singing,
The bells in the playground ringing and ringing.

All the bees whizzing around,
Everyone hearing their busy buzzing sounds.
Lots of birds are tweeting softly,
Loads of adults drinking morning coffee.

The spring season is March, April, May,
Each spindle of grass dancing all day,
The gentle spring breeze is blowing
And the winter snowflakes have stopped snowing.

So we have stepped into the season spring,
Children laughing, playing, having a sing.
Now I know that spring is fun
And I know what joy will come.

Jessica Rowe (11)
St Edmund's Catholic Primary School, Whitton

What Is Spring?

Spring is a time for flowers,
That is like humans growing.
Spring is a time for leaves,
To not fall off the trees.

Spring is a time for bees,
To fly all over the world.
Spring is a time for love
And everyone can share.

Spring is a time for rain to cry
And for all the stars to come
Out in the night sky.
Spring is like a flower
That's beautiful in every way.

Emily Everett (10)
St Edmund's Catholic Primary School, Whitton

Spring Comes Early

As new life comes
leaves start to grow
flowers come up
emerald-green grass comes again

as new life comes
sun shines out
daffodils grow
and out come all the colours

as new life comes
the wind blows
roses red, violets blue
and the pond shining in the distance.

Jack McQuillan-Butt (10)
St Edmund's Catholic Primary School, Whitton

Spring's Room

Spring is opening its smooth doors,
Where children play and birds will sing,
Blossom will fall and leaves will grow,
Oh, spring is such a wonderful thing!

People look at all the pretty flowers
And new baby chicks will see light,
Birds will soar over the trees
And it will be warmer at night.

Naomi Bower (11)
St Edmund's Catholic Primary School, Whitton

As Spring Blooms

Springtime is a time where everything's joyful,
The wonderful daffodils waken and all amazing things
This only happens in the graceful months of spring.

Newborn lambs prance up and down on their wobbly legs,
The months of winter suddenly transform
And the sun wakes up early and brightly dawns.

Chicks wake up early and noisily chirp,
Quietly, the trickling sound of splashing rain,
As it patters down the windowpane.

Butterflies daintily dance to the fresh breeze,
Bees buzz busily to and fro,
Collecting sweet pollen as they go.

The months of spring are joyful months,
As birds fly in the open breeze,
Noisy insects, collecting pollen, which makes most people sneeze.

Tara Proudfoot (11)
St Edmund's Catholic Primary School, Whitton

Anger

It gleamed like blood dripping from a tiger
It tasted like a really sour sweet,
making someone's head turn purple and red.
Anger sounds like someone has taken a tiger and is killing it,
whilst still alive and roaring.
It smells like someone has just been sick.
It's a tiger.

Joseph Sloan (9)
St Edmund's Catholic Primary School, Whitton

Spring Daze

As I watch the golden sun jump through the fluffy clouds,
I think what it would be like
Being the soft, soundless wind,
Not whistling through the night.

As I walk through the blossoming park,
I think of what it would be like
Being the smooth and silky leaves,
Feeding the new wildlife.

As I relax in the shimmering, glimmering pool,
I think of what it'd be like
Being the scaly, glittering fish,
Swimming from dusk 'til light.

As I think of spring, each day and night,
I know what it is like
Staring at the deep pink sky,
Dusk until the morning twilight.

Lauren Phillips (11)
St Edmund's Catholic Primary School, Whitton

Springtime

The blazing sun
Piercing through the sky,
Clouds as white as sheep fur,
The sky as blue as the sea.

The grass is a sharp blade,
The rain's beginning to subside,
The tree is a giant hand,
The flowers as colourful as the rainbow.

The trees starting to blossom,
The blossom's as pink as the pink panther,
The branches as long as a ladder,
The birds swaying in the sky.

Lance Fernando (10)
St Edmund's Catholic Primary School, Whitton

Blossoming Spring

Spring is a happy season,
Full of laughter and smiles,
Everywhere you look around,
There is joy for miles and miles.

All around the world is new,
Just go and have a look,
The daffodil in my garden,
Starts to open like a book.

Spring is like a leaping lamb,
Jumping into the sky,
All the birds, the newborn chicks,
Take from their nests and start to fly.

The blossom starts to open its eyes,
To all the new life in spring,
The beautiful lake the colour of sapphire,
There's a cute new little duckling.

The cute little duck just hatched from its egg,
The mother kept safe and warm,
That's what the beauty of spring is,
It's when new life is born.

Gabriella Rutzler (10)
St Edmund's Catholic Primary School, Whitton

Love

Love is the shimmering light of God Almighty,
Love smells like a lush rose rising from the ground.
Love tastes like a beautiful strawberry ice cream melting in the sun.
A dolphin is the glorious animal of love.
Love is the magenta-pink pillow.
Love smells like a glossy cherry tree,
Blossoming in the gorgeous sun.

Oscar Goodenough (9)
St Edmund's Catholic Primary School, Whitton

In Springtime

Everything starts to grow
In spring there's no snow
The sun cooks me like toast
In springtime I start to roast.

The flowers start to sprout
In springtime I love to go out
All the children play
In springtime it's a jolly good day.

Some trees have nothing to wear
In springtime there's no cold air
The children go to school
In spring they obey the rules.

Springtime is my favourite season
Read this poem, I have three reasons
Oh, I enjoy every hour of spring
In the morning all the birds sing.

Pierce Kavanagh (10)
St Edmund's Catholic Primary School, Whitton

Wonderful Spring

Spring is full of luscious flowers,
The air is fresh and the trees are yawning,
Birds are born, they sing with glee,
Spring is as lovely as the deep blue sea.

Yellow daffodils, as bright as the sun,
Blossom, as pink as a flamingo,
Trees are growing perfect leaves,
Spring is as lovely as the deep blue sea.

Spring is the season before summer's glow,
It opens its doors and gives us a show,
Everyone is as busy as a buzzing bee,
Spring is as lovely as the deep blue sea.

Esme Soiza (11)
St Edmund's Catholic Primary School, Whitton

Spring Is Here

Spring is a great season,
A season of new life.
All the birds are cheeping loud,
As loud as the wind's whistle.

The flowers are so bright,
As bright as the morning sun,
The leaves are awakening,
Opening their bright eyes.

Rivers flow so slow,
As slow as the moon moves.
The sun is so bright
As bright as the stars in the night sky.

Joseph Bonnichon (11)
St Edmund's Catholic Primary School, Whitton

Springtime

As we play outside
And stay till night,
As the days get bright,
The sun gives light.

As the leaves jump down,
The children start to glide around,
As the leaves start to wave,
They fall onto the ground.

As the day goes by,
The sun starts to rise,
Spring is a great season,
Because it's like a paradise.

Nigel Tate (11)
St Edmund's Catholic Primary School, Whitton

Oh How I Love Spring

Spring is lovely, spring is sweet,
It makes me feel happy,
Like I'm being swept off my feet.

The bees start to buzz
And the flowers start to bloom,
The birds start to sing
And give us a tune.

The leaves start to grow,
In the early spring dew,

Spring makes me happy,
What about you?

Daniel Power (10)
St Edmund's Catholic Primary School, Whitton

My Mum

My mother, Olga O'Brien
Can be as fierce as a lion,
But other times she can be kind,
I don't know what goes on in her mind!

She can get on my nerves,
But deep inside she plays on my curves,
I know sometimes I say I hate her,
But it's kind of like a cat purr.
What I means is I say one thing bad
But it always means another!
So when I say I hate her
She knows I mean I love her!

Niamh O'Brien (10)
St Edmund's Catholic Primary School, Whitton

Spring Is Here

Winter's disappearing
The wind's calming
The sun's awakening
Spring is here!

Great, gold beauty shines
As daffodils bloom
They sit and stare
Spring is here!

Leaves green, oh so great
Grow on copper chocolate-coloured trees
Gentle and gracefully dancing in the light breeze
Spring is here!

Baby white lambs
Newborn just today
Squinting for first sight
Spring is here!

Time walks by
The sun's snoozy and sleepy
The flowers yawn with tiredness
Spring is over!

Holly Harding (11)
St Edmund's Catholic Primary School, Whitton

The Magical Meadow

In the magical meadow
Flowers of rose, sapphire and violet glow
The emerald-green grass is sprinkled with dew
Oak trees grow ninety feet in the air
With roots as thick as elephants' trunks
Animals frolic around the meadow
And the sun always shines
So come to the magical meadow
Where fun can always be found.

Alexander Bartrip (11)
St Edmund's Catholic Primary School, Whitton

A Happy Time Of Year

Spring is the time of year
When we celebrate new life,
The flowers are awakened by the blinding sun
And the sky turns from a miserable grey
To a cheerful blue!

Roses, daisies and daffodils too,
Shoot up from the ground like rockets
Travelling through space,
Their gentle petals open wide
Showing off their amazing figures.

The tiny lambs are new life,
The joyful sun watches them
As they cuddle up to their cushiony mother.
Children gather round
As the small lambs stumble clumsily
Across the fluorescent, green grass.

Fionnuala Conway (10)
St Edmund's Catholic Primary School, Whitton

Spring Is Known When . . .

A lamb is born,
Baby chicks tweet
And the rabbits are seen.
Spring is known.

Laughter and joy's heard,
New budded flowers
And when the summer's sun's seen.
Spring is known.

When children eat chocolate eggs,
When the parents dance and play.
Spring is known.

Elliot Stahlmann (11)
St Edmund's Catholic Primary School, Whitton

In The Playground

In the playground I see people talking,
While they are walking,
In the sun, having fun.

Some are running very fast,
Until they have to stop at last,
In the sun, having fun.

Some are walking very slow,
Because they have nowhere to go,
In the sun, having fun.

Skipping and jumping, having a laugh,
When we get home we'll have a bath,
In the sun, having fun.

Children gathered all as one,
Under the sun, having fun.

Alana Hewitt (9)
St John's CE Primary School, Penge

Playtime

In the corridor I don't shout
I get my coat and then I go out,
The boys who play basketball
Are very tall,
The thing that does not shine is the sun
But I still have a lot of fun,
With my friends we start to walk
But at the same time we start to talk,
The thing that rings is the bell
And the teachers start to *yell!*

Olivia Tizie (8)
St John's CE Primary School, Penge

Cats Sleep Anywhere

(Inspired by 'Cats Sleep Anywhere' by Eleanor Farjeon)

Cats may sleep on mats
and they doze away.
They can sleep in hats
and they don't even care.

Cats could sleep on beds,
they will sleep wherever.
May sleep right on your head
but that would be very fluffy.

Cats might sleep on chairs
and curl into a ball.
Could be on the stairs
to lie down and relax.

They don't care,
sleep may cats,
but you also know,
they chase rats.

Tilly Sullivan (8)
St John's CE Primary School, Penge

My Friends And I

My friends are kind and caring,
We love chatting and sharing,
Our toys, our pens, our magazines,
Our feelings and our dreams.

My friends aren't always happy,
Some days they can be quite snappy,
My friends are sometimes sad,
But I try to understand.

My friends and I love having fun,
The best bit is when the party has just begun,
We enjoy spending time together
And pray that this will last forever.

Toyin Orelaja (9)
St John's CE Primary School, Penge

Bugs

In the shallows,
deep blue seas,
underground
or top of trees,
you can look anywhere -
bugs are everywhere!

Locust, spider and leech
are enough to make you screech,
mantis and scorpion will make you stare -
but bugs are everywhere!

Creepy-crawly,
scuttly, scrawly,
spider in the bath,
why do you make
the grown-ups scream
and to babies
you are a laugh?

Centipedes, snails and slugs,
butterflies - all kinds of bugs,
aphids, ants and all the rest
all come crawling
down your vest!

Niko Kristic (7)
St John's CE Primary School, Penge

A Windy Night

A windy night, more than a breeze
A windy night gusting through the trees
Sweeping through the country
While we dream.

The day breaks in silence
No birds singing today
I wonder, but I hope not,
If the wind has blown them away.

The garden is a sorry state
The flowers stand no more
The petals and leaves
Strewn on the floor.

The sun is now shining
The wind gone with the day
I'm glad I was sleeping
And not blown away.

Tess Wellfair (10)
St John's CE Primary School, Penge

The Four Stages Of Life

The doctor says you have given birth,
You are so happy you are crying.
The staff are happy for you,
The nurse thought you weren't trying.

Now the baby is a toddler,
You are so shocked he is walking.
Dad can see you in the future,
He sees you and your friends talking.

Dad says you are a teen now
And his vision has come true.
Tests are round the corner,
The house is empty except for you.

You look into the mirror and see you're an adult
And you thank God that you're alive.
People say you should get a girlfriend,
All you want to do is go to the ballroom and jive.

Joseph Adusei (10)
St John's CE Primary School, Penge

A River Of Haikus

River is your life,
Flowing mysteriously,
It will never end.

End is where things stop,
The curtains finally close,
At end, a shut door.

Door opens, new world,
But door shuts, path now blocked off,
Possibilities.

Possibilities,
Everyone has so many,
No dreams? That's nonsense!

Nonsense is pure fun,
It's great to have a laugh with,
Just go really wild!

Wild is . . . slight madness,
Wild is . . . truly muddled mind,
Wild is . . . dense jungle!

Jungle filled with trees,
Listen to the lion's roar,
The home of nature.

Nature is so pure,
The blue rivers and green grass,
It stays forever.

Forever is long,
It is an eternity,
But let's not worry.

Worry is a curse,
Though it is very scary,
Preparing for life.

Haiku has three lines,
With seventeen syllables,
Five, seven, then five.

Freya Soar Wilson (8)
St Peter's Eaton Square CE Primary School, Westminster

Seasons - Ever Changing

Spring is soft and gentle,
with newborn baby lambs.
The birds are up and singing
and call throughout the land.
The seasons ever changing,
are warm or damp or clear.
Spring is bright and merry: the
first season of the year.

Summer - hot and noisy,
holidays and fun!
On beaches adults sit and read -
while children swim and run!
The seasons ever changing,
are warm or damp or clear.
The second season 'Summer'
is the brightest of the year.

Autumn is more chilly,
with showers of leaves of gold.
The air is rather bitter
and the ground is much more cold.
The seasons ever changing
are warm or damp or clear.
Autumn is the harvest time: the third
season of the year.

Winter, full of cold and snow,
frost wonders that are real.
Nativity and crackers
and a tasty Christmas meal!
The seasons ever changing,
are warm or damp or clear.
Winter shows that we have found
the end of one more year.

Caitlin Walsh (11)
St Peter's Eaton Square CE Primary School, Westminster

Season - Haikus

Winter
Birds are migrating
Children drinking hot cocoa
Staying warm inside.

Spring
Flowers blossoming
Birds are singing once again
The sun is shining.

Summer
Children playing games
Happy faces all around
Summer has now come.

Autumn
The summer has gone
Tree leaves are now rustling
The cold has now come.

Harry Amoo (9)
St Peter's Eaton Square CE Primary School, Westminster

Winter And Its Ways

W inter is the depth of snow
I cy in the heart of life
N ice for the kid who likes to play
T inkling at the bottom of your feet
E choes of laughter from far and wide
R adiance for all mankind.

Matthew Ward-Perkins (8)
St Peter's Eaton Square CE Primary School, Westminster

Bringing People Together

I love to play football every day,
It is one of the few things where you don't have to pay.

You can play it everywhere, from Africa to Bombay,
It brings the world together in a more positive way.

It's a universal sport that is here to stay,
So go outside with a ball and try it today.

Luca James Buddenhagen (8)
St Peter's Eaton Square CE Primary School, Westminster

The Balloon Poem

I was floating in the sky,
When I saw a pigeon pass by.
I was going to say hello
But then I thought . . . no.

As I was floating in the sky above,
I saw a passing dove.
She looked very lonely,
So I asked if she was holy!

She got angry and flew away,
Just as the sky began turning grey.
I felt my knot begin to loosen,
And then came Hurricane Huston!

After the hurricane had gone,
I felt a sneeze coming on!
Weee! I went,
Over the sea, the land and Kent!

As I began to fall,
I flew past the city wall.
Then I went through a window
And landed on a patch of snow.

Zahra Taruvinga (9)
St Peter's Eaton Square CE Primary School, Westminster

Spy On The Run

A gun in my pocket, a poison pill under my tongue,
There's no doubt about it, I'm a spy on the run.

I lurk in the shadows, my life is all lies,
Even my hair is a spy's disguise.

I fly in planes that look like kites
And jump from them in the dead of night.

Once in a silver jet I flew,
To find an important assignment clue.

My kit is clean, my mission is coded,
I'm ready to go, my gun is loaded.

A gun in my pocket a poison pill under my tongue,
It's no fun being a spy on the run.

Barnaby Papadopulos (9)
St Peter's Eaton Square CE Primary School, Westminster

Love Letter

I'm in love in a serious way
I think about you every day
You are filled with every grace
I dream about your lovely face
I would hate it if we were not near
It would break my heart to see a tear
Streaming down your gorgeous face
We're going to meet in a love-filled place
Where I will take that one last glance
So we can build up our romance.

Isaac Semple (9)
St Peter's Eaton Square CE Primary School, Westminster

Or Maybe . . .

Winter is the best
It has Christmas Day
Look up high for Santa Claus
See the reindeer play
Or maybe . . .

Spring is very pretty
All the flowers grow
Then they spread around the park
What a lovely show!
Or maybe . . .

Summer is so sunny
Playing on the beach
When your ball goes in the sea
Try and try to reach
Or maybe . . .

Autumn is so windy
Go to fly a kite
Watch it glide into the sky
See its special flight
Or maybe . . .

Kate Wyncoll (9)
St Peter's Eaton Square CE Primary School, Westminster

Countryside Senses

The countryside smells damp and fresh.
It sounds beautiful and peaceful.
It looks like a kind of paradise,
In a sea of green.

Francesca Fitzgerald (10)
St Peter's Eaton Square CE Primary School, Westminster

My Cat

My cat has fluffy grey fur,
She has a lovely motorbike purr;
She has colour-changing eyes,
And of course she has nine lives!
She gives us some very bad scratches,
That, without Germolene, leave red patches;
However, she is awfully sweet,
And has lovely soft padded feet!
She sleeps on my bed at night,
And will stay there until it is light;
Oh my dear, beautiful cat!

Georgina Lawson (7)
St Peter's Eaton Square CE Primary School, Westminster

Love

Love is pretty
Love is red
Love is warm like a cosy bed
Love is a rose
Love is calm
Love is always in your heart.

Florence Chua (8)
St Peter's Eaton Square CE Primary School, Westminster

Late For School

This morning I got lost,
In the middle of town.
A dragon offered to help me
And he took me to his lair.
I thought that he would eat me,
Things were so unfair!
Then he sat me on a stool . . .
That's why I am late for school!

Rose Gentle (8)
St Peter's Eaton Square CE Primary School, Westminster

My Doll's House

My doll's house is as neat as the Queen's palace,
The sitting room is pristine
And on the wall there is a picture of the Queen.

My doll's house is as neat as the Queen's palace,
The baby's room is as quiet as a mouse,
At night the baby can't be heard through the house.

My doll's house is as neat as the Queen's palace,
The kids' room is the best,
Although the oldest is a pest.

My doll's house is as neat as the Queen's palace,
The parents' room is also the dining room,
They sleep and eat in the same room.

My doll's house is as neat as the Queen's palace,
The kitchen is dull,
So use your brain and skull.

My doll's house is as neat as the Queen's palace,
The bathroom has a shower,
Which uses up lots of power.

My doll's house is as neat as the Queen's palace,
The dad's office is small,
When the dad works there he looks like he's going to a ball.

Sophie Norman (8)
St Peter's Eaton Square CE Primary School, Westminster

Witch's Spell

Rubber dabber, make the potion with all the creatures in the ocean.
Sea monster and fish eye, a frog's body and shark pie.
Sea slugs and cat legs, frog's tail with chicken eggs.
A witch's toenail and a whale.
A shark's tail with a snail, *ha, ha, ha.*
Steamy, steamy, a rat's tail with a big fat whale.

Ronke Awonaya Daniella (8)
St Peter's Eaton Square CE Primary School, Westminster

Skateboarding

It looks easy!
You just need the knack
Look at the front
Or be flat on your back
Bend your hips
And learn any tips
It's scary
It's dodgy
But practise every day
You'll soon do the ramp and be flying away.

James Booth (7)
St Peter's Eaton Square CE Primary School, Westminster

Witches Spell

Witches at the sea making spells on me.
Dead bodies and smelly dogs' poo
Then a warthog's tongue.
Head of a snake and blood of a cat.
A frog's bottom and a tail from a rat.
Witches at the sea making spells on me.

Harry Johnson (8)
St Peter's Eaton Square CE Primary School, Westminster

Chocolate

Chocolate is very yummy
And definitely very scrummy
It all goes funny
Especially in my tummy.

Penelope Waltham (7)
St Peter's Eaton Square CE Primary School, Westminster

My Brother

Who almost ate a bear?
Who plucked all my doll's hair?
Who said my bed was a secret lair?
My brother!

Why did he eat all my sweets?
How did he snap a leek?
Who said my daddy was very weak?
My brother!

Lauren Marshall (8)
St Peter's Eaton Square CE Primary School, Westminster

Wizard's Spell

Kill, kill Lord Voldemort,
You shall die when you are fought.

Eye of frog and dung of cat,
Little wood shavings and an old rotten hat.

A pig's bladder and a big fat bun,
One dad and one mum.

Some potatoes and a smelly snail,
A falcon's wing and a rat's tail.

Kill, kill Lord Voldemort,
You shall die when you are fought.

Edmund Ramsey (7)
St Peter's Eaton Square CE Primary School, Westminster

Feelings

Happiness is blue like a big whale in the salty sea.
Fear is black like the roar of the dragon from its den.
Excitement is blue like a salty sea.
Love is red like anger.

Jose Angelo Pilar (7)
St Peter's Eaton Square CE Primary School, Westminster

My Magic Box

(Inspired by 'Magic Box' by Kit Wright)

In my box . . .
I will put my little spotty puppy and a little white kitten.
My big black bicycle that my grandad taught me how to ride.
My sister's first laugh when I push ball.
My story that I wrote by myself.
My 5th birthday.
My brother's aeroplane.
My sister's car.

Maria Sycheva (7)
St Peter's Eaton Square CE Primary School, Westminster

My New Year's Resolutions

I will not cut my dolly's hair
Or scare the pigeons in my garden,
I will not slam the doors in my house
Nor put a saucepan on my head.

I shall try to be early for school,
And I will try to remember when Romeo died,
I will try to remember to brush my teeth
And be more kind.

Milla McKenzie (8)
St Peter's Eaton Square CE Primary School, Westminster

There Once Was A Man In White

There once was a man in white
Who flew away on his kite
He let go of the string
And fell down with a ping
And by the time he got back it was night.

Ruskin Springer-Hughes (10)
St Peter's Eaton Square CE Primary School, Westminster

The Adventures Of Isabel

(Inspired by 'The Adventures of Isabel' by Ogden Nash)

Isabel is seven and has red hair.
While on holiday when she was swimming in the sea,
A sea monster came up from the depths' deep blue.
It roared at Isabel, 'I'll have you for tea!'
Isabel said, 'Now don't you dare!'
She pulled at his tail and tied him in a bow
Then she chopped him up to make a fishy stew.
Well, if you met a sea monster, isn't that what you'd do?

Isabel is seven and has red hair.
While going to the shops she met a mean old wizard.
To Isabel the wizard said, 'I'm going to turn you into a bright green lizard!'
Isabel muttered a spell she once learnt from her brother
And immediately turned that mean old wizard into a saucepan
Which she gave to her mother.
She said, 'Will you please use this to boil an egg for my tea?'
Isabel loved boiled eggs and soldiers you see.

Isabel is seven and has red hair.
While taking a walk in the park on a sunny day
A girl-eating tiger got in her way.
The tiger snarled and got ready to pounce.
Isabel stayed totally calm and quickly uttered a taming charm.
Isabel rode the tiger to school the next day.
She said it was very relaxing to travel that way.

Isabel is seven and has red hair.
Her mum is calling her saying, 'Haven't you lots of exciting homework to do?'
So Isabel scowls and makes a face.
Her mother puts her in her place.
Now Isabel is in bed
Where she can have more adventures in her head.

Isabel Elkington (7)
St Peter's Eaton Square CE Primary School, Westminster

Excitement

Excitement is pink like the sunset on a summer day.
Excitement sounds like someone splashing in the swimming pool.
Excitement tastes like strawberry ice cream.
Excitement smells like fish and chips.
Excitement looks like a red strawberry.
Excitement feels like a newborn baby.
Excitement reminds me of the water park.

Jessica Maya Lochan-Jenkinson (7)
St Peter's Eaton Square CE Primary School, Westminster

Colours Of Life

Red is for blood, trickling down my knee.
Orange is for the fruit, a sweet taste in my mouth.
Yellow is for the sun, shining brightly outside.
Green is for the grass, waving gently in the breeze.
Blue is for the stream, gurgling quickly downhill.
Indigo is for ink, a dark blotch on my work.
Violet is for the flower, a piece of life in nature.

Gabrielle Burton (9)
St Peter's Eaton Square CE Primary School, Westminster

Love

Love is pink like a heart.
It sounds like a friendly conversation.
It tastes like lipstick.
It smells like perfume.
It looks like a heart.
It feels like petals.
It reminds me of when I go to bed.

Giulio Satkuru-Granzella (7)
St Peter's Eaton Square CE Primary School, Westminster

Names For Princesses

A princess should have an unusual name,
That plays in your mind like a musical game.

Karamalinda, Tangly Hair,
Rozamatina, Lacey-the-Fair,

Marzana Mazey, Star-of-the-Skies,
Dorinda Daisy, Emerald Eyes,

Little Cozetta, Ebony Locks,
Shy Sarabetta, Fifi-de-Fox,

Tiger Truella, Pearl-from-the-Sea,
Silvery Belly, Sweet Annalee.

A princess should have a remarkable name,
That glows in your mind like a flickering flame!

Eleanor Burton (11)
St Peter's Eaton Square CE Primary School, Westminster

Friendship

Friendship is when . . .
You care about each other,
You're always there for one another,
Always sticking together, forever!
This is the real meaning of friendship!
To care and to share,
To cry and never say goodbye!
To argue who's first in the queue
And to say I love your shoe!
If you have more than one of these in common
You have a true friend.
To criticise the boy who broke your heart.
And with this, you and your friend will never . . . part.

Chloe Lindsay (11)
Timbercroft Primary School, Plumstead

The Christmas Poem

Christmas is jolly
Merry holly
The mistletoe out
Now everybody's about.

Start eating humbugs
Grandma giving out hugs
Everyone getting kissed
Grandad missed.

Out comes the sun
Everyone eating a sticky bun
Yule logs are the best
Better than the rest.

The sun goes in
All the rubbish in the bin
It starts to snow
The Christmas tree glows.

The twinkly light
In the moonlight
People awake
Some start to shake.

The food lies on the table
The horse lies in the stable
The clouds of joy come out
And everyone shouts, 'It's Christmas!'

Ranna Ameer (10)
Timbercroft Primary School, Plumstead

Out On The Street

Out on the street
Where crumbling houses
Fall like packs of playing cards

Flames through his veins
Like the hot burning sun

Flames the children of the Devil
Known as the death

A frightened man waits here
Not knowing what to do

As the smoke appears
The siren begins

It gives the man
An obvious clue

When the frozen man
Comes to the door

Let him in!
Let him in!
Let him in!

Doesn't cause any trouble
The man is already in danger.

Shoulder to shoulder
Bones to bones

It's likely that they'll
Come again sometime.

Leanne Swain (11)
Timbercroft Primary School, Plumstead

The Fire

Out on the street,
there is a dilapidated building.

Planes dipping down,
and booming as they go back up.

The dark night filled with the enemy,
destroying our town.

Sirens booming,
ear-splitting but drowned out by the planes

The town is engulfed in panic,
death is everywhere.

My family in the burning building,
are soon going to die.

Curse that enemy,
why attack?

Why?
Why?
Why?

The fire is almost upon me,
it is licking at my legs.

These are the children of the Devil,
am I on Earth on the sun?

My mouth is drying up,
darkness is closing in.

The windows are shattered
and engulfed in flames.

Shall I jump?
Am I high?

It's too late now,
I might as well say goodbye.

That enemy is evil,
pure, pure evil.

All that's to say now,
is . . .

Goodbye,
goodbye,
goodbye.

Baljinder Singh Manak (11)
Timbercroft Primary School, Plumstead

The Beauty Of Nepal

The snowcapped mountains,
Were ribbons of beauty,
    This is Nepal.

The green hills were high and low,
There was no pollution in sight,
    This is Nepal.

There are many rivers and lakes
And stunning beauty of nature,
    This is Nepal.

There are different types of cultures,
There are different types of religions,
But people love each other,
    This is Nepal.

World's highest mountain,
Full of natural beauty,
Many historical places,
Full of interesting history,
This is known as . . .
    My country Nepal.

Bibek Gurung (11)
Timbercroft Primary School, Plumstead

Out On The Road

Out on the road
Where all the buildings burn

Then fall with the Devil's children
And exploding bombs

People flee to the underground, petrified
While others try to get out of buildings

And a man scatters across the road
Then trembles into a building

He sees panicking and choking people
And hears the screams blending with air raid siren

He tastes the disgusting taste of fear
So if he comes to your station

Let him in
Let him in
Let him in

Now he's in the underground
As terrified as a mouse

Everyone sits silently
As still as boulders

The air raid alarm is still going
With the constant screaming

In every bed
A groan will begin

And then a noise can be heard
So people stand up

Ring
Ring
Ring . . .

Jack Cole (10)
Timbercroft Primary School, Plumstead

Alert

Out on the street
Where crumbling houses

Fall like packs of playing cards
Landing on the ground

And frozen children
In their own shadows

Sirens blend with
The horrid screams

And the breath of the
Smoke clutters the sky

Alerted of the danger
Another owner trembles

A passer-by stares
With fear in their eyes

World burns and burns

Here at safety
Down underground

Imagining hot gold fire
Burning their ankles

But at last as we all stare,
You're not alone

You can hear screams
But only faint as a whisper

When you hear
A loud bang, a bomb . . .

Boom!
Boom!
Boom!

Amy Vardy (11)
Timbercroft Primary School, Plumstead

Out On The Street

Out on the street
Where crumbling houses
Fall like packs of playing cards

Smoke rises
Beyond the misty sky

Flames through his veins like
The hot burning sun

The breath of the smoke
Turns to fire

The cries from baby children
Not knowing what's going on

A man walks along
Completely full of fear

When the terrified man comes
To the door

Run away
Run away
Run away!

Charlie-Jane Smith (10)
Timbercroft Primary School, Plumstead

Spring's Coming

Spring's coming, spring's coming
Hooray, hooray, hooray
Spring's coming, spring's coming
A start to a new day.

Spring showers
Rise the flowers
And make them look like rainbows.

Watch the hares
Watch the rabbits
Come out of their burrow.

See the grass
As soft as velvet
And we run to and fro.

We see the sun
That is bright
And so . . .

Spring's coming, spring's coming
Hooray, hooray, hooray
Spring's coming, spring's coming
And I hope it stays that way!

Elisha Grant (9)
Timbercroft Primary School, Plumstead

The Blitz

Out on the street
Where crumpling houses
Fall like playing cards

Like matching scars on fingers
With flames burning and licking them up between

Fire brigades are sounding in the distance,
Fearfully and fiercely coming to the rescue
Their shadows following behind

Mouths are screaming
Bombs, bombs, fire, help

I run as though competing in the Olympic Games
Where am I going? I'm looking behind. What do I see?

A man is limping as fast as he can
Alone and searching for his family

The burning flames reaching up to the skies
Incredible heat flying high

Tiny feet prancing around
Not sure where to go - just making ring after ring

Here in the underground amongst smoke and rubble
The heart of the town is at stake

Flames up above burning bright
From red and yellow and gold and blue

It's so hot you can almost hear it
Pet cats snarling and screeching back at it

My marathon nearly complete
Where can I go to escape this heat?

Safe to hide out - I hear them cry
Let him in
Let him in
Let him in.

Hasina Simms (10)
Timbercroft Primary School, Plumstead

World War II

Out on the street
Where crumbling houses

Fall like packs of playing cards
And windows smash like little pieces of candy

And sirens blast
And bombers attack

Fires burning
Yellow as the sun

Smoke rises
Ashes remain

Bang!
Boom!
Bang!

People running underground
Squashed in the dark

Silence
Followed by whistle and bang

Sirens sound again
All clear

Walking through the rubble
Homes and lives destroyed

Crying
Sobbing
Crying.

Douglas Bassett (11)
Timbercroft Primary School, Plumstead

The Blitz

Out on the street
where crumbling houses
fall like rows of dominoes

searing into bursts of flames
in the smoky mist of air

and plants burn
on their life

and the coughs of families
choke like a chip
stuck in the windpipe

hangs in rags
under the dark cloudy sky.

A petrified man is
cautiously creeping alone

on the dilapidated tar
his sweaty feet
pound and pound.

Here in a gloomy tunnel
in the heart of the city

the blankets are snug, warm,
soft and comfortable.

Feel the cosiness,
like a dog in the sunshine

breathing heavily
all over the garden.

When the petrified man
creeps to the tunnel

calm him down
calm him down
calm him down.

Kamil Bhagwathpersad (11)
Timbercroft Primary School, Plumstead

World War II

Out on the streets
Where crumbling houses
Fall like packs of playing cards,

In the foggy smoke
The cars and houses burn,

The breath of the smoke
Turns to fire,

Hangs till
Someone puts it out,

The people are walking
Alone,

On the bombed street
There,

Rags
Drag and drag.

Here in the underground
At the edge of town,

We're huddled up
And cold,

You can feel the cold
Like a cut,

Breathe quietly
You can hear,

When the Germans
Are gone,

When the siren
Stops . . .

Come out
Come out
Come out.

Emma Small (10)
Timbercroft Primary School, Plumstead

The Intimidated Man

Out on the gloomy road
Where collapsing buildings

Crack their teeth hastily
With the bomb's heated children

And people are intimidated
By the flaming houses

And the breath of charred objects
Rises like hot steam from coffee

The fear never ceases
Running through his veins

A petrified man
Is sprinting alone

On the liquorice-black road
His cold

Mind
And
Brain.

Here in a snug underground
In the heart of the railway

People are waving
With warm, welcoming smiles

Breathe softly
Under the cosy blankets

When the intimidated man
Arrives at a dull hole

Let him in
Let him in
Let him in.

Harman Gainda (10)
Timbercroft Primary School, Plumstead

The Blitzed

Out on the street
Where crumbling houses
Fall like packs of playing cards

People run, scream and yell,
The icy wind whistles around.

The smell of fire, the thoughts,
The taste of fear and danger rushing through.

The breath of the fire and smoke,
The darting of the flames.

Smoke rises
From charred remains.

Hangs in rags
Under the rolling moon.

A man is trembling
And stumbling alone!

On a cola-black road
It is bare.

Sirens
Ring and ring!

Here in a cold but safe underground
Under the earth

People cry, whimper and sob,
Play, stare and laugh.

You can hear the bombs
Like an aggressive dog.

Breathe deeply,
Stay alive.

But when a man knocks
On the underground door

Let him in,
Let him in,
Let him in!

Lucy Dean (11)
Timbercroft Primary School, Plumstead

Blitz Road

Down in South London,
Where ancient houses

Burn amongst the market
In the smoky town

Which forces people
To delay moving to their shelters

As they taste the fear
Like murky saltwater of the Thames

Which hangs in rags
Beneath the midnight moon

A man is walking,
Soon to run.

On the cobbled avenue
Cold as ice

And he runs
And runs.

But down in the dripping, damp underground
In the heart of London

People are sleeping
With blankets and pillows

You can taste the horror above
Like a scary film.

Tension everywhere,
Every room.

When the man has made it
He hammers the door

Let him in,
Let him in,
Let him in.

Luke McBride (10)
Timbercroft Primary School, Plumstead

Blitz - Out On The Street

Out on the street
where crumbling houses

fall like dominoes
as bombs scatter

and then explode.
Flames as hot as the sun

burn and flash
through everything they touch.

Smoke licking the buildings
gathers no one around.

A man is walking,
walking alone:

On the ash road
his cold

body
shivers
and shivers.

As the siren stops
still nothing freezes.

Everyone is still afraid,
the fear is still rising.

The man is walking alone,
he needs to find help.

Bang, bang, bang!
Someone knocks on the door.

Let him in,
let him in,
let him in.

Simran Sembi (11)
Timbercroft Primary School, Plumstead

Out On The Street

Out on the street
Where houses

Fall like
Packs of playing cards

And houses burn
Like toast in a volcano

Hangs in rags
Under the bellowing sirens

A man is running
Running away

On the battered black road
His trembling

Feet
Run away
And away

Here in a burnt house
At the heart of the street

The fire is burning
Red, yellow and gold

You can hear the bombs
Like a burning lion

He is breathing slightly
In every room

When the man
Comes to the underground

Let him in
Let him in
Let him in.

Andrew Barrett (10)
Timbercroft Primary School, Plumstead

World War II

Out on the street
Where crumbling houses

Fall like packs of playing cards
And the windows smash into little pieces

And sirens drone
Blend with the fire brigade

And fire rises
From the building

A panicking man
Waits alone.

Bang!
Bang!
Bang!

Here in a crowded tunnel
At the underground

The tunnel is freezing
Black, white and dirty

You can hear the bombing
Like a mummy lion

Breathe softly
In every place.

When the panicking man
Comes to the door,

Let him in,
Let him in,
Let him in.

Jonathan Sinda (10)
Timbercroft Primary School, Plumstead

Summertime

Summertime is finally here now,
Everybody's going to shout out wow!
Summertime should take a bow.

1, 2, 3, 4, what time do we adore? . . . Summertime.
4, 5, 6, 7, summer's as bright as a lemon,
7, 8, 9, 10, summer's better than the old Big Ben!

Let's all go to the beach,
And then we can reach,
A nice ripe peach!

1, 2, 3, 4, what time do we adore? . . . Summertime.
4, 5, 6, 7, summer's as bright as a lemon,
7, 8, 9, 10, summer's better than the old Big Ben!

We will have fun,
In the nice bright sun,
Because all the hard work has been done!

1, 2, 3, 4, what time do we adore? . . . Summertime.
4, 5, 6, 7, summer's as bright as a lemon,
7, 8, 9, 10, summer's better than the old Big Ben!

Rupinder Kaur Sembhi (11)
Timbercroft Primary School, Plumstead

The World Around Us

The world around us is fading so quick it's unbelievable
Which is my point, no one does believe it!
I made this poem to spread my word!

Forests are dying
Animals are crying
Some of us are sighing
Where happy things used to be
There is no sound in the last tree
We, we, we . . .
We are the ones to blame
People came
And they are still not ashamed
Of what they did and are doing now.

Emily Wallace (9)
Waltham St Lawrence Primary School, Reading

SATs

Hard work. No fun. Just tests,
That's all that Year 6 gets.
Sharpening pencils till it's 1 inch small.
Children get overloaded and then start to bawl.

Pupils are obsessed with getting level 5s,
So that they can become doctors and try to save lives.
But what will happen when they reach high school?
Will they turn bad or try to stay cool?

100% is an impossible score.
So revision is becoming more and more.
We all believe
That we can achieve!

Teachers give us so much support.
We're very thankful for what they taught.
SATs are hard for a bit,
But eventually, you'll get used to it.

Shivani Nathu (11)
Wembley Primary School, Wembley

A School Day

Come on children,
Take off your bags and coat,
I am your new teacher
And I like to boast!

If you come through the door,
You'll see I have a jigsaw,
Break it up,
Put it together again,
It's playtime but you have to stay indoors,
It's starting to rain.

Stop playing,
It's maths time now,
Let's add together,
Could you tell me how?

Now it's lunchtime,
Eat your food,
Hurry up or I won't be in a good mood.

Hurry up,
Lunch is finished,
Have you had fun?
I ate a sugar bun.
Now it's art, tear the newspaper apart!
Now it's home time,
Get in line.

Alexandra Wilkie
Wembley Primary School, Wembley

Birthday Poem

A birthday party for a teacher,
Is the best thing we can do,
And if you are very good,
We might invite you.

We even had a birthday cake
And music we hope she would like,
She is 28 today
And I hope she can ride a bike.

Everyone knows,
That we like her the best,
We like Miss Mafrica,
Better than the rest!

Sabina Lichacz (8)
Wembley Primary School, Wembley

My Star

My star . . .
My star holds . . .
A rose as red as blood,
A rainbow shimmering about,
A sapphire's eye as blue as the sky,
A stream of sunlight passing through,
As golden as a jewel.
My star holds . . .
A frosty snowflake from the Arctic
And the flow of the ocean,
My star gleams everywhere
In the pitch-black sky.

Delaram Imantalab-Kordmahaleh (9)
Wembley Primary School, Wembley

The Sun

The sun came up so that the moon could rest,
Its golden light made me feel the best!
Then the clouds came and they said to me,
'We'll spoil this day, just wait and see!'
Then the sun came and chased them out to sea,
He said, 'They're only scared of me!'
Then the moon came up so the sun could rest
And he said, 'That sun really is the best . . .'

Joseph McGovern (10)
Wembley Primary School, Wembley

A Fierce Lion

Your mane is like trees in the wind.
Your tail wags like a shaggy rug.
Your teeth are like daggers.
Your nose is wet like a sponge
And your roar sounds like thunder.
You terrify me!

Jelisa Johnson (9)
Wembley Primary School, Wembley

Shimmery Sea

Salty, salty sea, you inspire me.
How salty you can be.
Glorious sea you make me scream!
The sea in Jamaica is wonderful to me.
The sea sounds like it's going to cover me.

Gem-Jeni Findlater (8)
Wembley Primary School, Wembley

The Gloomy Forest

A deep, dark forest
Deep as the sea
Gloomy green creature as scary as can be
You think it is a cute creature
But it is dangerous and it can give you poison
But you can be a mythical creature and beware.

Nisharan Raja (9)
Wembley Primary School, Wembley

Winter Snow - Haiku

I am freezing cold,
I am happy winter came,
I am glad right now.

Sahar Ezzat (8)
Wembley Primary School, Wembley

Just One Question

There is something inside
Which I cannot describe
Like something out of a dream
Haunting me
A true passion
A feeling of the unknown
An ache in my heart
Paining me
Thoughts in my brain
But trust and faith in my heart
Tears in my eyes
Showing emotion.

Just one question, what is this feeling?

Fiona Beeby (10)
Wembley Primary School, Wembley

Mathematics

M ean, mode, medium
A re so hard
T asty and sweet
H ard but more difficult
E njoyable and sometimes fun
M arvellous and good
A mazing but tricky
T ired and exhausted
I nteresting
C hallenging and the best
S hining.

Angel (10)
Wembley Primary School, Wembley

My Love

You are my pure amour.
As we kiss it is tender.
You are the only one I can adore.
You are my true love sender.

When you leave my house I cry.
Our love is true.
I want to die.
We will get through.

I cannot bare to part.
You are fantastic.
You are my jam tart.
Without you I'm frantic.

I truly love you.
I hope you love me too.

Natalie Marie Barracliffe (11)
Wembley Primary School, Wembley

I Am . . .

Sports, intelligence, friendship.
I like surprises and dancing around.
Success, image and having fun
Are all important to me.
I like to achieve anything I am capable of doing.
I can achieve anything if I believe in myself.
I am perfect in my world
But I can change when it all gets to my head.
I like a neat and organised life.
I hate messy places.
I hate traitors.

This is me.

Urvi Shah (11)
Wembley Primary School, Wembley

Vampires

V illainous creatures
A dventurous monsters
M angy vampires
P reposterous bats
I ncredible speed
R ats for dinner
E xtraordinary flight
S weep down at night

Frazer Mahoney Pitter (10)
Wembley Primary School, Wembley

Afghanistan

The Afghan government should ban bombs and guns
That's why our people die in war,
Why don't you just let the kids have fun?
So please answer my question, why do you do this?

In Afghanistan you used to see flowers
But now you will only see exploded tanks,
Most of the poor people would like a warm shower,
Mostly people die because of explosions.

Sayed Tabibi (11)
Wembley Primary School, Wembley

Winter - Cinquain

Winter
Snowflakes falling
Making giant snowmen
Freezing cold and enjoyable
Coldness.

Fahad Khawaja (8)
Wembley Primary School, Wembley

Man Utd

M agnificent teamwork
A wesome speed
N ever losers

U nbeatable
T echnique
D efenders of all titles.

Ahmed Mohamed (11)
Wembley Primary School, Wembley

Going To High School

Going to high school is a nervous thing to do,
Because at the same time you're leaving your best friends too.
This is the time you are meant to move on,
From now on primary school is gone!

Going to high school may be hard,
It may cover over 50,000 yards!
In September we will go frequently,
For we will be as busy as a bee!

Going to high school is saying bye to your primary teachers,
As a present, I gave them their favourite book, Special Features.
On the last day I'll say farewell,
And when they see me, it will hopefully ring a bell!

Rohisha Luchun (11)
Wembley Primary School, Wembley

Fool Brothers

Brothers are always fools,
They think that they are cool,
They always tell us lies,
But they are never shy.

Sometimes they are kind,
But they watch us all the time,
They are the ones who make us laugh,
They are the ones who make us cry.

I like my brother very much,
Though he is so annoying,
I like my brother very much,
Though he is not sharing.

Sakshi Amit Shastri (10)
Wembley Primary School, Wembley

In The Streets Of India

In the streets of India, lonely and sad I sit.
Day and night, tears roll down my cheeks
My heart is filled with anguish.
I clutch a bundle of newspapers and matchsticks,
As I see the great women with luxury saris pass
And men with silk, rich turbans also carrying a boastful tongue.
I stare at the rajas on their elephants with their servants.
Dogs lick my wounds and steal the dry bread the baker
put in the refuse.
I lose heart and courage.
I lie awake at night and watch the fireworks and the starry heavens.
I count the stars and dream that one day I will be married
To a merchant and wear a colourful sari with pearls and
wear bangles.
I dream that I will sit on an elephant and ride in the city square
with my head up.
My soul bursts with sorrow and my eyes grow weary.
My bones grow weak and my body grows tired
But tomorrow is a new day, let us rejoice!
Let's not be downcast for we do not know what surprises it holds.

Jessica Julien (11)
Wembley Primary School, Wembley

Parrots - Haiku

Parrots are nice birds
Parrots repeat what you say
Parrots are so bright.

Bakhtawar Malik (8)
Wembley Primary School, Wembley

Young Writers Information

We hope you have enjoyed reading this book - and that you will continue to enjoy it in the coming years.

If you like reading and writing poetry drop us a line, or give us a call, and we'll send you a free information pack.

Alternatively if you would like to order further copies of this book or any of our other titles, then please give us a call or log onto our website at www.youngwriters.co.uk

Young Writers Information
Remus House
Coltsfoot Drive
Peterborough
PE2 9JX

(01733) 890066

FOREWORD

Over three decades ago, I left Edinburgh's Royal Mile for Aberdeen to further my career with Tennent Caledonian Breweries. My first-floor flat, located diagonally opposite John Knox's House, still holds special memories. At 24, the purchase was my debut into the property market and it proved beneficial. Not in terms of monetary value upon its sale, but also nostalgia. As a consequence, Awakening was written. Although the third novel in The **Adventures In time series, it's a personal favourite.**

DM

DEDICATION

This book is dedicated to the church I attended as a boy and teenager in Granton, Edinburgh. Thank you for Christian teachings and development.

Special thanks to Elaine Stone.

CHAPTER 1

JUNE 1967

On an amiable Saturday morning, Charlie Carsell-Brown and his eight-year-old son, James, sat outside their home in the family car. Whilst Charlie waited for his wife, Debbie, he tapped a forefinger on the steering wheel. James, in the rear passenger seat, fidgeted with a chrome window handle. As he glanced up, Charlie observed Debbie lock the door and then walk towards the car. He leaned sideways and pushed down the front passenger door handle. Debbie stepped inside and closed the door.

"At last!" Charlie sighed. "We want to get there today."

"You're too impatient." Debbie smiled. "Besides, I want to look my best for your aunt."

"Is it far to her house, Mum?" asked James.

"We'll arrive in Ardrishaig around lunchtime." Charlie turned the Ford Corsair's ignition key.

"Hopefully, just before."

As Charlie glanced at his wife, she wound down the window handle, and the car moved off. Debbie observed, "It's plush this car isn't it? Much better than the Anglia."

"It's a reliable car." Charlie tapped the dashboard. "No more breakdowns, I hope."

"Stop at the newsagent, I'll buy comics for James." Debbie looked back. "What would you like?"

"The Hotspur, and Victor, please, Mum. Oh, and the Valiant."

Debbie smiled. "Anything else?"

"A packet of Mintollas."

The car slowed down, and stopped outside the newsagent, where a display of assorted sweets and chocolate bars could be seen. James put his nose against the car window.

"No time for a chat." Charlie grinned.

"I won't be long." Debbie opened the door, and stepped out.

"Dad, why did you buy another car? I liked the Anglia.'

"This is faster." Charlie looked back at James. "It'll take us to Ardrishaig in less time than what the Anglia would have."

Debbie returned with a brown carrier bag, and as she closed the door, Charlie raised his dark eyebrows: "That was quick."

"I'll be longer next time."

Charlie laughed.

Debbie gave James his comics and sweets, then took out two magazines, plus a newspaper. Folding the empty bag, she laid it at her feet. James put two comics aside, and started to read his favourite.

"Charlie, what route have you decided on?"

"Head for Glasgow, then Crianlarich, and onto Inveraray. Ardrishaig is only a short distance from Inveraray. The journey should take us about three and a half hours."

James looked at his dad. "That's a long time."

Charlie opened the glove compartment. "Where's the road map?"

James put down his comic then picked up a yellow booklet off the black floor mat.

"Here it is, Dad."

"Let me have a look at it."

James handed the map to his dad who opened it at a particular page. "That appears the best route." Charlie glanced at Debbie. "I'll leave the map on the dashboard, just in case we get lost."

"Lost?" Debbie raised her thin blonde eyebrows.

After leaving the newsagent, a once-popular location came into view, prompting Debbie to glance sideways. "James, there's the old Granton railway station."

"Where?" He lifted his head, looking around.

Debbie pointed. "Back there, we've just passed it."

"It shouldn't have been closed, especially, with more car users." Charlie glanced at Debbie. "A local train service would be an ideal alternative." He paused. "Dr Beeching has a lot to answer for."

"Perhaps the trams should also have been retained."

"You never know what the future holds, trams may become popular again."

Debbie smiled. "Like men's double-breasted jackets, and wide ties?"

"Don't exaggerate, they won't return."

"As with the trams, Charlie."

"Dad, could we have taken the train today?"

"There are no trains to Ardrishaig, James."

When stopping at the traffic lights on congested Queensferry Road, Charlie looked at Debbie.

"Which magazines did you buy?"

"Vogue and Rolling Stone."

"Let's have some music." Charlie leaned forward, and turned the left-hand knob.

"Why did a radio not come with the car?"

As Charlie shrugged his shoulders, the lights changed, and he drove off. "It would have saved me the trouble."

"Perhaps, in the future, all new cars will be fitted with a radio." Debbie licked her forefinger and turned a page.

"Why did you buy a newspaper, there's not much in a Saturday edition?"

"The 'Express' has a fashion supplement."

James looked up. "Dad, The Saint is on tonight."

Charlie glanced at James's reflection in the front mirror.

"Will we be home in time to watch it?"

"Maybe, what's on TV tonight, Debbie?"

"Hold on." She put down her magazine, and picked up the newspaper. "The Saint is on at seven o'clock, followed by The Fugitive at eight. On BBC 2, it's a repeat of The

"What does stress mean, Mum?"

"I'll explain later." Debbie wound down the window handle further. "Ah, that's better."

James touched the window handle beside him.

Charlie glanced in the front mirror. "Leave the window closed, James."

James picked up a comic.

"At your uncle's funeral, Olivia looked well, considering."

"She's a strong individual. As a young child, she lost her father in the First World War." Charlie glanced at Debbie. "Never knew him, perhaps that made her independent."

"At the funeral, your mother and father called her Ann."

"Ann is her middle name."

Debbie looked behind.

"Almost finished my comics." James turned a page.

"It won't be long until we reach Ardrishaig."

"Given the length of journey, James hasn't been restless. Whenever I was in my parent's car, I couldn't sit still."

"No comment."

Following a trouble-free drive through sunny picturesque Argyll, James started to rub his stomach. "Mum, I don't feel well."

Debbie looked back.

"I'll stop at this lay-by," suggested Charlie.

When the car came to a halt, Debbie and James got out, followed by Charlie. Whilst Debbie took James for a walk around the lay-by, Charlie stood admiring the lochside view of lush green valleys. A short time later, Debbie and James returned to the car, and the family resumed their journey.

Debbie glanced back at James. "Feeling better?"

He nodded.

As Charlie wound down the driver's window, Debbie's magazines flew off the dashboard. "Not too far down!" She picked them up, and gazed out her window. "The view is stunning." Debbie looked at James. "Not be long now." He's still as white as a sheet. She turned to Charlie. "Your aunt stays just outside Ardrishaig, doesn't she?"

"About half a mile."

Debbie kept a watchful eye on James, and the car sped towards the family's destination, and then a signpost came into view.

"Here we are at last - Dochar." Charlie sighed.

"Dad, isn't it Ardrishaig?"

"Your great-aunt lives half a mile from Ardrishaig."

"Does the property have a name, Charlie?"

"Docharnea."

"There it is!" Debbie pointed.

Charlie slowed the car down, then turned into a long narrow driveway with trees on either side. Forty yards later, he stopped outside a cream villa.

"Your aunt must have a fit gardener." Debbie looked around. "There's Olivia, she must have heard the car."

Charlie, Debbie and James, got out, and approached the main entrance.

"Good afternoon," said Charlie.

"It's lovely to see you again." Olivia hugged her nephew. "You too, Deborah."

"Olivia, this is our son, James." Debbie put her hands on his shoulders.

Olivia bent down. "Hello, young man, how are you?"

"Fine, thank you."

"How old are you now?" Olivia smiled.

"Eight. Nine in December."

Olivia glanced at Debbie. "Informative, as well as polite. Come inside, Pearl will soon serve us tea in the lounge."

James looked at his mother.

Olivia led her guests into the reception area, through a hallway and then into a large bright public room. Debbie cast her gaze around the room. "It's fabulous, especially, the cornice." She stared upwards.

"The property is over seventy years old, however, I like

to keep it in the Victorian mould. I must admit, it takes a lot of upkeep, but worth the time and expense. If you wish, Deborah, I will let you see other parts of the villa later."

"This property is a complete contrast to our house. I adore character in a building and tell Charlie there's nothing like a traditional property."

"Wait until the maintenance bills appear."

Charlie laughed.

"It's nice, isn't it, Charlie?" Debbie continued to gaze.

He nodded.

"Please, have a seat."

Debbie, Charlie and James sat on a beige coloured couch and Olivia opposite on a matching two-seater. "How are your mother and father, Charlie?"

"They're both well. Father has started playing bowls at a local club. He's tried to get mother interested."

"Does she still paint?"

"Last year she painted a scene of the Fife coastline, and it now hangs above our living room fireplace."

"Your mother is a talented lady. I advised her many years ago to rent a studio and sell paintings. She can have my coach house free of charge."

"Too far from Newhaven."

Debbie smiled.

James fiddled with his sandal strap.

"True, I can't envisage your parents moving, they have lived in that house all of their married life."

"They love that house, and it's close to father's office."

"Do you use the coach house?" asked Debbie.

"No, Deborah, it has lain dormant for many years. Charlie's grandfather used it to store old furniture. When William and I moved here, the items were sent to a charity shop, coincidently, the one I now run."

Charlie gave a wide grin.

James whispered, "What's a coach house, Mum?"

"A long time ago, large properties like this had someone

who stayed in a separate house, called a coach house. People did not have cars in those days, and this person drove a coach pulled by horses."

"How fast would it go?"

"Adequate for the Victorians, but not us," said Charlie.

Olivia leaned towards James. "Would you like to see the coach house?"

James nodded.

Olivia looked at Debbie. "I will take James to see it, and in the meantime, have a look round Docharnea."

"Terrific." Debbie smiled.

Olivia took James's hand, led him out of the rear entrance and across a grey gravel courtyard. James stared at the distinctive black and white two-storey building.

"Would you like to look around inside?"

James nodded. "Yes."

Olivia opened the main door, which led to an upstairs floor. Taking James's hand, they climbed a creaky wooden staircase, and entered an empty room.

"This is where hay was stored for two horses." Olivia looked at James. "The old stable is underneath this room."

"Can I see it?"

"When we go back downstairs."

James was taken into another room, which had a fireplace, two dark wooden chairs, and a wall mirror. It also contained a musty smell.

"This is where the coachman lived, James."

At that moment, a woman's voice could be heard from the downstairs entrance. Olivia went to the top of the stairs. "Yes, Pearl?" shouted Olivia.

"An urgent call," Pearl shouted, "it's about your trip to London."

Olivia looked at James. "I will be back in a jiffy, stay here."

James nodded.

After his great-aunt walked downstairs, James cast his

The woman again glanced at the driver. "What is your name?"

"James."

The woman whispered to the driver, "I haven't seen those types of clothes before." She looked at James. "Would you like us to try and find your parents, James?"

He nodded.

The driver and his passenger stepped out of the vehicle and closed their respective doors. The woman loosened the pink bow under her neck, and the driver raised his goggles. James stared at their strange attire. "Why do you tie a bow round your neck?" He looked up at the woman.

She smiled. "It's so my hat won't blow off."

"Why do you wear a cap?" James looked at the driver's head.

"To keep my head warm." The driver gave a slight grin.

"Do people not wear hats where you come from?" said the woman in a curious tone of voice.

"Sometimes."

The woman whispered to the driver, "is this boy ill, maybe he has had an accident? He appears delirious."

James walked with both adults up the driveway to the villa's main door. The driver pulled on the brass doorbell handle and it rang. With no answer, he tried again. He looked at the woman. "Nobody appears to be at home."

The woman looked at James. "This is the property?"

"Yes, then my great aunt took me into the coach house."

"The coach house?" asked the driver.

"Where is the coach house, James?"

"At the back. I will take you there."

The driver and woman followed James to the coach house. When they arrived, one of the doors was ajar. The woman looked at James. "Here?"

James nodded. "My great-aunt took me upstairs to look around, then had to leave."

"Why?" said the driver.

"The housekeeper called to her from downstairs."

"What did she say to your great-aunt, James?"

"A person from London was on the telephone."

"Telephone?" The driver frowned.

"What is your great-aunt's name, James?"

"Olivia."

"And your parents?" said the driver.

"Charlie and Debbie." James's voice grew raspy. "Where did they go?" He sniffed.

The woman knelt down beside him. "Don't worry, James, we will find them." She looked at the driver, then James. "We will take you to the local police station."

James stared at the woman.

She smiled. "They will find your parents, and your great-aunt." The woman brought out a white handkerchief from her jacket pocket, and wiped James's eyes.

He sniffed.

"Better?" She smiled.

James nodded.

"My name is Rosalind, and this is my husband, Edward."

Rosalind took James's hand, and all three returned to the vehicle. Edward opened the rear door, and James entered. He sat on a cream leather double-seat, then fidgeted. Rosalind sat in the front passenger seat and tied a bow under her neck. After starting the engine, Edward got into the vehicle, and resumed his driver's position. He replaced his goggles, and Rosalind sat upright with hands clasped together on her lap. As the vehicle moved off, she glanced back at James. "Did your parents bring you here, James?"

"My dad drove us here."

"When did you leave Edinburgh?" said Edward.

"This morning, at eight-thirty."

"When did you arrive here, James?" said Rosalind.

"One o'clock, I think." James looked towards Rosalind. "Will the policemen find my parents?"

"They will do their best," said Rosalind.

"Does your father have a fast vehicle?" said Edward.

"It's a Ford Corsair."

"A Ford Corsair?" said Edward.

James nodded. "It's much faster than the Anglia."

"Does it look similar to this vehicle, James?" said Rosalind.

James shook his head. "No."

Edward glanced at Rosalind.

"Why does the engine need a handle to start it?" said James.

Edward glanced back at James. "It causes a spark and then ignites the engine."

Rosalind turned around. "Does your mother wear similar clothes to me?"

James shook his head. "A smaller dress, and no jacket or hat."

Rosalind looked at Edward.

"What does your father wear?" said Edward.

"Just a shirt, and trousers."

"No necktie, jacket or cap!" said Edward.

"Does he wear driving goggles, James?" said Rosalind.

"No." James cast his gaze around the vehicle. "I have seen a car like this in old films."

"A car?" said Edward.

"At a cinema where you stay?"

"No, at home on our television set."

Rosalind looked back at James. "A television set! What's that?"

"I watch films and other programmes on it."

"Programmes?" said Edward.

"The Saint, Man in a Suitcase, also The Prisoner. The Saint is on tonight, hope I won't miss it!"

Edward and Rosalind looked at each other with bemused expressions.

The 1914 shiny maroon Rover arrived at Ardrishaig's police station. Edward and his wife got out, however, James was reluctant to follow. Rosalind took his hand and smiled: "Let's try and find your parents and great-aunt."

Holding onto her hand, James stepped out of the vehicle and followed Rosalind and Edward into the building. As no one was about, Edward knocked on the polished wooden reception desk. A tall well-built police sergeant appeared from a back room and acknowledged them. "Good afternoon, how can I help?"

Rosalind glanced at James. "Sergeant, this boy has lost his parents and great-aunt."

The sergeant looked over the desk, then downwards.

James stared upwards.

"As I drove through Dochar, he was alone outside one of the properties," said Edward.

"Which one, sir?"

"Docharnea."

The sergeant looked at him. "The family who live there are on holiday in Inverness." Staring at James, he added, "those are unusual clothes."

"That is how we found him," said Rosalind.

"Has he run away from a circus?"

"There is no circus in Argyll this summer," said Edward.

"What is your name, son?" The sergeant grabbed a pencil and piece of paper.

"James."

The sergeant wrote it down. "Surname?"

Rosalind looked at James and smiled. "Last name."

"Carsell-Brown."

The sergeant looked up, then at the couple. "That's the name of the family who live at Docharnea."

"Then he is a relative," said Edward.

The sergeant stayed silent.

"They have a boy?" asked Rosalind.

The sergeant nodded.

James looked at Rosalind. "I'm thirsty."

"Would you like a glass of lemonade?" said the sergeant.

James nodded. "Please."

A constable appeared from the back room, and then lifted documents from a wooden table. The sergeant turned to face him. "Sandy, can you take this young lad into the kitchen, and give him a glass of lemonade?"

"Will do." The constable looked at James. "Come this way, son."

After James followed him into a kitchen, the sergeant shook his head. "He isn't from around here with that accent!"

"He told us that his parents came here from Edinburgh in a car, a Ford something," said Rosalind.

"A car?" The sergeant frowned.

"I believe it is another name for automobile, Sergeant," said Edward, "perhaps, an Edinburgh term."

"He talked about a televising."

Edward smiled. "Television, darling."

Rosalind nodded. "A device that screens programmes." She looked at her husband. "The Saint, Prisoner and some other name."

"Man in a Suitcase, I think," added Edward.

The sergeant laughed. "That sounds like the sort of act in a circus. Maybe a show is on tour in the region."

Edward glanced at his wife. "It's a plausible explanation."

She nodded. "Indeed."

"We'll investigate the matter, no doubt someone from a touring show, or circus will report a missing boy."

"What about his parents and great aunt, Sergeant?" asked Rosalind.

"I'm sure they will turn up." He cleared his throat.

She smiled.

"How did he know the name of the family who stay at Docharnea, Sergeant? It is an unusual one."

"Maybe he had spoken to a passer-by, and they mentioned who stayed at the property? In my experience, young boys are notorious for making up stories. We'll look after the boy until a relative or guardian comes along."

"Thank you, Sergeant," said Rosalind.

"Yes, thanks," added Edward.

Rosalind looked at the sergeant. "Can I say goodbye to the boy?"

"Of course, go ahead."

Rosalind thanked the sergeant and then went into the kitchen. The sergeant looked kindly at Edward. "How is Lady Beaumont, sir?"

"My mother is fine, Sergeant, as is my wife."

The sergeant grinned. "Boy or a girl?"

"If it's a boy, Andrew. A girl, Olivia. Hopefully a boy, Sergeant." Edward smiled. "He can follow me into the military."

"Are you on leave for long, sir?"

"Afraid not, Sergeant. I have to report back to my regiment next week."

As his wife returned, Edward adjusted his cap. Rosalind looked at the sergeant. "He enjoys lemonade, you may require another bottle!"

"We'll look after him, Mrs Beaumont."

When the couple departed, the sergeant went into his office, opened a drawer, and took out a file. After browsing through it, he put the file back into the drawer. Lifting his cap from a wooden stand, the sergeant put it on. "Sandy, I'm going out, be back in about an hour."

Sergeant Buchan left the station, retrieved his bicycle, and applied metal leg clips to his black uniform trousers. Manoeuvring onto the road, the village sergeant acknowledged the greetings from passers-by.

Fifteen minutes later, he arrived at a small red sandstone cottage, which overlooked Loch Fyne. After he dismounted, Sergeant Buchan removed the metal trouser clips, put them into his pocket and then approached the front door. A short grey-haired woman answered his authoritative knock.

"Hello, Sergeant, what brings you here?"

Sergeant Buchan tipped his cap. "I'm doing my rounds, Nancy, and thought I'd call in for a chat."

"That's kind of you, come inside."

Following Nancy into the compact living room, Sergeant Buchan closed the door and removed his cap.

"I trust you will have a cup of tea, Sergeant?"

"I never refuse one, Nancy."

She smiled. "Please, sit down."

"Thanks."

Nancy went into the kitchen, and Sergeant Buchan made himself comfortable on a cream floral two-seater couch. Whilst waiting, he studied landscape paintings of Loch Fyne and Ardrishaig, paying particular attention to a portrait of a young man. Several minutes later, Nancy returned with a brown wicker tray, which she laid, on a wooden side table.

Sergeant Buchan cleared his throat.

"Do you take milk and sugar, Sergeant?"

"Only milk, please."

Whilst Nancy poured milk into her guest's cup, Sergeant Buchan once more, looked at a portrait on the wall.

"That's the coachman at Docharnea. It was a parting gift from Elizabeth." Nancy sat down.

"What became of him?"

"He went to Edinburgh."

"Did he come from there?"

Nancy nodded. "He left Docharnea just prior to Elizabeth and her husband moving to New York."

"Do you keep in touch with them?" Sergeant Buchan lifted his blue patterned cup and took a sip.

"I receive an occasional letter."

"Do they enjoy living there?"

"From her letters, it would appear so. Elizabeth's husband works in Wall Street, for an accountancy firm, and she paints."

Sergeant Buchan grinned. "You like her paintings?"

Nancy nodded. "However, she won't have valleys and lochs to paint in New York."

Sergeant Buchan laughed as Nancy sipped her tea. He looked at the plate of digestive biscuits on the table.

"Take one, Sergeant."

He lifted one from the plate. "How is the new family at Docharnea, do they enjoy their surrounds?"

"I believe so, but with me being off sick, Charlotte has to carry out the housekeeping duties."

Sergeant Buchan grinned. "As does my wife."

Nancy laughed, and set her cup on the saucer. "Their current vacation came at an ideal time."

"When do they return?"

"In three days."

The sergeant lifted another biscuit.

"Have there been any unusual occurrences in the village?" Nancy enquired.

Chewing his digestive biscuit, the sergeant shook his head, and took another sip of tea. "However, we do have a boy at the station who has lost his parents."

"Lost his parents!"

Sergeant Buchan nodded. "I'm sure they'll soon appear to collect him."

"A local boy?"

"From Edinburgh."

"Why was he in the area?" Nancy moved forward on her chair.

"Visiting a relative, at Docharnea." Sergeant Buchan set his empty cup on the blue patterned saucer.

Nancy stared at her guest. "Strange, Charlotte didn't mention she was expecting visitors. What is the boy's name?"

"James." The sergeant stood up. "Thanks for the tea and biscuits, Nancy."

Nancy rose from her chair and escorted her guest to the front door. The sergeant opened the door and stood on the grey concrete step. "When do you return to work?"

"A week on Monday. Charlotte will be pleased."

Sergeant Buchan laughed.

"Is the boy at the station?"

"Yes." The sergeant put on his cap. "See you, Nancy."

"Bye, Sergeant."

As Sergeant Buchan cycled off, Nancy closed the door, and pondered. A boy called James, and from Edinburgh, had appeared at Docharnea? Could there be a connection to that other James she had met in 1896?

Two hours after Sergeant Buchan departed; Nancy made her way to Ardrishaig's police station with a package. It included a small bowl of elderflower fruit jelly, an apple tart, plus a book.

When she entered the station, Constable Fraser standing behind the reception desk looked up. "Hello, Nancy, is it Sergeant Buchan you're after? He's out and about doing his rounds."

"No, Sandy, I've come to see the boy." Nancy put a package on the desk.

The constable raised his dark eyebrows. "Lucky him."

Nancy smiled. "It's just a pudding, small cake and something to read."

"A book?"

"Sergeant Buchan said the boy came from Edinburgh, therefore, I've brought him a book by an author born there."

Nancy took a hardback out of the brown package, and showed it to Constable Fraser.

"A Study of Scarlet by Arthur Conan Doyle." Constable Fraser frowned. "The boy is only eight years old."

"Maybe he is intelligent." She laid the book down. "Can I meet him, Sandy?"

"Yes, of course. He is in the back room reading a comic."

After Constable Fraser left reception, Nancy took out the bowl of elderflower fruit jelly and an apple tart. She put them beside the book, and waited. The constable brought James through. "This is Nancy, she has something to give you."

James smiled.

Nancy crouched down. "Do you enjoy jelly pudding, James?"

He nodded.

"And, apple tart?"

His smile got wider.

Nancy stood up, took the pudding and apple tart off the desk, then handed them to James. As he took them, Nancy lifted the book and asked, "have you read this, James?"

He stared at the book.

"It's by Arthur Conan Doyle."

"Has it been made into a film, or a TV series?"

Nancy looked at Constable Fraser.

He shrugged his shoulders.

"I saw a film called Sherlock Holmes last year."

"At a cinema in Edinburgh?" Nancy glanced at Constable Fraser.

James shook his head. "In our house, the film was shown on television." James looked up at Constable Fraser. "My father told me it had been made in 1939."

The puzzled constable looked at Nancy, who had a bemused expression on her rounded face.

James held the book. "Do you have any science-fiction ones? What about The Time Machine? My father saw the film seven years ago and enjoyed it."

"On television?" said Nancy.

James shook his head. "In a cinema."

"I'll see what I can do, James."

"Thank you."

James returned to the back room, complete with Nancy's generous gifts. He continued to read his comic and munched on an apple tart. Nancy smiled at Constable Fraser.

"He has a creative imagination."

Nancy stared towards the back room, then at Constable Fraser. "Has no parent reported a missing boy?"

He shook his head. "Not yet."

"That is strange."

"Sergeant Buchan is investigating."

"What if by tonight, no parent has come forward?"

"He can stay with my wife and daughter."

"Given that the poor boy has lost his parents, he appears fine."

Constable Fraser nodded. "Indeed."

Nancy said goodbye, and left the police station. The boy had a charm, similar to an older person, also called James that Nancy had encountered in the past. Could James the man, and this boy, be the same person? Nancy's instinct leaned towards a positive perception. The boy appeared genuine, and sincere in his peculiar answers to questions. Whilst Nancy walked home, her train of thought turned to a piece of literature from the past. A book, which she had found in the coachman's quarters, sixteen years ago, titled, The Time Machine, by HG Wells.

Nancy entered her cottage, closed the door and went straight to her mahogany writing desk. Opening the drawer, she searched through notepads and letters for two particular diaries. Since becoming the housekeeper at Docharnea in 1896, Nancy had kept them for sentimental reasons. The diaries included instances, which referred to an enigmatic individual called James, who began working as a coachman in 1896. However, several months later, he disappeared. Then, sixteen years later, and not aged in any shape or form, he reappeared seeking his coachman job. As the property had a coachman, no vacancy existed. Then, as fate would have it, the coachman took ill. Thus, James once more filled the role. Nancy found the diaries from 1896 and 1912. She sat down on her fireside chair and started to read the oldest diary. James arrived in the month of April, departing in August. No explanation had been given to Charles or Mary,

Docharnea's owners. Nancy smiled, just as well a different person had taken ownership in 1912. She recalled that James's arrival on both occasions intrigued her. In 1896, he noticed a faulty axle on the coach, and had it repaired. If not, a nasty accident could have ensued. Nancy imagined the steep embankment, on the road from Dochar to Ardrishaig. If an axle broke, and the coach toppled over, it would career down the embankment, with serious injury to the occupants. Nancy put aside the diary, and picked up its counterpart from 1912. She found an entry of interest, and studied it. Hit by a runaway horse, James had ended up in Lochgilphead Hospital. He sustained concussion and severe bruising. However, he had saved Elizabeth, the owner's wife, from serious injury. James had pushed Elizabeth out of the horse's path in the nick of time. Nancy laid down the diary and smiled. Weeks later, when discharged from hospital, James returned to a redundant position. The purchase of an automobile by the owner had rendered Docharnea's coach and two horses obsolete. Nancy looked out of her cottage living room window. Not long after, James vanished for a second time. She speculated, and hoped, that he would one day reappear. Had James done so, albeit, as a boy?

CHAPTER 3

THE ENIGMATIC BOY

The following day, a tall well-groomed lady strutted into the Ardrishaig police station. When she approached the front desk, Constable Fraser looked up and put down his pencil. "Good morning, Mrs Lawson."

"Sergeant Buchan asked me to call round at my convenience."

"About the lost boy?"

The lady nodded. "Until he is spoken for, I am more than happy to look after him."

"That's kind of you, Mrs Lawson. We appreciate your compassion."

The lady looked around the spartan police station. "This is no place for a boy. Besides, my young nephew is staying with me, therefore, the two boys will be company for each other."

"I'll fetch James, he's reading Comic Cuts in our office."

"Then, my nephew and he will have a common interest. Alan looks forward to every new edition."

As Constable Fraser left reception, the lady adjusted her white wide-brimmed hat and then brushed a brown hair off her cream jacket. A young boy with blond hair and unusual clothes appeared with Constable Fraser. Mrs Lawson stared at his white T-shirt, blue shorts and white socks.

"This is James, Mrs Lawson."

Mrs Lawson bent down. "Hello, James. I have a comfortable bedroom for you."

"What about my parents and great-aunt, where are they?" James looked up at Constable Fraser.

"Sergeant Buchan is looking for them, James. When found, he'll let them know where you are."

"My nephew is staying with me and is about the same

age as you. He has lots of Comic Cuts, which you can read."

James grinned up at Constable Fraser. "Terrific."

Mrs Lawson glanced at the constable. "See you later, Sandy."

"Bye."

Mrs Lawson took James's hand, and led him out of the police station. Parked nearby was a shiny burgundy automobile, whose driver adjusted his beige cap. Mrs Lawson walked James to the automobile. "George, you shouldn't keep the engine running, we have to preserve petrol."

"I don't want to start it again, turning the handle gives me a painful wrist."

Mrs Lawson opened the rear passenger door, and James got in, taking a seat on the black leather upholstery. Mrs Lawson closed the door and sat in the front passenger seat. Whilst George put on his driving goggles, Mrs Lawson tied a white bow under her chin. James stared at her unusual hat. The automobile moved off, and headed into the centre of Ardrishaig.

A short time later, the vehicle arrived at a detached property surrounded by well-trimmed green hedges. The driver and his two passengers got out, and entered through the front door. Mr Lawson went upstairs, whilst his wife took James into the kitchen, and sat him down at a wooden table. She smiled his way. "Would you like a glass of lemonade, James?"

"Please."

Whilst Mrs Lawson poured lemonade from a jug into a tumbler, James cast his gaze around the kitchen, and noted an array of silver pots and pans on polished brass hooks. Mrs Lawson set the tumbler in front of James. After he took a sip, she smiled. "Is that good?"

James nodded, and took another sip.

A boy, taller than James, walked into the kitchen. He wore navy blue bell-bottom trousers with a navy blue and white top. James set down his tumbler, and the two boys took stock of each other.

"Alan, this is James," said Mrs Lawson, "he will be staying with us for a short while."

"Splendid."

James stared at Alan.

Alan stared at James's T-shirt.

"James is a visitor to Ardrishaig, Alan."

Alan looked at his aunt. "Can I have some lemonade too, please?"

"Of course."

"And a piece of ginger cake?"

"It will soon be time for dinner, Alan."

"After dinner?"

"Perhaps."

Whilst his aunt poured lemonade, Alan sat opposite James. Once more, he looked at his T-shirt. "Where are you from, James?"

"Edinburgh."

"Does anyone wear similar outfits to mine in Edinburgh?"

James shook his head. "Boys are too young to be sailors."

Listening, Mrs Lawson laid a tumbler of lemonade on the table. Going to a wall cupboard she took out a full bottle of lemonade and filled the jug.

"Why is there no collar on your shirt, James?" asked Alan as he picked up his tumbler and took a sip.

"T-shirts don't have collars."

"Why is it called that?" Alan set his tumbler on the table.

James shrugged his shoulders.

"Your hair is rather short."

"I was at the hairdresser last week."

"What is a hairdresser?" Alan glanced at his aunt.

"Where you go to get a haircut." James sipped his lemonade.

"You mean a barber shop?"

"That name is old-fashioned, they are now called hairdressers. Most barbers have closed. Where I stay, the barber shop is now a baker."

Mrs Lawson looked at James. "Where do you now go for a haircut, James?"

"My mum takes me to Leith, there are lots of hairdressers there."

Mum? "Does she buy clothes for you in Leith?"

James nodded. "Also, B Hyams."

"Where is that?" said Alan.

"The Royal Mile."

Alan looked at his aunt. "Perhaps mother could take me there."

She smiled.

"Father could buy a new top hat, Auntie!"

"A top hat?" said James, with a bemused expression.

"What type of hat does your father wear?" said Alan.

"He never wears one!"

"Not even a bowler?"

James shook his head.

"Does your mother wear a dress like mine, James?"

"It's shorter, and you can see her arms."

Alan looked at his aunt, then James.

"Shorter, and the arms are not covered!" Mrs Lawson raised her eyebrows.

James nodded.

Mrs Lawson looked at her nephew. "Alan, take James into the garden, show him your new swing."

Both boys finished their lemonade, and James followed Alan into a large garden, with a play area. Alan approached the swing, sat on the wooden seat, and was soon moving back and forward. Meanwhile, James stared at a small hut at the edge of the garden.

"My uncle keeps gardening equipment in there." Alan got off the swing. "You have a go."

James sat on the seat, gaining momentum. Soon, the

swing came to a halt, and he got off.

"What's wrong?"

James put a hand on his stomach. "I feel sick."

"Take a deep breath, that's what I do."

As James breathed in and out, Alan returned to the swing. James sat down on the dry grass.

"Do you play rugby, James?" said Alan as he swung back and forward.

"No, I play football," said James as he looked up at Alan. "Have you ever played?"

Alan shook his head. "Our school only has rugby teams."

"Our school only has football teams."

"Is it a private school?"

"Private?"

"Does your father pay school fees?"

"I don't think so."

"My father does, each year." Alan stopped swinging.

"Even when you attend secondary school?"

Alan frowned. "Secondary school, what is that?"

"After I leave primary, I'll attend a secondary school."

"At what age?"

"When I'm twelve. I've four years left at primary school."

"How long do you stay at a secondary school?"

"At least three years."

"I will soon be in my final year at school, then I'll go to Grammar, followed by University."

"What do you want to be when you grow up?"

"My mother would like me to become a lawyer, but I want to be a politician, like father."

"What's a politician?"

Alan stared at James. "A Member of Parliament."

"Guy Fawkes wanted to blow up the Houses of Parliament."

Alan stared. "What do you want to become, James?"

"A football player."

Mrs Lawson stood watching at the kitchen window, and turned to her husband, George, who had just entered. "That young boy has sparked my curiosity."

"In what way?"

Mrs Lawson stared at the garden. "When speaking to Alan, he mentioned that after the age of twelve, he attends a secondary school."

"Secondary school?"

Mrs Lawson nodded. "For at least three years."

Her husband approached the window, and observed James cross-legged on the grass, speaking to Alan. "It must be a fee-paying school. Children leave school at twelve and then have to work unless the family is wealthy."

"Similar to Susan, next door. She learns from her mother on how to become a future good wife." Mrs Lawson glanced at her husband. "My brother-in-law's royal connections should assist Alan's ambition."

"No doubt."

"A Member of Parliament beckons."

"I wager Alan is unaware of his mother's Suffragette activities."

Mrs Lawson put a finger to her mouth.

Her husband smiled.

Alan got off the swing and then sat on the grass beside James. "What games do you play, apart from football?"

"Monopoly."

"What type of game is that?"

"You buy as much property as you can, and the person who has the most, wins."

"How many play?"

"As much as five, boys and girls."

"Girls play it!"

James nodded.

"Where do you get the money from - your father?"

James shook his head. "Money is included with the game."

"It must be an expensive game to buy."

James stared at Alan. "It's not real money."

"Not real?"

"Imitation."

Alan hesitated. "I play Snakes and Ladders and marbles."

"My friends and I play marbles on our school breaks, morning and afternoon."

"Do you play tennis?"

"There are no tennis courts at our school."

Alan raised his head and smirked. "Our school has two tennis courts, a rugby and cricket pitch."

Mrs Lawson came into the garden and Alan looked towards his aunt. "It will soon be time for dinner, please show James where the bathroom is, and he can wash his hands."

"Yes, Auntie." Alan stood up. "This way, James."

James followed, and as he entered the kitchen, spotted a comic on the table and went over for a closer look. Alan paused then handed it to him. "You can read it after dinner."

James looked at the front page. "Comic Cuts."

Alan grinned. "It is the best-selling comic. Comes out every week!"

James turned the pages.

"Have you ever read it?"

"In the police station."

Alan stared.

"I like to read the Hotspur, Valiant and Tiger."

"Are they on sale each week?"

James nodded.

"Is the Tiger about a zoo?"

"It's a sports and adventure comic. My favourite character is Roy of the Rovers!"

"The Rovers?"

James glanced at Alan. "Yes, Melchester Rovers."

"After dinner, you must tell me all about Roy, and his football team."

"Also, Captain Hurricane."

"Being a fast footballer, no doubt that is why he is in charge of the team."

James laughed. "He's an army captain in the Valiant."

When both boys departed the kitchen, Mr Lawson smiled at his wife as she returned from the garden.

"Have you heard of comics called Valiant, Hotspur and Tiger?"

Mrs Lawson shook her head.

"They are on sale in Edinburgh."

"As well as an unusual style of clothes."

Alan returned to the kitchen, approached his aunt and stood still. Turning round to face him, she asked, "what is wrong?"

Alan whispered, "Was James was apprehended?"

"Do not worry. Edward Beaumont and his wife found James all by himself in Dochar, and took him to the police station." Mrs Lawson smiled. "He hasn't been in any trouble."

Alan sighed. "Phew!"

Alan and James kicked a ball to each other in the garden, watched by Mr Lawson and his wife through the kitchen window. "Aren't they supposed to throw a rugby ball at each other?" said Mrs Lawson.

"Since James doesn't play rugby, the oval ball is being used for football."

"One kick in the wrong direction and a window will require a replacement."

Mr Lawson grinned. "At least the ball is a child's size."

His wife remained silent.

"It won't be our young guest who breaks a window, he's adept at kicking an oval ball."

"Snakes and ladders would be less noisy."

Mr Lawson laughed. "The boys may soon tire."

"Hopefully, before my nerves are shattered!"

Several minutes later, Alan picked up the ball, and took a couple of deep breaths. James stood and waited.

"How about a game of marbles?"

"We played this morning."

"Tennis?"

"I haven't played tennis."

"I will show you."

Mrs Lawson looked at her husband sitting at a table reading the Sunday Times. "I will give the boys lemonade."

Mr Lawson raised his head. "Do they appear thirsty?"

"No, but I don't want a tennis ball heading this way."

Mr Lawson laughed, and continued to read the broadsheet newspaper. His wife poured lemonade into two tumblers then took them outside. Receiving them, James and Alan accepted with gratitude. Mrs Lawson returned to the kitchen, and sat opposite her husband.

"There's tension in the Balkans," he said.

"It was the main topic of conversation at the Post Office."

"It will be a welcome change from a discussion about certain locals."

Mrs Lawson laughed.

Mr Lawson murmured, "a volatile situation indeed."

"What's up?"

"This article refers to the Balkans as a 'powder keg' about to go off. There are a number of countries in the region at loggerheads with each other."

Mrs Lawson sat back on the wooden chair. "Thankfully, Britain is many miles away, a conflict will not affect us."

Her husband lowered the newspaper. "If a conflict begins with the smaller countries of Bosnia and Serbia, others could be drawn in."

"Which countries?"

"Russia has an allegiance to Serbia, and Austria with Bosnia."

"Will the larger countries not try to avert a major conflict?"

"You would expect them to, however, this article adds that when a large country mobilises, it is difficult to reverse."

"Thank goodness we are not involved." Mrs Lawson sighed. "At present, our Liberal Government has enough problems."

"Prime Minister Asquith has his hands full with the Irish problem, plus further threats of strike action."

"Not to mention the Suffragettes."

Mr Lawson turned a page, and smiled.

"Why are you smiling?"

"The Football Federation of Brazil has been formed. Due to a lack of amenities, teams will have to play games on the country's beaches." Mr Lawson shook his head. "I can't see Brazil being a force to be reckoned with."

Mrs Lawson got up, and walked to the window, then returned to her seat. Her husband lowered the newspaper.

"The boys are sitting and drinking their lemonade."

"The window panes will remain intact?"

Mrs Lawson nodded.

"James appears fine."

"He's an active boy, who will help keep his mind preoccupied until his parents are traced."

A few minutes later, Alan and James came into the kitchen with their empty tumblers. Alan looked at his uncle, then his aunt.

"Do you want more lemonade?" Mrs Lawson took both tumblers.

"Can we go to the park, Auntie?"

"There are no ball games allowed on a Sunday."

"We can visit the play area."

Mrs Lawson looked at her husband.

He nodded.

Both boys left the property and then headed for the park. When they arrived, June's glorious warm sunshine had brought out the crowds, resulting in queues for the swings and seesaw.

Alan turned to James. "We will have to wait a while."

James sighed.

Alan smiled at James. "It's just as well Auntie didn't dispose of my old togs."

James looked at his outfit, and rolled up the cuffs. As two children came off the seesaw, Alan and James dashed forward. They sat opposite each other, and started to move up and down.

"This is better than my garden swing."

James grinned.

After several minutes, Alan moaned. James stared at his friend and the seesaw came to a standstill.

"What's wrong?"

"I don't feel well."

"Your face has gone white!"

Alan held his stomach.

"Take deep breaths."

Alan managed a wry smile, and both boys got off the seesaw, much to the delight of queuing children. Alan and James left the play area, and sat down on a nearby wooden bench. Alan took several deep breaths.

"How do you feel?"

"Not as bad."

"Let's go down to the canal. My gran told me that sea air is good for you."

"Does she live close to the sea?"

James nodded. "Newhaven."

"In England?"

James shook his head. "Leith."

The boys left Ardrishaig's public park, and made for the canal. When they arrived, as with the park, families had converged in large numbers. Alan looked around, then at his friend. "It took seven years to build."

"Why did they build it?"

"So that commercial boats could make quicker journeys

to other parts of Scotland."

James stared at Alan. "What does commercial mean?"

"Provide food and coal for families and businesses."

"Why don't you have a railway to do that?"

Alan shrugged his shoulders.

"My gran has a railway close to her house!"

"Where does it go?"

"From Granton Harbour to Leith Docks."

"Have you travelled on it?"

James shook his head. "It's not a passenger train."

"Are there any passenger stations in Edinburgh?"

"Waverley and Haymarket. The others are closed."

"Why?"

"Because of Dr Beeching."

"Is he a GP?"

"I'm not sure. I enjoyed my trips to Princes Street on the train."

"It's also closed?"

James nodded. "Two years ago."

"Let's head home, my appetite has returned."

Two young teenage girls with straw boater hats accompanied by parents had stood next to the boys. The father looked at James, then his wife.

"What's up Bill?" She adjusted her cream hat.

"The blond-haired boy with an Edinburgh accent."

"What about him?" The woman glanced back.

"He said that Edinburgh had only two stations, and Princes Street had been closed."

"We went shopping in Princes Street last week."

The husband smiled. "The boy referred to its railway station."

"That remains open too, we took the train from Princes Street to Glasgow."

The husband nodded, looking at James in the distance. "There is also a suburban railway network in and around Edinburgh."

"I'm certain it will still be there!"

"Daddy, can Mary and I have an ice cream cone, please?"

The father turned around.

"A seller." The daughter pointed. "Over there."

The father lifted his dark hat, pulled out a white handkerchief from his flannels, and mopped his brow. "Good idea." He replaced the handkerchief, and replaced his hat. "Let's go."

The husband, wife and smiling daughters walked towards a queue of thirsty customers, which had grown longer.

As the boys left the park, James looked back, then at his friend. "Why do men look as if they're at work?"

Alan stared at James.

"Why do they wear suits to the park?"

Alan looked at the park.

"It's the weekend."

"When visiting a park, what do men in Edinburgh wear?"

"A shirt, and trousers."

"What, no hat?"

James shook his head.

A short while later, the boys arrived at Alan's aunt's house. After they entered from the back door, Mrs Lawson greeted them. James looked at her. "Have my mum and dad been found yet?"

"Sergeant Buchan is still searching, and when he finds them, I will let you know as soon as possible." Mrs Lawson gave James a comforting smile.

"Can we play football in the garden, please, Auntie?"

"It won't be long until dinner." Mrs Lawson glanced at James expression of anticipation. "Just for a short while."

"Thanks, Auntie!"

The boys went into the garden, but shortly after, Alan returned to the kitchen for a glass of water. When his aunt handed it to him, Alan took a sip.

"James appears fine."

"Edinburgh people are strange, Auntie."

"In what way?"

"James told me that men don't wear hats or suits to a park!"

"Oh?" Mrs Lawson raised her eyebrows.

Alan looked towards the garden. "He plays football with a rugby ball."

"Your uncle believes James may become a terrific rugby kicker."

"He is skillful."

Mrs Lawson glanced anxiously out the window.

CHAPTER 4

CAPTIVATED

After they left the vehicle, Edward and Ann walked to a secluded idyllic location. Situated outside Ardrishaig, and away from village glare, it allowed them to spend special times together. However, the couple's relationship remained complicated. Edward had not long been married, and soon he would become a father.

Four months earlier, Edward and Ann met by chance. She had been walking along the edge of a country road, on her way home from work. As Edward drove past in his new vehicle, mud splattered onto a young lady's white dress. When she screamed, the vehicle came to a halt, and Edward got out. Lifting his driving goggles, he walked up to the young lady and raised his cap. "I'm terribly sorry."

She examined her dress.

"I will pay to have it cleaned."

"It's okay." The young lady looked at Edward.

"No, it is my fault, I insist. Allow me to give you a lift home. Where do you stay?'

"A mile from here." The young lady stared. "You're the son of Lady Beaumont?"

"Yes, I am."

She glanced at Edward's vehicle.

"C'mon, you'll be home in a jiffy!"

"Is it new?"

"Not quite, I bought it six months ago."

Edward replaced his cap, and escorted the young lady to his vehicle. As he opened the passenger door, she stepped inside. Edward closed the door, got into the driver's seat, and replaced his goggles. The young lady looked at Edward, and he grinned. "Glad I left the engine running, it saves having to start the damn thing again. Where do you want dropped off?"

"Do you have the correct time, please?" The young lady removed a white hat, and adjusted her long black hair.

Edward stared. "You look younger without the hat, how old are you?"

"A gentleman does not ask a lady her age."

Edward glanced at her.

"I am in my twenties."

Edward took out a gold watch on a matching chain from his waistcoat pocket. He tapped it with his forefinger. "My watch has stopped!"

"Let us hope your vehicle performs better."

Edward laughed.

"I'll give you directions to where I live." The young lady put on her hat.

Edward nodded. "Splendid."

"If you carry on down this road and then turn left."

As the automobile moved off, Edward's passenger held onto her hat, amidst a slight breeze. She gazed at the surrounding countryside. After the vehicle turned left into a narrow road, the young lady looked at Edward. "This is fine, thank you."

"Here?" Edward glanced at his passenger.

She nodded.

Edward brought the vehicle to a halt. He looked around the vicinity, then at his passenger.

"Thank you for the lift."

Edward raised his goggles. "The nearest house is further down the road!"

"Being seen with a married man would not be prudent." The young lady smiled at Edward.

"I am escorting you home."

"My father would not approve."

Edward looked at the young lady, and sighed.

"What if your wife found out?"

"It is hardly a scandal. And, due to my driving, your

dress was stained."

The young lady smiled. "I'm aware of that. However, this is a village, and people gossip."

"Haven't they better things to do?" Edward shook his head. "I'll be glad to get back to my regiment in Edinburgh."

"When do you return?"

"Soon."

"I must go."

Edward got out, and went around to open her door. He held out a hand, and the young lady stepped out. "Goodbye, and again, thank you."

"My pleasure, goodbye."

Edward got into the driver's seat and then gazed at his passenger walking away down the narrow road. He smiled, lowered his goggles and drove off.

Edward drove along the country road where he'd recently encountered a delightful young lady. Would their paths cross again? Then, he spotted her and brought the vehicle to an abrupt halt. "I've learned to drive in a careful manner."

"Thank you. It'll save me having to wash another dress!"

Edward laughed. "Get in, I'll give you a lift." He leaned over, and opened the passenger door.

"I'm not sure, kind sir. My older brother spotted me with you."

"Explain to him that I'm a friend."

"And, a married one!"

"I'm also a gentleman."

The young lady gave a faint smile, and got in.

"What type of work is it you do?" Edward asked as they drove off.

"I'm a maid to one of the families in Dochar."

"For how long?"

"Nine years. I started after leaving school."

Edward glanced at his beautiful young passenger. That

makes her around twenty-one.

"My family is not privileged as your family, sir. After school, my two brothers went to work on a farm. What about you, may I ask?"

"After school, I went to an academy and then onto university."

"In Glasgow?"

"Yes, old Glasgow town, then I joined the army. It's a family tradition, which stretches way back to fighting Napoleon."

He's younger than I thought.

Edward drove on to Ardrishaig, and a short time later, came to a halt. The young lady opened her door and stepped out.

"What is your name?"

"Ann."

"It's been a pleasure, Ann. Oh, and do tell your brother not to worry."

Ann gave a forced smile.

As Edward drove away, Ann hurried down the lane to her parent's cottage. After looking around, she walked slowly up the garden path. On entering the front door, Ann removed her hat, shaking out her long dark hair.

"I spotted you," said her older brother, a tall well-built individual, greeted her.

Ann jumped.

"He's a married man, Ann," he continued with a stern glare.

"Oh, Roy. It was only a lift."

"That's twice. Father and mother would not approve."

"I don't want to discuss the matter."

Roy scowled at his sister.

Ann hurried past him, went into her room, and shut the door. She took a couple of deep breaths, and then smiled as she threw her hat onto the bed.

Ann picked up a book, which lay on a brown wicker chair, sat down, and started to read DH Lawrence's, 'Sons and Lovers'.

Roy went into the garden, and lifted a large wooden handled axe off the ground. He made for a nearby cut-down thick tree trunk. Swinging the axe in a frantic manner, he chopped the trunk into small pieces. Roy's grunting and fierce swinging continued until he was forced to stop.

The following day, Edward and Ann's paths crossed once more. Two miles from Ardrishaig, he noticed her walking along the roadside. Hearing a vehicle, she turned around. It drew up beside her, and stopped. Edward raised his distinctive driving goggles. "A beautiful day, is it not?"

"Yes, lovely."

"Would you like to go for a spin?"

"Where is your wife?"

"She is staying with her mother in Inveraray."

Ann hesitated.

"I can show you a picturesque spot, not far from here."

"I have to be home within the hour."

"I will see to it."

Edward leaned forward, opened the passenger door, and Ann stepped inside. She closed the door, looked behind her, then at Edward.

"If it rains, the roof folds back into place."

"It would save the use of an umbrella."

Edward grinned.

The Rover headed for the outskirts of Ardrishaig and then onto a narrow road through woodland. From there, Loch Fyne came into view. After the vehicle came to a halt, Ann stepped out, and gazed around in awe. Edward removed his goggles and cap, and put them on the rear seat. He got out, closed the door, and walked towards Ann. She turned to face him, then at the loch.

"Glad you came?"

Ann nodded. "It's beautiful, I haven't seen the loch from this location." She turned to face Edward. "Do you bring your wife here?"

He shook his head.

Ann returned to the view and stood still for a few minutes, then she turned to face Edward and pointed to the slope. "There's a bench, would you like to sit?"

As she walked down the slope, Edward followed. Ann reached the bench, sat down and stared at Loch Fyne. Edward sat next to her, then admired the loch. She removed her hat, laid it on the bench and looked at Edward. "How did you discover this place?"

"I found out about it from someone who painted landscapes."

"From the village?"

"Dochar."

"What was his name?"

Edward grinned. "The artist was a lady, she stayed at Docharnea."

"I worked there for a short time, assisting Nancy, the housekeeper."

"Before moving to America, Elizabeth often came here to paint. I believe she once persuaded the coachman to pose." Edward grinned as he glanced at Ann.

"He left Docharnea in a hurry."

"Back to Edinburgh, from what I am aware."

"Edinburgh?"

"As a boy, I met him. I would ask all types of questions about Scotland's capital, and he would answer with enthusiasm."

"Was his portrayal of Edinburgh the reason you wanted to be based there?"

Edward nodded, then looked at Ann. "If not a maid, what would you have wanted to become?"

She sighed. "My family are not well-off, opportunities are limited."

"If people have money, are you suggesting opportunities will exist?"

"You know they do!"

Edward grinned.

Ann stared upwards, then at Edward. "I would love to have my own business, a dress shop."

"Sell dresses?"

"And design them."

"Ann, that is a splendid idea. What's stopping you?"

"Edward, there are various reasons."

"Tell me."

Once more, Ann sighed. "I have to work, and give my parents the income. Therefore, no money is available to purchase stock, or rent premises."

"You can still design them, and take your ideas to a manufacturer."

"My father would not approve, a woman's place is at home. We have no independence - women are not even allowed to vote."

"One day, that will change."

"Change, how?"

"The Suffragettes will prevail. It may take a decade; however, women will one day be able to vote."

"Promise?"

Edward nodded. "My mother has assured me!"

Ann whispered, "I've heard a rumour that all of her friends are Suffragettes."

Edward moved closer to Ann and whispered, "Do not reveal this to anyone." He grinned. "And you don't have to whisper, there is nobody else about."

She laughed.

Edward stood up. "I'd better take you home."

Ann got to her feet, lost her balance and stumbled. As Edward caught her, their eyes met.

As Monday morning arrived at the village police station,

Sergeant Buchan and Constable Fraser attended to their everyday duties. A strapping individual, Sergeant Buchan had joined the force thirty-five years earlier as a junior constable. Now in his fifty-third year, he remained content to work in Ardrishaig's law-abiding scenic surroundings. Also, as a respected member of the community, people looked up to him. To accept a promotion would mean relocating to another district, which did not enthuse. Colleague Constable Fraser was younger, and carried less weight on his broad shoulders. His short black wavy hair being a stark contrast to Sergeant Buchan's grey thinning crown. Constable Fraser not only preserved law and order within the community, but he also worked as a volunteer fireman. Loyalty for duty allowed him to carry out both roles with zest. Both officers were married to local women, as well as the emergency services.

Sergeant Buchan went to the filing cabinet, took out a folder, then sat at his desk. He opened it, and read a particular document. A clearing of the throat followed, plus a stare directed towards Constable Fraser.

"Tea is on its way."

Sergeant Buchan grinned.

Constable Fraser put aside a pencil and incident form, and went into the back room. A few minutes later, he came out with two mugs of tea. Sergeant Buchan glanced at his colleague.

"Yes?" Constable Fraser set a mug on his colleague's desk.

"Sandy, do you recall the owners of Docharnea?"

"Charles and Mary Carsell-Brown, then James and Elizabeth."

"The current family are Philip and Charlene?"

"Philip and Charlotte."

"Do you know them?"

"On my rounds, I've spoken to Mrs Carsell-Brown several times."

Constable Fraser grinned. "Being a family member must be beneficial."

"I wouldn't want to maintain the grounds." Sergeant Buchan sipped his tea.

"Having a gardener helps."

Sergeant Buchan glanced up. "If it keeps Angus out of mischief, fine."

Constable Fraser laughed. "He enjoys a tipple."

"And a large one!" Sergeant Buchan read the document. "The former coachman, he went to Edinburgh."

"I heard to work there." Constable Fraser sipped his tea.

"The boy staying with Mr and Mrs Lawson is from Edinburgh."

"He and the coachman have the same name."

Sergeant Buchan nodded.

"Why do we have the coachman on record?"

"In 1896, he was reported as a missing person by the owner of Docharnea." Sergeant Buchan looked at his colleague. "He vanished without a trace, however, reappeared sixteen years later."

"Was an explanation given for his disappearance?"

Sergeant Buchan shook his head. "I gather he didn't look a day older."

"Maybe I should apply for a transfer to Edinburgh and preserve my looks. My wife wouldn't disapprove."

Sergeant Buchan laughed. "Mine too, maybe my hair will grow back." Sergeant Buchan touched his stomach. "And lose a couple of stones."

Constable Fraser grinned.

Both officers finished their mugs of tea, and resumed routine duties, unaware of the link between coachman and boy.

CHAPTER 5

THE APPROACHING STORM

On a warm sunny afternoon in late June, Edward and Ann visited their favoured secret location. Due to its distance from the village, and as only a privileged few locals owned an automobile, it was ideal. Ann's older brother became aware of the relationship, but had remained tight-lipped. Edward's mother, Lady Beaumont, was prominent and respected within Ardrishaig's close-knit community, therefore, a scandal would bring shame upon the family.

Whilst the couple sat next to each other admiring Loch Fyne, Ann looked curiously at Edward. "You have that expression again."

He stared at her.

"Do you feel guilty? Driving here, you hardly uttered a word."

Edward took Ann's tender hand, and paused. "It's not you, or us, Ann."

"Well then, what?"

Edward sighed. "I believe Britain will soon be at war."

"War! With whom?"

"Austria, and perhaps, Germany."

"Why?"

Once more, Edward sighed.

"Britain has no conflict of interest with either country."

"Ann do not reveal what I am about to tell you, not even your family. Promise me?"

"I promise, Edward."

"I have been ordered back to my barracks in Edinburgh."

"When do you leave?"

"In three days. A crisis may be about to unfold in the Balkans."

"But Edward, that's thousands of miles from here!"

"In the Crimea, we fought the Russians for three years. Not to mention the Boer Wars."

Ann moved closer to Edward. "Are you certain?"

He nodded. "I also overheard mother in conversation with one of her friends, who is married to a Government Minister."

Ann stared at Edward.

"War is coming, Ann." Edward cast his gaze around the tranquil scenic setting. "Birds sing and the sun shines." He shook his head.

Ann put her head on Edward's shoulder. "If a war does start, it may finish within months." She looked at Edward. "Britain has the Royal Flying Corps, the Royal Navy and its Empire's resources."

Edward smiled at Ann. "You have a trait that I admire – optimism."

"Should war break out and conclude, you could be home by Christmas."

Edward understood that other countries with interests in the Balkans would join the conflict, and a short war would not materialise. Given his family's involvement in fighting for Britain, Edward believed war only produced heartache. He looked at Ann with sad eyes. "When I told mother I wanted to join the army, she disapproved."

"Why?"

"She said that in peacetime, sons bury their parents, but in war, parents bury their sons."

"Is it not a tradition within your family to sign up for the army?"

Edward nodded, looked towards Loch Fyne, then at Ann.

"There is something else on your mind, Edward."

"Tomorrow, Rosalind returns from Inveraray."

Ann remained silent.

"We can still keep in touch."

"How?"

"When I am on active service, I will write to you.

Nobody will suspect - you could be a relative."

Ann smiled. "I will have to ensure my family do not suspect."

Edward snapped his fingers. "When I sign the letter, I can use another name."

"What will you call yourself?"

"What name would you prefer?" Edward smiled.

Ann hesitated.

"If you had a son, what would you call him?"

"I'm not sure."

"After your father?"

"My father's name is Alfred."

Edward leaned back. "Alfred!" He shook his head.

"How about?" Ann paused, then smiled. "Andrew."

Edward nodded. "Andrew, it is!" He took Ann's hand. "We have the remainder of this afternoon."

"Yes, we do."

Several hours later, Edward and Ann returned to the automobile. As Ann sat in the passenger seat, Edward lifted a crimson rectangular box from behind his seat, and handed it to her. Ann's eyes lit up. After she opened the box, a white rose presented itself to her.

"It represents purity, innocence and secrecy."

Ann kissed Edward. "My choice for you would be red."

"For what reason?"

"Courage, respect and love." Ann laid the box on her pale blue dress.

Edward took Ann's hand. "This will be our last time, together."

"Only in the present, Edward. I'll await your return, no matter how long you're gone."

"Hopefully, not long."

Ann held Edward. "At least we can keep in touch."

Edward grinned. "Remember, always refer to me as Andrew from now on."

Ann laughed. "Only in a letter."

Edward laughed.

Ann gripped his hand. "Are you convinced there will be a war, Edward?"

"There is much unrest in Europe - and beyond. The German Kaiser wants his nation to expand. To do so, he will have to occupy other countries."

Ann sighed. "Why did we have to meet now?"

"I am not sure."

"I feel insecure."

Edward turned to face Ann. "Promise me you will be strong."

Her voice grew raspy. "As long as you will return."

Edward hugged her. "I promise."

Ann smiled.

"Perhaps this situation in the Balkans will come to a speedy end. As the Monarchs of Britain, Russia and Germany are related, they will not wish a conflict."

"Let's hope so."

The couple kissed, left their treasured location, and returned to Ardrishaig. After Edward left Ann, she clutched the box, and pondered over what the future would hold.

Mrs Lawson and four friends sat round a mahogany table in the living room sipping cups of tea with digestive biscuits. The host had regular Suffragette gatherings every fortnight, and in this era, the Government would perceive this as being radical! Husbands of attendees were unaware of meeting content and if so, would certainly disapprove.

A movement, which began in the late nineteenth century, the Suffragette's main grievance being, women could not vote. By June 1914, their profile had been raised through arson and violence. At a prestigious event at Epsom Racecourse, Surrey, in 1913, which involved the King's horse, a woman protester ran in front of it and was killed. This dramatic incident highlighted the Suffragette's determination to enhance publicity for their cause. To solidify their resolve, if a Suffragette was imprisoned, she would go on a hunger strike.

The Suffragettes of Ardrishaig, however, remained passive. Being residents of a quaint village in rural Argyll, it became prudent to remain discreet. They would discuss the movement behind closed doors, and propose an action that would not come to fruition. An acquaintance of Mrs Lawson, grey-haired and serene Mary Butler, attended the first gathering in 1896 at Lady Beaumont's residence. Guests at the current meeting did not only discuss the plight of Suffragettes, but also the matter of a possible crisis in the Balkans.

"If war breaks out," said Mary, "Britain will be drawn into the conflict."

"If such a situation occurs, the Movement may have to suspend militant action," said Mrs Lawson.

"Then," said Meg, "the Government may propose an amnesty for Suffragettes who are serving a prison sentence."

"That would be good!" said Catherine.

"The Government will hope a goodwill gesture may soften our resolve," said Jessica.

Mary lifted her cup and took a sip. "Let us hope war does not come." She set her blue patterned cup on its saucer. "If so, it could be on a grand scale."

The group spoke of how past loved ones had been taken in previous conflicts. Various battles fought overseas, which stretched back sixty years to the Crimean War. Due to a subdued tone, the gathering ended.

A short time later, Alan entered his aunt's house out of breath and distraught. His aunt, washing crockery in the kitchen's white ceramic sink, turned to face him. "What is wrong, Alan?"

"James." He took a deep breath.

"What about him?" Mrs Lawson wiped her hands on a towel.

"He has gone missing!"

"Calm yourself, tell me where you last saw him."

"In..." Alan took another deep breath. "In the park. I was on a swing, and minutes later he had disappeared."

"Did you have an argument?"

Alan shook his head. "No, Auntie."

"Did you try to find him?"

Alan nodded.

"We'll go back to the park, perhaps he wandered off and has now returned."

Mrs Lawson went into the hall, opened a closet door, took out a jacket and hat, then looked in the mirror.

"Should we not wait for Uncle to return home?"

Mrs Lawson glanced at the wall clock. "The bank does not close for another hour."

As she walked in a brisk manner towards the park, Alan kept pace. "Where could he have gone, Auntie?"

"Not sure, but as most boys in the village have dark hair, James will stand out." Mrs Lawson gave a comforting smile to her nephew.

Walking home from work, Ann observed a young boy coming towards her. She did not recognise this person, and why was he without a parent? When he approached, Ann stopped and then the boy looked up at her.

"Hello," said Ann, as she smiled.

The boy stared.

"Where is your mother?"

"I want to find her."

"Where are you headed?"

"Docharmea."

"Do you mean Docharnea?"

The boy nodded. "That's where I last saw her."

Ann looked back to nearby Dochar, then at the boy. "It's a long walk."

"I want to find my parents." James voice grew raspy.

Ann bent down and gave a warm smile. "What is your

name?"

The boy whispered, "James."

"My name is Ann, I will help you to find them."

"Thank you."

By giving assistance to the boy, Ann would arrive home late, and no doubt be quizzed by her older brother. If asked, she would admit to being with a younger man in need of comfort and assistance. As she walked alongside the boy, Ann became aware of his stamina. Even with a longer stride, she had to keep up with him. "Do you play any sports, James?"

He nodded. "Football."

"In a public park?"

"And in my parent's back garden."

"Where is your parent's house?"

"Edinburgh."

"Edinburgh!" Ann stared at James.

Looking up, he nodded.

"Did you travel to Ardrishaig by paddle steamer?"

"My dad drove us here."

"That must have been a long journey."

"Dad had to stop on the way, I felt sick."

"Do you not like to travel?"

"On my way here, I ate too much chocolate."

Ann smiled. "What else do you enjoy?"

"Music."

"What kind?"

"I like the Monkees and the Beatles."

"Are they Scottish Folk groups?"

James stared upwards at Ann. "They are pop groups."

Pop groups?

"I listen to their records in my bedroom."

Ann glanced at James. "You have a gramophone player?"

James gave Ann a puzzled look.

"Your family are privileged."

"Do you not have records?"

"No, I go to the village public house. That's where I listen to music."

"Do they play records?"

Ann laughed. "The public house has a folk group."

"What kind of group is that?"

"A trio of musicians who play the bagpipes, violin, and a harp."

"Have you been to any music concerts?"

Ann shook her head. "I'd like to visit Glasgow, they've not long opened the West End Playhouse."

"There's a Playhouse in Edinburgh." James smiled at Ann.

"Is it a music hall?"

"It's a cinema."

"What's that?"

"It shows films. Have you never been to one?"

Once more, Ann shook her head. He has a vivid imagination.

"Do you play any instrument?"

"I have no spare time to learn or play an instrument."

"Why not?"

"I work six days a week from seven-thirty until six o'clock in the evening. After arriving home, I help my mother prepare dinner and then tend to other duties."

"That's not fair."

Ann smiled at James.

"Why do you start work so early in the morning?"

"That's what my employer demands." Ann looked at James. "What time does your mother start work?"

"She doesn't work."

Ann raised her thin dark eyebrows. "Does your father work?"

James nodded. "He leaves the house about eight-thirty."

Lucky him.

James looked up at Ann. "What do you work as?"

"I'm a maid for a local family. They have a large

property, which is not far from here." He's a curious one.

"Do you have children?" James stubbed his toe, and looked at the ground.

Ann stopped. "Are you okay?"

James nodded, and continued.

Ann started to walk, then glanced at James. "No, I don't have children, I'm not married."

James looked up at Ann. "Will you get married?"

She smiled. "I hope so."

"Do you have a boyfriend?"

"There is a special person."

Minutes later, Ann and James reached Dochar, and soon after, Docharnea. Ann stood at the foot of its driveway, and looked at James. "Let's try the main door."

James nodded.

They walked up to the front entrance, then Ann pulled the brass doorbell handle. As it rang, she looked at James, waiting in anticipation. Ann rang it a second time, waited and sighed. "It appears nobody is home."

"Where can they be?"

"When were you here?

"Three days ago."

"Three days!" Ann stared at James. "Where have you been for that length of time?"

"Staying with a Mr and Mrs Lawson."

"In Ardrishaig?"

"Yes."

Ann was aware that Philip and Charlotte Carsell-Brown lived here, however, given his Edinburgh accent and appearance, James did not belong here. He looked up at Ann.

"How did you become separated from your parents, James?"

James took Ann's hand, and led her to the coach house. He stopped and pointed to a black painted door. "My great-aunt took me through the door and then upstairs. She left me to answer a telephone call."

"A telephone call?"

James nodded. "I then looked into a mirror and felt unwell. Went downstairs, and when I opened the door, everything looked different." He stared at Ann. "Everybody had disappeared."

Ann turned the door handle. "It's locked." She looked at James. "What was different?"

James pointed to the garden. "The trees were much taller, twice as big." James stared at the villa. "It was a different colour."

Ann bent down and faced James. "As no one is here, we should return to Ardrishaig. Mr and Mrs Lawson will be worried."

"What about my mum, dad and great-aunt?"

Ann remained silent.

James started to sob, and Ann brought out a handkerchief from her jacket pocket, then wiped his eyes "I will take you back to Mr and Mrs Lawson." Ann smiled. "Until your parents and great-aunt return, they will care for you."

James sniffed and then Ann gave him a warm hug. She took his hand, led him out of the property, and towards Ardrishaig. Feeling disconsolate, James remained silent on the way back.

On the final Friday in June, Alice Lawson and her four friends, Mary, Jessica, Meg and Catherine sailed to Glasgow. They had travelled by paddle steamer from their village port to Govan Wharf, filled with anticipation about their visit to the West End Playhouse Theatre, St George's Cross. As it lay on several tram routes, transport from Govan was no problem.

Acts scheduled to appear included a comedian, ventriloquist, magician, fire-eater, knife-thrower and singer. Upon reaching the theatre, a long queue had formed. As the five ladies took their place, Mary read a billboard poster, then looked at Alice. "Perhaps the magician could conjure up a new British Government?"

"One that would give us the vote," said Alice, as she looked at her friends.

Whilst they laughed, directly behind them, a tall gentleman dressed in a black top hat and dark suit frowned at the group.

"Is this a theatre or a music hall?" said Mary. She looked at Alice.

The gentleman leaned forward. "It is a theatre, madam."

Mary turned around. "Thank you for that, sir."

He raised his top hat, and smiled. "You are welcome, madam."

Catherine whispered to Meg, "He's posh with that accent."

"The dark moustache and long beard give it away," said Meg.

"Similar to King George?" said Jessica.

Meg nodded, then tucked her jet-black hair under a pink hat.

"Alice?" Jessica turned to her.

"Yes?"

"Why don't we go to George Square tomorrow?"

"There's attractions in the West End to visit, replied Alice.

"We could demonstrate, and get publicity," said Jessica with enthusiasm.

"I've heard it's a popular place to congregate," added Catherine.

Once again, the gentleman behind leaned forward, and stared down at fair-skinned Catherine. "Do you want to end up in prison, madam?"

Catherine turned. "If sent to prison, I'll go on a hunger strike."

"That is what Ethel Moorhead said, and she was force fed!"

"Huh!" Catherine looked away.

"At last." Alice sighed. "We are moving."

"Have your two shillings and three pennies ready," cried Mary.

Each opened their trim bags, and brought out the required coins. They entered a crowded foyer, paid their admission, and went into the arena.

"Five empty seats, over there!" Catherine pointed.

"Ideal," said Alice, "quick, before they are taken."

The ladies sat down and within fifteen minutes, no empty seats remained. In front of the wooden stage, sat an orchestra. This comprised an organist, cellist, violinist, trumpeter, clarinet player and drummer, complete with cymbals. The musicians looked presentable in black formal suits, white shirts and black ties. Meg, sitting beside Mary, whispered, "The young woman next to me has had a skinful."

Mary glanced at the woman, then looked at Meg. "She appears okay."

Meg whispered, "Her breath stinks of gin."

When the young woman burped, and repeated her action, Mary nodded. Then, to the sound of a drum roll, the Master of Ceremonies walked onto the stage. His attire being a black tailcoat, trousers and red waistcoat over a white shirt and white bow tie. Applause from all parts of the theatre followed, and he gave a polite acknowledgement, then went to a table and chair next to the stage. On the table lay a small well-crafted hammer, which was thumped twice. "For your pleasure, one of the country's utmost quintessential comedians."

"There's enough comedians already in Glasgow," shouted the young women next to Meg, amidst audience laughter.

The Master of Ceremonies looked at Meg. "Nevertheless, madam, one more won't do any harm! Ladies and gentlemen, please welcome, Jimmy Bell." He hit the table once with his hammer.

As the audience cheered, Meg glanced at each of her four friends, then at the Master of Ceremonies. The young woman giggled, and nudged Meg. "He thought it was you."

The orchestra played an upbeat tune, and the burgundy curtain went up. A short bald man wearing a brown checked suit held a tiny brass bell in his hand. "You won't forget my name!" He rang it, and chuckles ensued. Putting the bell into his jacket pocket, Jimmy addressed the audience. "I complained to the landlady about my digs - especially the bed. She asked, what's the problem? I said, there's a dead flea in the bed. She replied, one dead flea won't cause you harm. I stated, no, but 40,000 fleas came to its funeral!" Laughter followed from all parts of the hall. Jimmy Bell continued with his repertoire of jokes, then received rapturous applause. As the curtain came down to a short tune, the young woman turned to Meg. "My old man is just as funny." She burped. "My mammy says he should be on the stage." The young woman giggled.

Meg looked at Mary, who had a wide grin.

Next, a ventriloquist introduced as Jack Thom and Henry. Both individuals wore a tuxedo with white collared shirt and black bow tie. Jack Thom sat the dummy on his leg, and asked questions on politics, the economy and Glasgow. Henry fired wisecracks at the red-haired ventriloquist, whose finale featured him drinking a glass of water whilst Henry recited a short poem. No water spluttered out of the ventriloquist's mouth. As they left the stage, a warm round of applause ensued.

"Mystical, magical and sensational!" said the Master of Ceremonies, as he described dark-suited Marvel the Magician.

"Good evening, ladies and gentlemen." He bowed.

"So far," shouted a man in the front row.

The magician smiled. "Don't hold your breath."

"Can you make my second husband disappear?" cried a

middle-aged woman in the stalls.

"What happened to your first husband, madam?" said the magician.

"He disappeared on his own accord!"

Laughter erupted, and once more, the magician showed his white teeth. He performed a series of tricks which included a white dove and an empty bottle disappearing. A man shouted. "Can you bring back the bottle full of beer?"

"Would a bottle of ale brewed by J&R Tennent suffice, sir? It's a Glasgow company."

"Any type of alcohol is fine by me!"

The magician held a silver tray in his left hand, and with his right, held a small white sheet in front of the bottle. With a flick of his wrist, the sheet was taken away, and a full bottle of ale stood. Marvel left the stage, approached the man and gave him the bottle. As the man took it, he gave a 'thumbs up' to the magician. Marvel returned to the stage, and gave a farewell bow.

A dramatic short piece of music played, and the next act announced on stage was a man who ate fire. He ignited a fire in his mouth, and transferred the flames to various parts of his body, then extinguished them. The audience gasped in awe of the fire-eater's feats.

After he left, the Master of Ceremonies praised the fire-eater's bravery. He thumped his hammer twice, and a man in a black suit with matching cloak appeared. A scantily dressed young woman with long platinum-blonde hair accompanied him. She took position in front of a board, which encompassed her body. As the knife-thrower took his stance, she stood motionless. When four knives struck the board on each side of the assistant's torso, the audience applauded. A further four landed next to her head. As applause diminished, the knife-thrower approached the board and removed his eight shiny knives. He laid them on a small circular table, then lifted up a large dagger. Accompanied by a drum roll, the knife-thrower steadied himself, and paused. He threw the dagger towards his assistant. When she opened her eyes, it had rested above her head. Following loud applause, the knife-thrower walked forward, and addressed the audience. "Can I have a volunteer from the audience?"

The five Ardrishaig ladies looked at each other in a sheepish manner, however, the young woman next to Meg raised her hand. "I'll do it!"

Cheers rang out, and she walked down a narrow aisle, then stepped onto the stage. The knife-thrower led her to the board. His assistant removed the dagger, then handed it to the knife-thrower. The young woman stood still, and closed her eyes. The hall remained silent then came a roll on the drums. When it stopped, the dagger left the knife-thrower's hand, and as it lodged next to the young woman's ear, she broke wind. The audience laughed, applauded and then cheered. The assistant led her off the stage. When she returned to her seat, Meg received a grin. "Your turn next."

To Meg's relief, the knife-thrower continued with his assistant until the act finished. The Master of Ceremonies stood, and announced the evening's finale. Following moans, he grinned. "You can always return next week."

Scattered cheers echoed around the hall, and the curtain rose to melodic music. A tall elegant dark-haired man introduced as Danny Lyne stood smiling. His green jacket, black trousers and pale green cravat contrasted well with a crisp white collared shirt. A neat side parting and moustache completed the singer's presentation. Singing You Made Me Love You and Who Were You With Last Night endeared Danny to the audience. His final song, Danny Boy, ended the evening on a high. The Master of Ceremonies gave way to an encore, then an audience sing-along of Meet Me in St Louis.

People poured out of the venue, and into St George's Cross. Here, they could catch a tram home to various parts of the city. The Ardrishaig ladies walked the short distance to Bath Street, where they could catch a tram to their overnight accommodation in Partick. Whilst they waited, Catherine beamed. "I loved that show, we have to plan another visit."

"An illusionist is appearing in September," said Jessica, "I overheard a woman in the foyer."

"Did you catch his name?" said Meg.

"John Nevil, I think."

"Harry Houdini would be a star attraction," said Alice.

"Wouldn't he just!" said Mary.

Before sailing home on Saturday afternoon, a visit to Kelvingrove Park favoured the majority. Being a short distance from their guest house, made it an ideal choice. When they arrived, joyful mothers and playful children savoured the sunny calm conditions. The Ardrishaig ladies found a vacant wooden bench, sat down and discussed the location. Meg revealed that the park had been opened in 1852, and was known as the West End Park. In 1888, it hosted the International Science Arts and Industry Exhibition, which had five and a half million visitors.

"Did you attend the exhibition, Meg?" asked Catherine.

Meg nodded. "I came with my parents. Dad spent a good hour in the shooting gallery."

"Then it's not only about exhibits?" said Jessica.

Meg shook her head. "An assortment of visitor attractions." She pointed to a grassy area where young women played croquet. "I recall a temporary bandstand with musical performances." She smiled. "After he had been at the shooting gallery, Dad wanted to attend a football match at a local club's ground. However, Mum ruled it out of bounds!"

"Most of the proceeds went towards building the Kelvingrove Art Gallery and Museum," said Alice.

Meg nodded. "It opened in time for the city's next International Exhibition, in 1901."

"I visited the Scottish Exhibition held here in 1911," said Mary, "my husband exhibited his animal ornaments."

"Did he sell many?" asked Catherine.

"Enough to cover his costs." Mary raised her grey eyebrows.

Meg stood up. "Let's go to the Art Gallery and Museum."

"What about the Botanic Gardens?" said Catherine, "there's a wide variety of different plants and flowers."

"The Art Gallery and Museum has more culture," stated Meg.

"A show of hands for the Botanic Gardens!" said Alice as she observed the group. "Sorry Catherine, perhaps next time."

On the way to Meg's choice, they stopped at a stall, which sold ice cream cones. All five bought one from a jovial attendant, who handed over three strawberry cones and two vanillas, then took two pennies from each lady. As they enjoyed their cones, Mary looked at Alice. "How is the boy from Edinburgh?"

"He is fine, a composed boy." Alice licked her cone. "George's sister is bringing her nephews over today, therefore, James will have another two playmates."

"Strange, he was left on his own?" said Meg.

"He must have wandered off," said Alice.

"But from where?" said Meg.

Alice shrugged her shoulders.

"It's not as if there are any new families in the area," said Mary.

"James mentioned his parents had visited a relative at Docharnea." Alice licked her lips.

"There have been eerie goings-on at that property," said Mary, "the coachman vanished and reappeared sixteen years later."

"And he hadn't aged!" said Jessica, as she licked her lips.

"He vanished again – two years ago!" said Meg.

Catherine adjusted her hat. "Docharnea is haunted, is it

not?"

"Or, it's a gateway through time," said Jessica.

"Haunted is more plausible," said Alice, "time travel is for writers of fiction."

"I enjoyed HG Wells' book," said Jessica. She licked her fingers.

"If a time machine exists," said Alice, "we could travel into the future and discover when women will be allowed to vote."

All five ladies laughed, then made their way to the Art Gallery and Museum. The red sandstone exterior in a Spanish Baroque style looked impressive. At the entrance, a woman wearing a long black dress and floppy grey hat handed out leaflets to female passers-by. Mary took one, and read it.

"What does it say?" asked Meg.

"It's about a rally in George Square this afternoon at four o'clock."

"A rally?" said Jessica.

Mary smiled. "For women to get the vote."

As the five ladies went into the building with distinctive black and white floor tiles, Alice looked upwards at a large hanging clock. "We only have one and a half hours until our sail."

Catherine observed a concert pipe organ located below it. "I hope the clock is secure."

Jessica looked upwards.

The second floor displayed a variety of distinguished works of art. As the ladies admired them, shouts could be heard from a lower section of the gallery. An attendant rushed towards a woman who held a pot in her hand, about to throw its liquid contents onto a painting. He grabbed the pot, and red paint spilled onto his dark blue uniform. A second attendant arrived, and restrained the woman who was yelling, "give women the vote, give it to us now!"

When led away by stern-faced attendants, the ladies

looked at each other and then Catherine stated, "That wouldn't have happened in the Botanic Gardens."

"It is not worthwhile to damage a plant," said Meg, "no drama!"

As onlookers dispersed, Mary glanced at Alice, and gave her a wry smile. "The movement is alive and well in Glasgow."

"I agree, however, we are not about to ruin any work of art."

Jessica looked at Mary and tutted. "It may have been a Rembrandt."

The ladies resumed their tour, and later walked to Partick Cross to catch a tram. Whilst she passed the local subway station, Catherine stopped. "Let's take the train."

Jessica stared at the signage.

Inside, they observed a man in a dark blue suit and peaked cap sitting at the ticket desk.

"Has it been a busy Saturday?" said Meg.

"The employee looked up with a broad smile. "Not too bad, miss."

Each lady purchased a ticket, then walked with caution down steep grey concrete steps to the platform.

"If he had to work on a Sunday, we wouldn't have been cheery."

"The only person I know who enjoys working on Sunday is our church minister," said Mary.

"He will expect us tomorrow morning, 10.30, sharp!" said Meg.

An echo of laughter could be heard from the platform, where the five ladies joined several other passengers.

Meg looked around. "The light is subdued."

Catherine sniffed the air. "It has a musty smell."

"The subway has been here for twenty years," said Mary.

"It must have been a huge project to build stations below ground level," said Alice.

Jessica stared at the entrance and exit tunnels.

"It should be quicker than the tram," added Alice.

A rumble of wheels came from within a tunnel, and soon two brown and cream carriages appeared at the platform. Catherine looked at her friends. "We'll be at Govan in no time."

After a stop at Merkland Street, the ladies reached their destination. As they left the train, Alice stared at Jessica. "You are as white as a ghost."

Jessica sighed. "I am claustrophobic."

"Sigmund Freud is the person to cure you," said Catherine.

"Who's he?" said Jessica.

"A Psychoanalyst, I've read about his studies."

"What sort of studies?" asked Jessica.

"On our way home, I'll explain."

"Catherine is well-read," whispered Meg to Mary.

Mary nodded.

Passengers climbed the steep steps and departed Govan Cross station. When she emerged into the daylight, Jessica removed her hat, and took a deep breath. After a brisk walk, the ladies arrived at Govan Wharf, and awaited their transport home. Already, families congregated. Jessica glanced at Catherine, then the groups.

"Glasgow is popular for a Saturday excursion."

At that moment, a ship came into view, and stopped at the quayside. After arrivals disembarked from a wooden passageway, waiting passengers boarded. Ten minutes later, the Duchess of Argyll left port. Being pleasant, people sat on deck to admire the sea view. A slight breeze did exist, however, welcome on this warm final Saturday of June. After Jessica got up and walked around, Meg stared in her direction. "The sea air will do her good." She looked at Mary. "Hopefully, Jessica doesn't suffer from sea-sickness!"

Mary sighed. "It's bad enough being claustrophobic."

"At least some colour has returned to her cheeks," said Alice.

Jessica returned to her four friends and sat next to Alice. "I'm glad Ardrishaig has no subway."

"It doesn't even have a railway station!" said Mary.

As they laughed, a Caledonian Steam Packet employee started to check tickets. A stern expression and uniform represented officialdom.

Jessica whispered to Meg, "He doesn't appear to enjoy a Saturday shift."

Meg gave a wry smile.

The ladies duly produced their return tickets, and each one was scrutinised.

"How old is the vessel?" said Alice.

"Eight years, built at Dumbarton. It's equipped with turbine engines, one of the first to have 'em." The employee checked other passengers' tickets.

A nearby group of adults discussed tensions in the Balkans. One woman explained she had received a letter from a relative in Austria. They had maintained that a recent minor conflict between their country and Serbia could escalate and involve countries which border the two.

"In what way?" said an acquaintance.

"Germany is allied to Austria, and Russia to Serbia."

Alice whispered to her four attentive friends, "I believe Edward Beaumont has been ordered back to his regiment in Edinburgh."

"Britain is a long distance from the Balkans," said Mary, "a conflict wouldn't affect us."

"Our Royal Family has links with the Tsar," said Catherine, "Nicholas may seek assistance."

"The French can assist Russia, they don't like the Germans," stated Mary.

"It's not that long since the Boer Wars ended," said Meg, "we don't want any more conflicts." She sighed.

"Let us change the subject," said Alice, "when shall we schedule our next meeting for?"

Mary whispered, "Discuss disrupting a village activity?"

"Our sewing club?" asked Alice.

As Meg, Jessica and Catherine laughed, the steamer arrived at its first point of call. Several passengers disembarked, and a group of young adults boarded. They sat close to the Ardrishaig ladies, then started to chat. Their topic also related to the Serbian-Austrian situation. The company employee approached them to check their tickets. A young woman asked if the weather would remain calm until Inveraray.

"It should do Miss, to my knowledge, nothing unpleasant is forecast."

An adult in the group pondered.

Constable Fraser attended to paperwork at his desk, then took several documents to the filing cabinet. As he opened a drawer, Sergeant Buchan entered. "Anything of interest, Sandy?"

"Just after you left, a relative came into the station to collect James."

Sergeant Buchan removed his trouser bicycle clips. "His mother?"

"His cousin, a young woman."

"Definitely a relative?" Sergeant Buchan put the clips on his desk.

"Before giving directions to Alice Lawson's house, I made sure. Also, she had similar features to James, also, an Edinburgh accent."

Sergeant Buchan nodded his approval.

"She would return James to his parents' time."

Sergeant Buchan frowned. "His parents' time?"

"Probably meant parents in quick time, it must be an Edinburgh expression."

"Did she mention how the boy became separated?"

"The family had been camping near Loch Fyne, and James wandered off."

Sergeant Buchan shook his head. "Campers! Adults

should keep an eye on the children."

Constable Fraser nodded.

Sergeant Buchan noticed a package on the reception desk. He picked it up, and looked at his colleague.

"Nancy brought it round."

"What's in it?"

"Cakes and a pudding."

Sergeant Buchan grinned.

"For James."

"Could do with a cup of tea, Sandy."

"And a cake, Sergeant?"

"Mustn't let them go to waste."

Constable Fraser acknowledged, and went into the back room. Whilst listening for the kettle to whistle, he reflected on what Nancy had said. She believed that in the future, James would reappear.

After putting down the telephone, Olivia returned to the coach house. Entering a door leading to the upstairs floor, she climbed its steep wooden staircase, then took a deep breath. In the coachman's quarters, Olivia found James sitting on a chair, and staring up at the wall mirror. She smiled. "It is very old."

James gazed in her direction.

"Gothic, a style from the distant past."

James stood up, and became unsteady. Olivia rushed towards him and held his arm. He had a dazed expression.

"Are you okay?"

"I feel dizzy."

Olivia looked at the chair in front of the mirror.

"I was about to stand on it."

"Just as well you didn't!"

James managed a smile.

"Did you want to look at yourself in the mirror?"

James hesitated, then nodded.

Olivia took his hand. "Let us go back to the villa, your

mother and father will think you have wandered off."

Olivia and James walked with caution down the staircase, and after leaving the coach house, Olivia closed the door behind her. Whilst he walked across the courtyard, James looked back.

"The next time you visit, I will show you a secret compartment in the coach house."

When his great-aunt led James into the living room, Debbie rose from her seat, and approached him. "You look pale, what did you get up to in the coach house?"

Olivia glanced at Debbie. "I found James in one of the upstairs rooms." She glanced at Charlie. "He must have a curious nature."

"We are well aware," said Charlie, smiling at Debbie.

Debbie put a hand on James's forehead. "You're warm, how do you feel?"

"Tired, Mum."

"He'll sleep all the way to Edinburgh," said Charlie.

James sneezed.

Debbie looked at Charlie, then James. "Perhaps you've caught a cold."

"He felt dizzy in the coach house," said Olivia.

"It may be a bug," said Debbie.

Charlie looked at Olivia. "We had to stop at a lay-by, James felt woozy."

"I will get a tissue," said Olivia.

She left the living room, and returned with a paper handkerchief. After she gave it to James, he blew his nose, then put the tissue into his trouser pocket. Debbie looked at her son. "Give the tissue to me."

As James pulled it out of his pocket, several coloured marbles dropped onto the carpet, and rolled towards Debbie.

She stared. "Where did they come from?"

James hesitated. "I don't know, Mum."

Debbie glanced at Olivia. "The coach house?"

Olivia shook her head.

Charlie laughed. "The coach house is a place of magic!"

Debbie looked at Charlie. "Maybe it can conjure up a pools win."

Whilst Charlie and Olivia laughed, James retrieved the marbles, stared, and examined them.

CHAPTER 6

A FUTURE RETURN

When his great-aunt passed away in 1999, James inherited her elegant Victorian property overlooking Loch Fyne. He took the decision to leave France, where he lived and worked, and return to Scotland. The new Millennium would herald a new chapter in James's life.

One afternoon, he went into the property's traditional coach house to reminisce, recalling his visit as a boy in 1967. However, James also remembered that visit was blighted by giddiness and nausea. He looked around three of the four rooms, and left a particular one till last. In 1896, the owner employed a coachman, and this room would have been a treasured habitat. From the window, a large garden and Loch Fyne were in full view. The coachman's quarters had forever intrigued James, and he examined several items of crafted furniture. One being the wooden chair he stood on to look at himself in the wall mirror. James glanced at it and smiled.

Although a beautiful property in an idyllic setting, Docharnea had a dark and disturbing past. Members of James's family had suffered misfortune, trauma and death. Local folk maintained a former coachman haunted the property. After being dismissed, poverty and depression followed, then he took his life. Legend has it, that with his dying breath, the coachman cursed Docharnea. James did not believe in spirits, but a mysterious power did exist within the coach house. This would transport him back in time to avert the tragedies that had beset his family. Following a series of thrilling adventures, James longed for a return to his own timeline.

I opened my eyes, blinked, and stared at the mirror. Both

of my legs felt fragile, however, I kept my balance. I looked at my watch, and as in previous time shifts, it had stopped. Casting my gaze around the coachman's quarters, it appeared different from my previous time travel venture to 1930. The room had been repainted, and items of furniture were missing. Warm bright rays of sunlight shone through the window. After having to endure a chilly 1930's winter, it was a relief to feel warm again. In February of that year, the weather was severe due to below freezing temperatures and snowdrifts. I went to the window, and surveyed the garden below. Could it be late spring? Certainly, trees were full of leaves, with hedges and bushes in need of a trim. I observed bundles of brown leaves scattered around the garden, and the green lawn resembled an overgrown field! Shaking my head, I put the watch back into my pocket. Whilst walking down the creaky wooden staircase, I stumbled, but grabbed hold of the wooden bannister. Reaching the bottom, I opened the door, then stepped into a courtyard full of weeds. Prior to my travels, the courtyard surface had small grey gravel stones. Now, more green than grey existed! The exterior of the villa looked similar to when I came to live here. Nevertheless, a lick of paint would not go amiss. Everything that could grow had, and at great speed. Traffic noise from the road outside had diminished. Perhaps the council renewed the road surface, or has the combustion engine been upgraded? I walked round the property, and discovered that both back and front entrances were locked. Is the rear entrance key still under the disused water well? I went to the well, lifted a small slab of concrete, and smiled. Picking up the silver key, I approached the door, however, after inserting the key, it wouldn't open. With my shoulder, I applied pressure, and the door flew open. Upon entering, a musty smell hit me, plus a feeling of emptiness. Typical of a property that had been deserted and required warmth and a purpose. I walked through the downstairs hallway, and observed no change, although, the spider had enjoyed being the solitary occupant. After removing several webs, I went into the main public room, where Mary Carsell-Brown interviewed me for a coachman's position. On that occasion, bulky furniture and stuffed birds filled the room. At present, the furniture is minimal. If Mary had travelled from her Victorian era, how would she perceive it? Certainly, Mary would have recognised the large dark stone fireplace, which retains its dignity. That interview took place in 1896, however, for me, only a year has passed. In a historical context, I have experienced six timelines and witnessed memorable sights.

I went upstairs to familiarise myself with the remaining rooms. I gazed at my favoured bedroom and gave a sigh of relief. No more sleepless nights in uncomfortable and unfamiliar spartan accommodation. Walking back down the white wooden staircase, the thought of delivered mail struck. I walked into reception, and was confronted by a pile of letters that would fill a postman's sack! I picked up a bundle, and checked the postmarks. The first was 2011, another being 2013. My goodness, I have arrived in the future! I am not back in my own timeline of 2000. The next letter, 1st April 2014, brought a smile. Then, my mindset changed. Since the Millennium, I've missed fourteen years. I looked at another postmark - 23rd May 2014. Sifting through the pile, I concluded that this was the latest date. With a sense of apprehension, I opened a letter marked URGENT. It had been sent by Argyll and Bute Council, referring to unpaid tax. The letter stated that they would restore my water supply if I paid monies due. I studied an attached statement for fourteen years - £28,672.75! Maybe I should have remained in 1930. Since I haven't stayed here, at least there will be no energy usage. I picked up another letter marked URGENT which, coincidentally, was from my energy supplier. As their representative could not gain entry to read gas and electricity meters, they had been cut off. I went into the hall, and lifted the landline handset. I listened, and smiled - disconnected. My trusty cell phone will have suffered the same fate.

Thoughts shifted from unpaid bills to food. I'll have to go into Ardrishaig and purchase supplies. Certainly, in this timeline, I can withdraw money from my bank account. Being home, at least I have a wardrobe of clothes, therefore, I won't have to rely on charity shops. Fashions will have changed in fourteen years, and in what way? I must catch up on lost years. It would have been ideal to switch on the television, radio or computer. And of the computer, how many emails should I have answered? With no power or razor blades, my 1930 beard will have to remain. Then again, it will make me look older, and mask a fourteen-year gap. My goodness, I am now fifty-six!

After a change of clothes, I locked the main door, and walked down my driveway. At the foot, I turned left towards Ardrishaig. Many cars, vans and lorries passed in both directions, looking not too dissimilar from those at the Millennium. Further along, I noticed that a once-empty plot of land now had six houses. Perhaps one day, Dochar's small hamlet status will be discarded. In 1896, I recall only four properties instead of the current fourteen. Due to progress, not much remains static. It's fascinating to witness a century of change in a single year.

Several minutes later, I came across an elderly lady attending to plants in her front garden. She looked up, and gave a warm smile. "Hello, out for an afternoon stroll?" She laid her trowel on the grey concrete dyke.

"Yes, a fine day for one."

"Let's hope there's a proper summer this year, we haven't had one for some time."

"When was the last good summer around this way?" Did I miss any?

"Have you been living overseas?"

"Yes, just returned."

"Where's your tan?" The woman smiled.

"It wasn't a warm sunny location." Here, in the depths of winter.

"We shouldn't complain about our summers, we no longer have severe winters."

It was in 1930.

"Do you stay local?"

I looked back, and pointed. "Dochar."

"Dochar?"

I nodded.

"Years ago, a chap went missing from one of the properties. People say it's haunted."

"Which property?"

"Docharnea. As far as I'm concerned, ghosts don't exist."

"I agree." However, time travellers do.

"It's good to meet a normal person."

I remained silent.

"Are you headed for the village?"

"Yes, to a bank."

"Lovely to speak with you." The woman picked up her trowel.

"Bye."

"Goodbye."

I soon reached Ardrishaig and reminisced. Is the retail revolution I experienced in the sixties still in progress? I entered the main street, and observed several closed shops with a 'To Let' sign. One is the boutique, which had an astute female sales assistant. I approached, and peeked through the window.

"It's been closed for years!"

I turned around.

A stocky grey-haired man grinned. "She made her money and scarpered up tae Glasgow."

"Has the shop remained empty all that time?"

He nodded. "People here now shop in Glasgow, or use the Internet."

Internet? Shopping culture has indeed changed.

"That's if they have money tae buy anythin', with benefits bein' cut."

"How is the economic situation around here?"

"Economic situation? It's a joke!"

What would he make of 1930?

The man shook his head, and walked on.

I continued along the main street, and came across a familiar sight - Macmillan Solicitors. Since I took ownership of Docharnea, don't I have stories to tell! As I started to walk away, a lady in a stylish dark blue outfit rushed out of the premises, and dropped a document.

"Miss!" I said.

She turned around.

I picked up the document, and handed it to her.

"Thanks." She smiled, then stared.

Jane Mackay. She dealt with my acquisition of Docharnea.

"Have we met?"

Yes, fourteen years ago. With my beard, she won't recognise me.

"Jane!" A woman came out of the premises. "Your smart phone." She handed it over.

Smart phone? The design is sophisticated compared to my cell phone, then again, mine is fourteen years old.

"Oh, thanks." Jane took the phone, put it into her black leather handbag and then looked at me. "Thanks, again."

"My pleasure." I walked on. Her size 12 has become a 16.

I reached the bank, entered and joined a long queue of patient customers. When an older teenager's phone rang, she took it out of her brown shoulder bag, then answered the call. Since she stood in front of me, I overheard the conversation. An application for a job at Inveraray's Burgess Hotel had been successful. Excited, she turned to me. "I've got it."

"Congratulations, well done."

"It's a receptionist position at the best hotel in Argyll!"

"A private hotel?"

She nodded. "A chain of twelve in Argyll and further afield."

"What is the company called?"

"The Carsell-White Group."

"Carsell-White?"

The older teenager nodded. "Named after the original directors. They started with one hotel and expanded. I have it on good authority that a take-over is about to happen with another company, and the estate will increase to thirty."

"Progress indeed." She's researched well.

The teenager beamed.

"Next customer, please," said a male bank employee.

The successful applicant approached the counter, signed a document and then received cash. I observed today's date in bold print at the counter - 20 May 2014. When she departed, the bank employee nodded in my direction. I approached the counter.

"Can I help you, sir?"

"I would like a current statement, please?"

"Account number, sir?"

After I supplied details, my account appeared on his computer screen. He studied it, then looked at me. "No activity for fourteen years, Mr Carsell-Brown?"

"I have been on my travels."

"I will need identification."

"A council tax reminder?"

"That will suffice, sir." The employee smiled.

I gave the letter to him. Glad I brought the reminders with me. "Now that I've returned, I want to settle my debts."

The employee entered details into his computer, then a printout of my statement appeared. He handed it to me, plus the council tax letter.

"Thanks."

"Will that be all, sir?"

"I require a new cheque book and wish to draw out cash."

"Please fill in your details, sir." He pushed a form towards me.

As I filled it in, the employee left and soon returned with a chequebook. I gave him the form, then I received cash, plus a chequebook. Picking up both, I put them into my jacket pocket.

"Is there anything else, Mr Carsell-Brown?"

"That's all, for now."

"Have a good day, sir."

Leaving the bank, I headed for a newsagent. Until my domestic power is restored, a newspaper will suffice for current events. Next, I had to make urgent calls, and came across the village's sole telephone box. Soon, cell phones will render them redundant. With my abundance of coins from the newsagent, I will contact the various providers. To breathe fresh air, I kept the door ajar with my size nine. Several speedy calls ensued.

Next, I headed for a familiar place throughout my travels - The Grey Gull Inn. Since water and power won't be restored until tomorrow, this will become my temporary home.

I waited in the foyer for a few minutes, then picked up one of many brochures from a table. It contained information about tourism throughout Argyll. In 1930, whilst I attended a meeting in Lochgilphead Town Hall, an entrepreneur raised the issue of visitor attraction, which raised eyebrows. He suggested a pro-active approach to promote the scenery, sea links and amenities. Eighty-four years later, it is good to see the marketing of local tourism.

"Good afternoon, sir, how are you today?"

I turned around.

"There are many attractions in the area - sailing, hillwalking and the establishment's fine beers."

An ambassador, as well as the receptionist.

"Do you require accommodation, sir?"

"A room for one, maybe two nights." I laid the brochure on the table.

The receptionist looked through a register book.

"A single room."

"You're in luck." He looked up. "With the Commonwealth Games, it's a busy time."

That reminds me, the World Cup will commence next month. "Where is the World Cup being held this year?"

"Brazil."

"Are Scotland involved?"

He shook his head.

"Pity."

"Andy Murray may retain his Wimbledon title, though."

"Andy Murray?"

The receptionist frowned. "Have you been in outer space for the last five years?"

The last fourteen.

"He won Wimbledon last year."

"Splendid." I must catch up on the past.

The receptionist handed me a key. "Room 13, on the first floor, sir."

"Thanks." I took the key. "Is there a radio or television in the room?"

"Both, sir. Dinner is served between eight and ten o'clock. The bar does snacks and is open till midnight."

"Terrific." I recall when it closed two hours earlier.

"Breakfast is seven till nine."

After a delicious evening meal, I left the dining room, and entered a traditional-style bar. The plain white walls contrasted with dark wooden furniture. A polished floor appeared spotless, as with the bar counter. An intriguing observation - no customer smoking, or ashtrays on tables. With clean air, it's not in keeping with a bar. Has the Government overtaxed tobacco? I approached the counter and a member of staff stepped forward. "Yes, sir?"

I looked at the shiny brass beer fonts. "A lager, please."

"Tennent's Lager or Stella, sir?"

I pointed to the appropriate font.

"A pint, sir?"

I nodded. It's been a while.

The bar person poured lager into a glass then laid it on the counter in front of me. It had a healthy froth on top - a good sign.

"£2.50, please, sir."

I handed over the correct amount.

"Thanks, sir." He pressed a series of buttons, and deposited the coins into a sophisticated electronic cash register.

When I paid for a drink in my previous timeline, as cash was rung up, the bulky metal till rang. Character, indeed. I sipped my pint - terrific! The best beer I've tasted in 118 years. A fellow customer at the bar looked my way. "Are you on holiday, sir?"

"I've been overseas and just returned." I cast my gaze around the vicinity. "Is this a non-smoking bar?"

The man grinned. "How long have you been gone?"

"Quite a while."

"A smoking ban in public places has been in force for nine years."

That explains it.

"However, since the ban, bar trade has fallen."

"There's a healthier atmosphere."

The man nodded.

I hope he's a football fan. "What is the latest in Scottish football?"

"Which league?"

"The Premier Division."

"It's now called the Premiership, and Rangers, Hearts and Hibs are not involved."

I lifted my pint and took a swig.

"Hibs were relegated last season."

I choked, then coughed. Not again! When I left in 2000, they had been promoted back to the top division!

"They reached consecutive Scottish Cup Finals in 2012 and 2013."

I put my glass on the bar and smiled. "Did they win both finals?" Please say they did.

The man shook his head.

"One of them?" Surely.

Once more, he shook his head.

My heart sank. Certain aspects of football remain unchanged. "Which teams did they play against?"

"Celtic and Hearts. Celtic beat them 3-0 and Hearts 5-1."

My heart sank further.

The man stared. "You look deflated."

Thank goodness I wasn't here. "What of Rangers and Hearts current situation?"

"Both went into Administration and received punishments."

"And the Scottish National team?"

"They are in power at Holyrood."

I smiled. "The football team?"

The man laughed. "Since 1998, they still haven't qualified for the latter stages of a tournament."

Oh, well. "How is the economy?"

He took a sip of his beer. "Improving, considering the Government had to rescue most of the large banks."

"What happened?"

"They went bust."

"Bust! How?"

"Lending to people who couldn't repay loans."

"Similar to 1929."

The man grinned. "Were you there?"

I laughed. Yes, just returned.

My fellow customer finished his drink, bade farewell, then left the bar. I picked up mine and finished it.

"Another lager, sir?" said the bar person.

"Just a half-pint."

Soon, a glass arrived, and I handed him two coins. He handed me a fifty-pence piece.

"Thanks." A pint is cheaper than two half-pints!

"On vacation, sir?"

"Just returned."

"An adventure holiday?"

I nodded. And more.

"My older brother went hot-air ballooning in France."

"Did he enjoy it?"

The bar person shook his head. "He's not keen on heights."

"Why choose ballooning?"

"For the thrill."

He'll enjoy time travel. "Could you recommend a local gardener? Since I've been away, my garden has gone wild."

He laughed. "There is a local firm whose premises are near the canal."

Could it be the same one, which began in 1896?

"Hold on, I'll get you their details."

He went into a back room, then returned with a small, printed card. After handing it to me, I read it.

"The firm carries out work throughout Argyll, however, their premises still remain in Ardrishaig. You can go onto their website and view what services they provide. If you wish, they can redesign your garden. Plants, flowers plus ornaments, can also be supplied." The bar person grinned. "For the affluent clients, they have installed garden fountains."

"Is there a particular reason why the premises remain in the village?" I put the card in my trouser pocket.

"A pledge the original owner made."

In 1896, young Angus mended his ways. Now a thriving company exists, a meaningful legacy.

"A refill, sir?"

"No, thanks." I put my glass on the counter.

"Night, sir."

I left the bar, then went to reception for my room key. With comfortable accommodation, and a couple of beers, I'll sleep well tonight.

I opened my eyes, and heard birds chirping in my left ear. Where am I? Raising my head, I looked around the room. This is not my hospital digs. I composed myself, and sighed. I'm at the Grey Gull Inn. Phew! I sat up, yawned, and then stretched my arms. Since my time travel exploits began, that's the best night's sleep I've had. I glanced at the bedside clock on a wooden cabinet – 8.30am. I've slept for ten blissful uninterrupted hours. I stared at the en-suite bathroom, how I have missed a long hot bath to relax in and a refreshing shower. Everyday luxuries that I took for granted and can now be enjoyed again. Once more I yawned, then glanced at the bedside clock. Damn! I'll have to rush or miss a cooked breakfast. I dashed into the bathroom, showered, then got dressed. I dashed downstairs, and upon entering the dining room, observed a woman wearing dark attire removing used cutlery and plates from a table. She turned to face me.

"My apologies, I had my best sleep in a long time."

She looked at a wall clock.

"I'm famished!"

"Be back soon to take your order." She left with a full tray.

I sat down at a set table, and picked up its menu card. Whilst reading, the waitress returned.

"A full breakfast with coffee, please."

"Toast, sir?"

I nodded. "Please."

"Marmalade or butter?"

"Marmalade, please."

The waitress smiled and left.

I sat back on a comfy chair, and stared out of the dining

room window. As the sun shone through, I reflected on recent travels, and the gift I had. However, could I ever go back in time again, and would I want to? Low pay for long laborious hours as a coachman and hospital porter, plus unhealthy living standards - no thanks. Especially, when one coachman task involved cleaning out a stable for two horses. I can still smell it. As for being a porter, my backache from pushing trolleys remains. Then again, I witnessed remarkable sights, and met my past relatives.

"Your breakfast, sir." The waitress paused. "Sir!"

I looked up.

She smiled. "Not fully awake yet?"

"Just thinking about the past."

After a delicious breakfast, I paid my accommodation bill, then walked back to the small hamlet of Dochar. Before leaving, the owner said he would contact the garden firm, recommended to me by one of his bar staff.

As I approached Docharnea, vehicles sped along the straight and narrow road. Due to the warm sunny weather, most had their driver's window down. No doubt an insect or two made a nuisance of themselves. Walking up the driveway, I shook my head. When I took ownership of the property, a blue sky could be seen, however, not anymore. I hope the garden firm arrives sooner, rather than later to trim those trees. I opened the door, and stepped into reception. The blush magnolia walls, white ceiling and skirting, still look fresh. I checked the mailbox, good, no postman this morning. To find out if power had been restored, I pressed the nearest light switch, and smiled. Now I can listen to music. When in the Grey Gull bar, I observed a young woman view programmes on her cell phone. I will be traditional and watch in front of a television. To ensure running water, I went into the bathroom and then turned on both chrome taps. After they spluttered, water flowed from each. I am now home.

Sifting through the remaining backlog of mail, I heard the sound of tyres come up the driveway. Moments later two doors closed, and the doorbell rang. I rose from my couch, went into reception, and opened the door. Standing, were two sturdy men dressed in grey sweatshirts and black trousers, each with a hearty grin.

"Good afternoon to you, sir," said the older man, "we're here to transform the grounds of your property into respectability."

I smiled. "It may take both of you some time."

"Don't concern yourself, sir, we've seen worse than this!"

"How much will it cost?"

"Give us ten minutes, we'll have a look around the property."

Both men surveyed the perimeter, and examined prime areas of growth. The older of the two shook his head, and his colleague nodded. After fifteen minutes, they returned with solemn expressions. I stood at the door, fearing the worse.

"A huge job, sir." The older man sighed. "We'll need an extra pair of hands."

"Our great-grandfathers knew each other."

He stared. "Did your relative stay here?"

"Yes, for a spell, he worked as a coachman."

Grinning, he shook my hand. "I'm Angus, named after my great-grandfather."

"Pleased to meet you, Angus. I am also named after my great-grandfather."

"Then you're James?"

I nodded.

He glanced at the younger man. "James, this is my son Alex."

I shook his hand.

He is named after my grandfather."

I met him in 1912.

"Is the property haunted by a ghost? We hear all sorts of

stories."

"If not, does the price come down?"

Angus laughed. "The cost for cutting, trimming and clearing is £1900, James." He cast his gaze around the area. "It'll take three of us three, maybe, four days."

I nodded. "Fine, when can you start?"

"Tomorrow morning."

"Splendid."

The two gardeners bid me farewell, and got into their white van. As it moved off, the older man waved. When the van left Docharnea, Alex looked at his father. "You estimated the job at £3000!"

Angus glanced at his son. "Our family owe a great debt to that man's great grandfather. Later, I'll tell you the story that my father revealed to me."

I returned to my backlog of mail, and after a while, put them aside. I grew tired of promotional literature for car insurance, domestic radiators and double-glazing. Does a company recoup marketing expenditure, or is it a reason why most go bust? I went into the kitchen, made a cup of coffee, and stood outside the back door. I stared at the coach house - a lick of paint is needed. Fourteen winter gales and heavy rain have taken their toll. I better check that all four rooms within the building are safe and secure. Hopefully, no wasps, birds or small animals have found it desirable. I drank my coffee, lifted the coach house keys off a wall hook, and walked across the courtyard. I went into the old stables, and looked about. As a coachman, I had to hold my nose each time. However, now it is an empty shell, and used for storage. I breathed out, and locked the door. Next, I checked a large room, where the coach could be left overnight, however, it usually lay outside. In those times, the courtyard consisted of grass, mud and weeds. Also, horse dung did not lend to its appeal. I shut the large double-door, and went to a door, which led upstairs. I inserted the key, and turned its black handle. The door did not open, I tried again with force, and it flew open. I'll ask Angus if he knows a good joiner. The wooden staircase, with its familiar creak, requires a sweep. At the top, both entrances on either side will also have to be tackled. To the right is where I stored fodder for both horses, apart from a spider's web over the small skylight, the room's empty. I entered the coachman's quarters, stopped, and cast my gaze around the room. I stared at a space where my makeshift bed used to be. The six o'clock morning starts still haunt me. I went to the window, and looked out, recalling when no trees existed. Whilst walking away, I glanced at the Gothic mirror. I am not staring into it ever again! Besides, past family trauma has been averted with no damage to the timeline. I went back down the staircase, and locked the door behind me. Looking around the vicinity, I pondered. Even in 1896, and throughout the ages, Docharnea retains its charm.

Before leaving for Ardrishaig, I stood and admired my revitalised garden. The Angus I met in 1896 would have been delighted with the result. Also, weeds had been cleared from the courtyard and driveway, plus years of autumn leaves had been removed. They filled the flattop lorry twice! Next on my list of urgent tasks - a cleaner to spruce up Docharnea's interior. In the village, I'll get a local newspaper and check out the advertised services. Rather than take transport into Ardrishaig, as previously, I'll walk. With my age now fifty-six, I should undertake more exercise.

Accompanied by warm sunshine, I strolled along the pavement, gazing at Loch Fyne in the distance. I've experienced the view for more than a century, yet the thrill doesn't diminish. Thirty minutes later, I entered a newsagent, and came out with an edition of the Argyllshire Advertiser. My next stop would be the village supermarket to stock up on food. Having discovered a cost-free delivery service, I made arrangements. To sit down and read my newspaper, I came across a coffee shop. Sitting down, I cast my gaze around the bright interior. I remember this place being the former tearoom where my great-aunt, Olivia, and I shared a pot of tea in 1940. The previous day, I had prevented my great-uncle from a fatal motor accident, and to convey her gratitude, she wanted to thank me. Unknown to Olivia, I was her future great-nephew! However, when we chatted, she appeared as if aware of a family connection. A woman's intuition?

"Yes, sir." The shop assistant paused. "Yes, sir!"

I looked up. "My apologies."

A tall slim woman smiled. "What can I get you?"

"A white coffee, please."

"Would you like a scone, cake or biscuits with your coffee?"

"Do you have any doughnuts?"

The shop assistant nodded.

"What do you have?"

"Jam, custard and plain."

"Plain, thanks."

"One or two?"

"I'll have two." I need to put on weight.

"Back soon."

The stocky waitress who served me in 1930 wore a plain black dress. This vibrant individual has a stylish red top and tight black trousers, therefore, pleasing on the eye. I turned to the sports section of my newspaper with interest. This summer would be a prominent one due to a World Cup tournament, and the Commonwealth Games in Glasgow. The city's hoteliers will be gearing up for this prestigious event, rubbing their hands in anticipation. As the shop assistant returned with my order, I came across 'Services', and an abundance of tradesmen, though, no domestic cleaner. Upon finishing my coffee, the shop assistant approached. "Can I get you anything else, sir?"

"Nothing to eat or drink, however, I'm in need of a domestic cleaner."

The shop assistant glanced at a nearby table. "That woman cleans for several local businesses. Shall I enquire for you?"

"Please do."

She went to speak with the woman, who then looked over, rose from her chair, and came across. "Can I sit down, please?"

"Certainly."

"My name is Nanette," she said smiling, "where is your property?"

"Dochar."

"Is it Docharnea?"

I nodded.

The curvy auburn-haired woman laid her hand on my arm. "My mother's great-aunt worked there a long time ago."

"What was her name?"

"Nancy."

Ardrishaig is indeed a small place.

"Three families employed her." Nanette beamed. "Is your surname Carsell-Brown?"

"I'm James Carsell-Brown."

"Nancy worked for a James Carsell-Brown, and his wife Elizabeth."

I remember them well.

"Poor James, being murdered in New York."

"What became of Elizabeth?"

"After returning from America, she bought a hotel in Inveraray, then acquired more. Later, Elizabeth sold her share of the company to a business partner."

"To retire?"

Nanette nodded. "Elizabeth and her second husband moved to the French Riviera."

"A local chap?"

"Yes, Adam Fraser."

Adam got his wish. "What year did they move to

France?"

Nanette paused. "1949. Unfortunately, Adam passed away five years later, but Elizabeth lived to the ripe old age of ninety."

Not if I hadn't pushed her out of a runaway horse's path.

"A penny for them."

"I lived in that part of France."

"When?"

"Fourteen years ago."

"Has your property been empty for all that time?"

"Sadly, yes."

"I may be there for a couple of days."

"I understand."

"Is it haunted? A rumour exists that the ghost of a coachman appears at night."

I laughed. "Only once a year – the 31st of October."

Nanette laughed.

"You won't be bothered for another five months!"

"That's okay, then." She smiled.

With starting that rumour, my grandfather and great-uncle have a lot to answer for.

"I could start the day after tomorrow."

"Splendid, see you then."

Nanette got up, and departed the coffee shop. I returned to my newspaper and turned to an article on the Glasgow Commonwealth Games. I attended the 1938 British Empire Exhibition in Glasgow's Bellahouston Park only last year! I folded my newspaper, went to the cash point, and paid the helpful assistant. Since my visit in 1930, the shop has had a makeover, and perhaps several times, but that damn doorbell still remains!

I walked along the main street, and approached the village hall. I observed a billboard poster and moved closer. It publicised a debate on Scotland's future, which would take place on Friday 6 June at 7.30pm. A date in 1944 that became synonymous for an allied invasion of Europe. Let's hope this will be a peaceful harmonious debate. Representing the 'yes' campaign would be Alistair Lambton, a Conservative councillor, and his opponent, Alec Struthers, a local Scottish Nationalist councillor. Could those individuals be descendants of people I have also encountered back in time? I must go to the meeting and find out.

I arrived at the village hall later than expected, but managed to find an empty seat. Interest on Scotland's future had gripped the residents of rural Ardrishaig, including teenagers. A well-groomed middle-aged lady next to me sighed. "I feel my age tonight."

I smiled. "Most of the teenagers don't look eighteen."

"Have you just returned to Scotland?"

I nodded.

"Sixteen-year-olds are now allowed to vote."

"Sixteen?"

She nodded.

That explains it.

"I am not against them being given a say, however, do they possess the knowledge and experience to decide Scotland's future?"

Good point.

A man sitting next to the lady leaned towards her, and shook his bald head. The wrinkles on his face highlighted a long existence. "They're too young. At eighteen, I fought Hitler."

I could hear noises of discontent from behind and glanced round. A group of teenagers in dark blue tops glared at the man.

The lady looked at the man. "This is the 70th anniversary of D-Day."

"I've the scars to prove it!"

A groan followed from one of the teenagers. I looked at the clock on a wall, and it showed a few minutes until the debate commenced. Having attended a rowdy meeting here in 1938, hopefully this time no eggs will be thrown.

Five minutes later, a lady and two gentlemen walked onto the wooden stage. The chairperson introduced both guest speakers and then announced this evening's format. Alistair Lambton would put forward the argument for a united Britain, and Alec Struthers an opposing view. I turned to the lady and whispered, "Do both men live in the village?"

"Yes," she whispered, "And Alistair Lambton is the grandson of Alan Lambton."

I nodded.

"Have you heard of him?"

"Yes." In 1912, I met him when he was a boy.

"The other chap is from a staunch Christian background. His family has been involved with the local church for many years. Alec is an excellent choirmaster, similar to his father and grandfather."

How will he conduct the audience?

"He resembles his grandfather, in a dignified way."

My thought also.

"There is a rumour that his grandfather did undercover work in the war."

It's not a rumour, as I found out to my cost in 1940.

Alistair Lambton spoke about financial stability relating to currency, pensions and the National Health Service. Alec Struthers advocated fulfilling Scotland's potential to become a richer nation. Alistair Lambton then emphasised a 'yes' vote could result in large companies relocating to England and many jobs lost. Alec Struthers highlighted further North Sea oil fields, which would create jobs. Arguments continued from each speaker, and once they had concluded, the chairperson asked for questions. A woman in the front row raised her hand. "What is plan B for the currency?" she said looking at Alan Struthers.

He did not give a direct answer, but added that Scotland

could retain the present currency. An elderly man raised his hand, and the chairperson acknowledged him.

"Will pensions and benefits be cut Mr Struthers, given there will have a smaller pot of cash?"

Alec Struthers shook his head. "If Scotland becomes richer, then benefits would be increased."

"And what of pensions?"

"I don't envisage any pension reduction."

A younger man raised his hand.

"Yes?" said the chairperson.

"Mr Lambton, will Scotland be devolved more powers from Westminster?"

Alistair Lambton straightened his tie. "I would say it is a distinct possibility."

A teenager raised his hand, then again.

"Go ahead," said the chairperson.

He stood up. "Mr Struthers, will more jobs be created in an independent Scotland?"

"Tax and DVLA Organisations will be based in Scotland, rather than centralised in England. Oil and gas research are a 'forte' for Scottish companies. The aforementioned will create jobs under an independent and entrepreneurial Scotland."

The teenager sat down, and whispered to a friend. "What does entrepreneurial mean?"

"The chance of a job." His friend grinned.

A gentleman in a dark suit, white shirt and sober tie got up. "Mr Struthers, your Party wants to rid Scotland of nuclear weapons?"

Alec Struthers nodded.

"Have nuclear weapons not prevented another major war? If we didn't have them, the Russians would bully us. A submarine loaded with nuclear missiles from Faslane patrolling the Atlantic, is a deterrent, is it not?"

Silver-haired members of the audience clapped, and in particular, the Normandy veteran.

"And you want to get rid of Faslane!" The gentleman shook his head, and sat down.

"Nuclear weapons have not stopped wars, Syria and the Ukraine are perfect examples," stated Alec Struthers.

Other sections of the audience cheered and clapped. A broad smile appeared on Alec Struther's face.

Twenty minutes later, the discussion ended in a peaceful and cordial manner. The audience appeared split on a 'yes' or 'no' vote. Thursday, September 18, would be an eventful day.

CHAPTER 7

A LOST LOVE

July brought glorious warm sunshine and clear blue skies. I may regret not replacing Docharnea's well-worn patched-up grey slated roof. Wet and windy weather could result in buckets at the ready for leaks. A benefit of the dry summer – my lawnmower is not overworked. Given the amount of grass, it is a welcome break. As for inside the property, a proficient domestic cleaner had added a sparkle.

Feeling content, I went for a late morning walk. After a short while, I approached the grey-haired lady's house. As before, she tended to her garden plants.

"Good morning," I said smiling.

She looked up. "Hello, again."

"Still busy, I see."

"My flowers are to blame."

I glanced at different shades of roses. "The weather has been kind to them?"

"And the weeds!"

I laughed.

"Where are you headed?" She laid her trowel on the dyke.

"Nowhere in particular, just out for a brisk walk."

"Rain or shine, a friend of mine would take regular walks along this road."

"For exercise?"

The lady shook her head. "She met a chap many years ago, then he suddenly disappeared, but maintained he would return as he left."

"Disappeared?"

The lady nodded. "I felt she nursed a broken heart."

"What was your friend's name?"

"Abigail." The lady looked into the distance. "She stayed

outside Dochar, about a quarter mile."

Abigail Anderson, whom I met in the mid-sixties. I have to pay her a visit.

"She kept active, until she passed away."

I paused. "How long ago?"

"Just last year." The lady sighed.

It would have been good to meet with Abigail again.

"She retained her good looks."

I smiled. "Who lives in the property now?"

"A retired couple."

"I'll let you tend to the flowers."

"My back gives way after an hour, I'll finish in a short while."

"See you, later."

"Bye."

As the lady picked up her trowel, I heard a buzzing sound, but dodged the yellow and black pollen-gatherer. I followed the pavement and recalled Abbie and myself going to Glasgow, for a pop concert forty-seven years ago. I will visit her place of rest to pay my belated respects.

I arrived at Ardrishaig's cemetery, and walked through two eight-foot tall grey iron gates.

An eerie silence engulfed the cemetery, and although fine weather, no birds sang. I spotted a woman with a long black dress and dark shawl, standing in front of a grave. I will ask her where Abbie has been laid to rest. As I walked towards her, she turned around, and the face of a young woman confronted me. She gripped the woolen shawl around her neck.

"Excuse me, I'm looking for the grave of Abigail Anderson."

She pointed.

I looked ahead. "Next to the tall headstone with a cross?" I take it a stare means 'yes'. "Thank you."

Her lifeless eyes made me feel uneasy, and the black

attire accentuated an ashen face and white neck. I walked to Abbie's grave, and bent down to read the headstone inscription.

'Abigail Syme Anderson, 1930 - 2013'.

I thought about our first encounter in 1938, accompanied by her mother in Dochar. Two years later, our paths crossed in the spring when I reappeared wearing a coachman's uniform, and Abbie remained unfazed! In 1967, when I sought accommodation at the Grey Gull Inn, she greeted me at reception. With my physical appearance unaltered, she recognised me. Abigail became the only person aware of my true identity. Disappearing after our friendship blossomed made me feel callous. Next time, I will bring flowers.

Upon leaving, I observed that I had the cemetery to myself. I looked at my watch, and headed for the village coffee shop.

When I reached it, other village residents shared my addiction. I spotted an empty chair, where a woman wearing a nurse's uniform underneath a jacket sat. I approached, and she looked up.

"Is this chair taken?" I touched it.

She shook her head. "It's all yours."

"The shop is busy today!" I sat down.

"A poet is reciting from her new book." The nurse glanced at her watch. "She's due to start in five minutes."

"A local poet?"

The nurse nodded.

"An excellent way to promote a new book."

"She has also done a recital at the hospital."

"Are you on a lunch break?" I glance at the uniform.

"No, my shift has finished." The nurse grinned.

"What is the poet's name?"

"Ella Lansbury, she's my mother. After retiring several years ago, she had time to spare, and made use of it."

"Did she secure a publishing deal?"

"Eventually, but my mother sent her work to many

publishers, plus several agents."

Maybe I should write about my time travel experiences.

The shop assistant approached. "Can I get you something before the recital starts?" She looked at both customers.

"A black coffee, please", said the nurse.

"White for me, please."

The shop assistant departed with a smile.

"Prior to retirement, what did your mother do?"

"Company Director. My grandmother began the company more than eighty years ago, and later, my mother became a director."

"And you?"

"I wanted to be a nurse, however, I paint in my spare time."

"What is your grandmother's name?" Have I met her in the past?

"Evelyn Stoddart, her maiden name was White."

Evelyn White, that name is familiar. Of course! She worked as a receptionist at the hotel in Inveraray, which held a Christmas Eve dance in 1929.

"Have you heard of her?"

I nodded. "An older relative met her at the Burgess Hotel, Inveraray."

"That was the first in a chain of hotels."

"Is Lansbury your mother's married name?" It's uncommon for Ardrishaig.

"No, it's Smith, she didn't want to use her real name. Incidentally, my name is Elizabeth Smith." She held out her hand. "Beth to my friends."

I shook it. "James, James Carsell-Brown."

Just as Ella Lansbury arrived, the shop assistant returned with two coffees. When the audience had settled, she introduced herself, then recited a selection of her favourite poems. Fifteen minutes later, she received an appreciative round of applause. I drank my coffee, bid farewell to Beth, and left to the sound of that bell.

I arrived home, checked the letterbox, and took out a leaflet. Too late, another garden maintenance firm beat you to it. I went into the kitchen, and put the leaflet into a drawer. Later, I will sit on my comfortable living room couch and watch football. Having experienced harsh and austere timelines, it's a luxury I took for granted. Tonight, Germany plays Brazil for a place in the prestigious World Cup final. Attack-minded Brazil, with a passionate home crowd behind them, should stroll to victory.

A dramatic one-sided encounter unfolded, though not for the favoured team. As someone once said, "Football can be a strange game." With a 7-0 score in favour of Germany, strange is an understatement! Brazil's supporters will have to drown their sorrows, rather than celebrate, in the streets of Rio.

Whilst about to fall asleep, sudden gusts of wind ensued, then noises from the coach house. A door banged to and fro, therefore, I hadn't secured it. Damn! Then, the faint sound of footsteps could be heard. I got up, pulled back the curtain, and observed a deserted courtyard. After making myself respectable, I went downstairs and searched for a torch. Finding one, I opened the back door, and shone the torch around the courtyard. With no one about, I approached the coach house, closed the door, and locked it. I cast my gaze around the calm surrounds, went back inside, and returned to bed.

Next day, I went into Ardrishaig, and bought flowers to lay at Abbie's grave. Upon entering the cemetery, I noticed another visitor. Getting closer, I recognised the young woman from my previous visit, and wearing the same attire. Also, a similar eerie silence still existed. I approached Abbie's grave, placed pink roses, and stood. After a period of reflection, I turned around to leave. Whilst I walked through the iron gates, a stocky, white-bearded man carrying a shovel approached. He stopped, and tipped his grey cap. "Mornin' to you, sir."

There's no dirt etched into his cuticles. "A pleasant day to tend the grounds."

"Aye, it is that, sir." The workman grinned.

"Do you have many visitors to the cemetery?"

The workman shook his head. "You're the only one I've seen in a week."

"On the two occasions I've been here, I saw a young woman."

"Are you sure, sir?"

"Positive, she left only a minute ago." I pointed. "She stood at the tall grey headstone."

The workman looked towards the headstone.

"She wore a black dress and shawl."

"A young woman, you say, sir?"

"Early to mid-twenties, she had long raven hair."

"Nobody passed me, sir." The workman grinned. "Maybe she's a quick walker."

I laughed.

"Must get to work, sir." He tipped his cap, and walked on.

I headed back to the main street, and glanced at my watch - time for a late morning coffee. Entering the outlet, I had my pick of tables, and chose a window view. Outside, people walked past in summer clothes with a smile. Warm sunny weather can boost trade for local retailers, with an influx of visitors. However, today's amiable weather won't entice them indoors! The economic revolution of five decades ago will be a distant memory to locals, although, I witnessed it less than a year ago.

"Hello again, sir," said the shop assistant, "a black coffee?"

"White, please."

She smiled. "Today, we have excellent chocolate fudge cake on special offer."

"Do you have any doughnuts?"

She nodded. "Yes, we do."

"I'll have two, please."

"Back soon." What's wrong with fudge cake.

I looked out the window and noticed two women with jackets on top of their nurses' uniforms. One is Beth, whom I spoke to at a recent poetry recital. The two women entered, and Beth looked at me, then came over with her colleague.

"Hello, again," I said.

"Can we join you?" said Beth.

"Of course, have a seat."

Both women sat opposite me, and looked towards the shop counter. The assistant acknowledged them and came over.

"Two black coffees, please," said Beth.

The shop assistant smiled and departed.

"James, this is Sarah, my friend and colleague."

Sarah held out her trim hand.

I shook it. She has a strong grip.

"Phew!" said Beth, "it's hot in here." She removed her dark blue jacket.

Sarah removed her cream jacket.

I grinned. "Customers who enter may think this is a casualty unit."

Both women laughed, looked at each other, then at several customers at their tables. Sarah flicked a dark hair off her pale blue uniform.

"How long does your shift last?" I looked at both women.

"Eight hours," said Beth.

Sarah removed a black shoe, and massaged her foot. "I must get a pair of larger ones." She replaced the shoe.

"You should wear softer ones," said Beth.

"My feet will be fine for the weekend." She smiled at Beth.

I looked at Beth.

"Sarah and I are going hill-walking this weekend."

"Far afield?"

"Lochgilphead," said Sarah, "the hills are not as steep."

Beth laughed. "The Munros in Argyll can be tackled later."

Sarah nodded. "When we become hardy and experienced, similar to my brother."

"When did Derek tackle his first Munro?" said Beth.

"Four years ago, and has climbed all nineteen within Argyll." Sarah looked towards the counter.

"What are your plans for this weekend, James?" said Beth.

"I have an idea for a novel, and will attempt to make a start."

"Sarah raised her eyebrows.

"What's it about?" said Beth.

"Time travel."

"Fiction?" said Sarah.

I nodded. Not really.

"Come hill-walking with us," said Beth, "the weather is ideal."

"Write your novel later," added Sarah.

The shop assistant returned, and lifted each white saucer and cup off a wooden tray onto the table. "If you require more coffee, let me know." She went to serve another customer.

Sarah lifted her cup, took a sip, and set it down. "That's better." She sat back.

As Beth and I followed, Sarah looked my way. "What did you do this morning, James?"

"I visited the cemetery."

"Paying your respects to someone?"

I nodded.

"You would have the cemetery to yourself," said Beth, as she sipped her coffee.

I shook my head. "There was another visitor, a young

woman."

Beth coughed, setting her cup on the saucer.

"Wearing a long black dress and shawl?" said Sarah.

"Why, yes, do you know her?" I sat back.

Sarah stared at Beth.

"What's up?" They have serious expressions.

"Have you not heard the cemetery is haunted by a young woman?" said Beth.

I smiled at both women. "Is this a wind-up?"

Sarah leaned forward. "We're not winding you up, James! She has haunted the cemetery for almost a century."

"Not many people have seen her," said Beth, "she appears at certain periods in time."

"I've seen her twice."

Beth stared at Sarah.

"When did someone last see her?"

"Ten years ago," said Sarah, "around this time of year."

I finished my coffee, and set the cup on its saucer. "I have a joiner due at one o'clock."

"See you later," said Beth.

I paid for my coffee at the counter, and whilst leaving, acknowledged Beth and Sarah's farewell gesture.

Beth lifted her cup, and looked at Sarah. "Glad you didn't mention the curse."

"Anyone who can see her, dies soon after." Sarah frowned. "Thankfully, not many have."

"Why James?"

Sarah shrugged her shoulders.

By August, rain had become a rarity, thus benefiting Scotland's inhabitants, retailers and tourists. Those who visited Glasgow's Commonwealth Games would perceive the country as a desirable destination, with its scenic charm and constant sunshine. For me, glorious weather or not, I wanted to start my novel - easier said than done. Does the story begin with me as a child in Edinburgh, or, an adult in

Aberdeen? Then there is my liaison in Nice with the French Secret Service, and their spy, pretty Michelle Duvallier. Having lived in Nice, knowledge of the city will be beneficial. I could start from when first entering the coach house, and being thrust back in time! I will go for a walk, ponder, and later decide.

Whilst walking, I recalled certain events. Before my travels began. I had visited great-aunt Olivia's grave. After I went back in time, I met her as a young woman! This being one of many surreal moments that I experienced. Further on, I came across the active lady at work in her garden. She spotted me, approached the garden wall, and removed her green gloves. "Dare I say it, some light rain would help."

I smiled. "It will arrive, soon enough."

She laughed. "Back to the village?"

"Yes, the cemetery."

"A relative?"

"Olivia Carsell-Brown."

"A lovely person, and did a lot of charity work for the local community."

"She enjoyed her work."

"What was the connection?"

"My great-aunt."

"Losing her father at such an early age." The lady shook her head.

I met Edward in 1896. "A charming individual."

The lady paused. "To the florist?"

"Yes, see you later."

"Unless it rains!"

I laughed.

"Bye." How would he have known Edward, he died in 1916.

I carried on and observed many shiny vehicles pass by. The car wash in the village garage has been busy.

After popping into the florist, I arrived at the cemetery. Even though the sun shone, a strange chill existed. I approached Olivia's place of rest, and laid white Gladiolus at the headstone. Since my previous visit to her grave, a year had passed, but fourteen years for others. Walking back to the gates, I pinpointed where the young woman had stood. Being curious, I went over to the grave, and stared at the headstone inscription - Edward Beaumont, 1884-1916. With Edward being an only child and Olivia having no children, the young woman isn't a close relative. Who is she?

As I left the cemetery, the grave worker approached, shovel on shoulder and whistling a merry tune. "Any young women around today, sir?" he said grinning.

"If so, they're invisible!"

He laughed, and walked on.

In Ardrishaig's main street, I spotted a board outside the Grey Gull Inn. It advertised a two-course lunch for £4.95, plus a drink. Hungry and a tad thirsty, I was hooked. I went up to the bar, and a curvaceous woman came forward. Her blonde hair in a ponytail added to a pleasant appearance. "What can I get you, sir?" she said smiling.

Lovely white teeth. "I saw your special offer on the advertising board."

She handed me a printed menu card.

Nothing appeals. "Any toasted sandwiches?"

"What would you like, sir?"

"Do you have ham and cheese?"

The woman nodded.

"Splendid."

"Something to drink, sir?"

"A lager."

"A pint?"

"Just a half-pint." A pint this early will send me to sleep.

The woman poured lager into a sparkling glass, and laid it on the counter. "When the toasted sandwiches are ready, I'll bring them over."

"Shall I pay now?"

"Later, is fine."

Lifting my glass, I sat at a nearby dark wooden table with two matching chairs. Noticing a newspaper on the next table, I reached over. I opened The Oban Times at its sports section, which highlighted the aftermath of Glasgow's successful Commonwealth Games, plus Andy Murray not retaining his Wimbledon title. As for football, a paragraph touched on Fort William's determination to win the Highland League title. However, the region's prominent sport of shinty, received wide coverage. My toasties appeared, and I put aside the newspaper.

Feeling refreshed, I left the Stag Inn, and strolled along the main street. Passing a charity shop, I observed a window poster with large bold letters - Food Bank. I moved closer, surely, not in 2014! When I travelled back to 1929, much hardship existed, what has transpired in the present? An unkempt man about my age approached, and stood beside me, then glared at the window. "That's due tae cuts in benefit," he said sharply. "People can't afford essentials." He shook his head. "I've had tae cut doon on ma beer and fags."

I continued along the main street, and whilst nearing the supermarket, spotted a black purse on the ground. Further on, a hunched white-haired woman carried a shopping bag. As I picked up the purse, she went into her jacket pocket, stopped and turned round.

I walked up to her, and gave her the purse.

The woman sighed. "Thanks, son." She put her hand on my arm, then swiftly removed it.

"Are you okay?"

The woman composed herself.

"Can I help?"

"No, I'm fine." She stared at me.

I handed over the purse and the woman put it into her pocket. She appeared upset, therefore, I made a suggestion. "Can I buy you a coffee or tea?"

The woman smiled. "Coffee, please."

We walked to the coffee shop, entered, and found a spare

table. A minute later, the shop assistant came across.

"A coffee, please," I said.

The shop assistant smiled. "White?"

I nodded.

"Black for me," said my guest.

As the shop assistant departed, the woman unbuttoned her beige jacket, and leaned forward. Her thick spectacle lenses and black rim put me on the defence.

"Touching your arm gave me a jolt!"

"Why?"

"I'm psychic, and sensed an unnatural presence." The woman sat back. "Has someone close to you passed away recently?"

"A year ago."

"Since then, have you experienced unusual occurrences?"

"When in the cemetery paying my respects to that person, I saw a young woman at a nearby grave, and moments later, she was gone. I asked a gravedigger if he had seen her."

"What did he say?"

"He hadn't."

"Describe her?"

"Long raven hair, black dress and shawl. Also, I have seen her more than once."

The woman stared.

"Do you know who she is?"

"You are not from here?"

"I came to live here fourteen years ago, left not long after, and have just returned."

The shop assistant brought both coffees, laid them on the table, and departed. The woman lifted her cup, took a sip, and set it on the saucer. As she did so, I noticed her wrinkled handshake. I lifted my cup, took a sip, then gripped it with both hands.

"The young woman is not of this world."

I set my cup on the saucer.

"She is caught between both worlds - the living and the dead."

"Why?"

"Following a broken heart, she took her own life, and her spirit cannot rest.

"What happened?"

"She was having an affair with a dashing army officer who came from an affluent family in the village. Before going off to fight in the Great War, he promised to write."

The First World War began exactly a century ago.

"However, unable to be with him, the young woman longed for the war to end and their relationship to resume. When she discovered he had been killed, it was devastating. She attended his morning funeral, then at one o'clock, returned to the grave with a kitchen knife and slit both wrists."

I shook my head. Tragic.

"When found, all colour had gone from her body." The woman sighed.

The haunted stare I received.

"Her parents could not accept that their only daughter had taken her life. Less than a year later, her mother passed away, and the father suffered constant ill health, until his death three years later."

"What was her name?"

"Ann Anderson." The woman paused. "My great-aunt."

I looked at the woman.

"My grandfather found letters from Edward neatly placed inside a box."

I drank what remained of my lukewarm coffee, and set it down. The shop assistant came over, and I shook my head.

"I've often been to the cemetery in the hope of catching a glimpse of Ann."

"Why me?"

"There must be a connection, perhaps a meeting in the

past." The woman smiled. "You wouldn't have been around a century ago."

Masquerading as a coachman, but our paths did not cross. "Since you are a Psychic, has contact ever been attempted?"

"On a number of occasions, but there's been no response. You remain the sole person I've met who's seen my great-aunt."

"What about others who have seen her?"

The woman stared. "They're dead."

The shop assistant reappeared.

The woman looked at her watch. "I must leave."

"I'll have another, please."

The shop assistant smiled and departed.

"Take care." The woman stood up.

"Why did Ann Anderson return to the cemetery at one o'clock?"

"The thirteenth hour of the day."

The woman lifted her bag, walked to the exit, and before leaving looked in my direction. Minutes later, the shop assistant came over, lifting empty cups and saucers.

"Did Susannah read your palm?"

"No, but she made it sweat."

The shop assistant laughed.

After she left, I reflected on what the Psychic had to say. After Edward Beaumont's death at the Somme, Ann Anderson could not face a life without him. A century on, she still mourns for her lost love. Why am I the only person she reveals herself to? Also, my great-aunt Olivia has the middle name of Ann.

September brought less daylight, and evening business-networking opportunities. As people returned from summer vacations, the local Business Club began a series of monthly meetings for Ardrishaig, Lochgilphead and Inveraray members. Ardrishaig's Grey Gull Inn hosted the initial meeting on Monday 1st September. Being a qualified marketing professional, perhaps I can obtain work. Writing a novel is all very well, but it doesn't put food on the table. If a business reference is required, I can mention a past example. Using 21st century marketing techniques, I advised my great grandfather in 1938 on how to promote his supplies of wine. Producing positive results, word spread to local entrepreneurs, resulting in a marketing revolution. As a consequence, prosperity within the area exploded.

I arrived at the Grey Gull in good time for the 7.30pm start. Whilst entering reception, I straightened my tie. The dark attired lady with short auburn hair sitting behind a desk looked up. "Business Club meeting, sir?"

I nodded.

"Your name, sir?"

"James Carsell-Brown."

From a guest list, the lady put a tick against my personal details with her silver pen. "You're the first to arrive."

"Are many expected?"

"We have thirty-two guests registered to attend."

"Splendid."

"Coffee, tea and sandwiches will be served at the event."

"How long has the Business Club existed?"

The receptionist smiled. "Long before my time." She laid her pen on the desk. "I believe it began in the 1950s."

"Sixty years, that is a long time."

"I'm sure someone with a similar surname to yourself started the club." The receptionist looked at the sheet of paper. "Yes, Carsell-Brown." She looked up. "During the 1960s, an upsurge in business success occurred. My grandmother's friend worked here as a receptionist at that time, and often spoke about the good old days!"

"What was her name?" Could it have been Abigail?

"My grandmother?"

I smiled. "The receptionist."

"Abigail Anderson. Robert, her father, worked here in

the bar."

He may have served me.

The receptionist glanced towards the entrance door.

As members arrived to register, I went into the function suite. A crisp white tablecloth covered a long narrow table with plates, crockery and paper napkins. A tall well-groomed lady dressed in a white blouse, navy pinstripe jacket and skirt appeared, and surveyed the table's contents. Members took their seats, and the guest speaker, a representative of Scottish Enterprise stood.

The talk related to export markets, and given the upcoming referendum, a relevant topic. When he finished answering a multitude of quick-fire questions, he slumped down, and mopped his brow with a handkerchief. A well-deserved round of applause followed, then members left their seats and dashed to the table. The well-groomed lady set down two silver pots. "Tea on the left, coffee to the right. Help yourselves to milk and sugar." The lady smiled. "Sausage rolls, sandwiches and assorted biscuits will follow."

I approached the table. "A good spread." I'm feeling hungry.

She leaned forward. "A lot of preparation, I'm glad it's only once every three months!"

"The next meeting is at a venue in Lochgilphead?"

She nodded. "Then Inveraray, and the following month, back to us." The lady flicked blonde hair off her jacket.

"Spread around the spread!"

She laughed.

"Where in Inveraray is the next venue?"

"The Burgess Hotel." She departed.

It's not that long ago I attended their Christmas Eve dance in 1929! Members helped themselves to tea and coffee, then as plates of 'finger food' arrived, they disappeared. Whilst drinking and eating, members mingled and discussed the forthcoming Scottish Referendum.

Uncertainty relating to partnerships with England and other countries were high on everyone's list, plus concerns if an independent Scotland could keep the same currency. If not, this may result in serious trade repercussions for Scottish businesses whose main customers are located outwith Scotland. A member next to me hinted the major Scottish banks could relocate to England, and would they still 'prop' up Scottish businesses? Looking around, members' concerns did not affect their appetites, and after more food appeared, it vanished. Drinking my coffee, I observed the business gender ratio had altered. When I attended a similar meeting fourteen years ago, businesswomen represented a quarter of members, it's now a third, and they're younger.

I left the suite, and being early evening, went into the bar for a beer. A barman who enjoyed hearty meals looked my way. "What can I get you, sir?"

"A lager, please."

"A pint?"

I nodded.

He filled my glass, and set it down. "£2.50 please, sir."

I handed him three coins. I remember when several pennies would suffice, however, the beer tasted like vinegar.

"Did you enjoy tonight's meeting, sir?" He wiped the countertop with a cloth.

"Yes, informative and interesting." I lifted my glass and took a sip.

"What type of business are you in, sir?"

"Advertising and marketing."

He grinned. "No need to market the lager you're drinking, even the foreign beers have been seen off."

"A quality lager." I took a swig, coughed, then set it on the counter.

"Okay, sir?"

I nodded. It's strong.

"No watered beer here, may I add!"

I believe you.

"Did many attend the meeting?"

"Around thirty."

"In recent years, it has not been well attended."

"Any particular reason?"

The barman shrugged his shoulders. "My son attended tonight's event."

"Oh?"

"He graduated from university and then started an information technology company."

"Where did he graduate from?"

"University of the West of Scotland."

I sipped my lager. "Have you worked here long?"

"I own the establishment," he said grinning. "I inherited it from my father."

That's a surprise.

"My grandfather started the business."

I set my glass on the counter. I stayed here in 1938, could that have been Mike, who loaned me a record player and several records?

The owner held out his hand. "I'm Mike, named after my grandfather."

I shook it. "James." His grandfather had a slimmer waistline. "A distant relative met a Robert Anderson who worked here, have you heard of him?"

"His daughter Abigail worked as a receptionist in the 1960s."

The owner excused himself to serve another customer, and I began to reminisce about my visit here in 1967, meeting Abigail. Minutes later, he returned and wiped the counter. "I recall my father telling me of a family trauma which concerned Robert Anderson's young sister."

"What happened?"

"She committed suicide."

"How long ago?"

He paused. "About two years after the First World War started."

My goodness, Ann Anderson.

"Robert's parents and brother never got over the tragedy."

When the owner once more excused himself, I took a swig. Interesting, a family connection between Abigail and the young woman. Still, the question remains, why am I the only person who can see her? I finished my drink, bade farewell to the owner, and headed home.

Two days later, I made my way to the cemetery hoping I would see Ann Anderson's ghost. Being aware of certain circumstances, my curiosity heightened. Will this mysterious young woman reappear again? After all, it has happened on two recent occasions.

Late morning, I approached the iron gates with anticipation, as well as apprehension. I entered, but the cemetery belonged to myself. I walked over to visit Abbie, stood for a short while, then glanced at Edward Beaumont's grave. I spoke to him 118 years ago! Time travel can indeed be a complicated experience. I retraced my steps to the exit and met a familiar individual. "You've usually gone by this time, sir, I must be early!" He took out a silver pocket-watch from his grey waistcoat pocket, and grinned.

His attire doesn't alter. "I tried to find the grave of a young woman who died a century ago."

"Her name, sir?"

Ann Anderson."

"I'll take you to it."

I followed him to the far end of the cemetery, where he pointed to a small grey headstone.

I stared.

"I'll leave you now, sir."

I looked at the workman. "Thank you."

He tipped his grey cap, and departed.

I walked over to Abbie's grave, lifted a flower, and laid it in front of Ann's headstone. A gust of wind appeared, however, the flower did not move.

After a stroll to the main street, I went for an early afternoon coffee. In the shop, I sat down at a window table, and waited. Thursday could be a momentous day in Scotland's history, and with only a couple of days, it was on everyone's lips. The shop assistant approached carrying a tray of used crockery. "The usual?"

"Please."

Beth entered, spotted me, and came across. I saw the shop assistant look our way, and nod.

"Still on night shift duties?"

"I need a strong cup of coffee!"

I laughed.

Whilst Beth removed her jacket, the shop assistant came across with two cups, and set them down. "Black and strong, Beth."

She looked at the shop assistant. "Thanks," she said, then turned to face me. "What did you do this morning, James?" Beth lifted her cup, and took a sip.

"I visited the cemetery hoping to get a glimpse of the ghost." I smiled.

"Which one?"

I paused.

"There are two."

"Two?"

"The young woman, and the gravedigger."

I lifted my cup, and took a sip.

"Don't tell me you've seen the gravedigger as well!"

"This morning, and on two other occasions."

"Beth set her cup on the saucer. "Nobody has seen either of them for decades, yet you've seen both!" Beth took another sip.

I moved forward. "I'm aware of what happened to the young woman, why the gravedigger?"

"It's reckoned he suffered a massive heart attack digging

a grave, and is buried where he collapsed."

"Poor chap." I sighed.

"His job meant everything to him."

"When did he die?"

"1926."

That would explain why he had a pocket-watch.

Beth looked towards the counter. "Ah good, here comes my refill."

The shop assistant laid another black coffee on the table, whilst looking at me. I shook my head, lifted my cup and took a sip.

"I haven't seen Abigail's daughter for some time."

I choked.

"Are you okay?"

I coughed.

"It must have gone down the wrong way."

In more ways than one. I set my cup on the saucer, then coughed.

"You've gone pale."

No wonder.

Beth finished her first cup, then lifted the second.

"How old is Abigail's daughter?"

Beth looked upwards. "I would say, about mid-forties."

Born in the late 1960's. "When did you last see her?"

Beth paused. "About five or six years ago." She sipped her coffee. "Never again did she visit her mother."

"Strange."

Beth shrugged her shoulders.

"For Abigail to visit her daughter, it involved a three hour coach journey into Glasgow, then a connection to Edinburgh."

Beth sipped her coffee. "It's a trek."

I nodded. I may be a father, and have a daughter who will be older!

Beth smiled. "Everything okay?"

"Yes." Not particularly. I drank the remaining coffee,

and glanced at my watch. "Must go, a workman is returning to complete repairs."

"See you later."

"Bye." Hopefully, the walk home will clear my head.

CHAPTER 8

INTERVENTION

I went upstairs and entered the computer room determined to start my book. If I delay any longer, it will never get started, and having discovered that I may be a parent, a distraction is welcome. Where to begin the story still ponders, however, I've gone for an ideal location. After all, I have authenticity at my disposal, therefore, I'll go into the coach house and get a 'feel' for its surroundings.

Walking across the courtyard, I observed the need for a strong weed-killer. How do they grow so fast? I opened the main door, put the key into my trouser pocket, and walked up the staircase with its familiar sound. I wandered round the coachman's quarters to reacquaint myself, then stared at the wall mirror. Why is there no reflection? Mystified, I moved closer, peered, then had to steady myself. Given my past experiences with this mirror, I should have known better. Scrutinising my surroundings, everything appeared normal, and I gave a sigh of relief. I walked down the staircase, and at the bottom, found the door locked. I held my breath and looked at my watch, it had stopped. Damn! I took the key out of my trouser pocket, and opened the door. After stepping outside, I shook my head. The trees around the property had not matured, and only the sound of small birds could be heard. The villa and courtyard looked similar to a previous visit in 1912. Instead of grey gravel, the courtyard combined grass and dirt. And I thought the courtyard in 2014 required attention! I gathered my thoughts, and stared at the coach house. Why have I been sent back? I had resumed a normal existence, and once more, it has been disrupted. As a rabbit ran across the courtyard, I followed its path. There are only tyre tracks, which confirms the timeline is after 1912, when a vehicle replaced the coach and horses. With no one about, and a summer climate, perhaps the residents are on vacation. I took a deep breath - the air is fresher. I approached the rear door that I had existed only minutes ago and found it locked. During this period, Nancy is the housekeeper and she'll no doubt remark that I require a good feed. I walked round the villa with caution. Not only is there a scarcity of vehicles, also properties. Dochar only had a few properties in 1912, Docharnea being the second property built in 1896. With my light-coloured shirt and dark trousers, at least I'm dressed for a traditional summer. Alas, in this era, collarless shirts were the norm, and trousers with turn-ups. My pair of stylish narrow shoes without laces could raise a few eyebrows, although, most people don't stare at the ground. It would be an easy solution to go back into the coach house and attempt to travel back to 2014, but would I arrive there? If as my instinct suggests, I'm here for a reason, therefore, I have to find out. Also, my previous interventions brought good fortune to others.

In the driveway, I heard a vehicle, and observed it going past. Moving at a slow pace, I had time to observe the chassis of an automobile, circa WW1. Also, the road had no pavement, therefore, this era does not take pedestrian welfare into consideration. I pondered on what to do. As the property is empty, should I take refuge in its coach house? Nancy may not appear for some time, and I have to eat. There may be food in the kitchen, however, I'm not going to break into my own property! I checked the cash in my pocket - £12. In this timeline, that could keep me in food and lodgings for at least a week. I won't be able to use the two £1 coins, but hopefully, my £10 note will blend in.

I walked with caution along the disjointed road's edge towards Ardrishaig. Never again will I complain about the poor state of its roadside pavement, because at least in the future, one exists! In this era, motor vehicles are a rarity in a rural village where only the wealthy can afford one.

After twenty minutes, only a single vehicle passed, and when it did, the driver waved. Such is the restricted speed of this era's vehicles, together with driver etiquette. Then, a coach and two horses came towards me with the driver perched on his seat smiling and waving. I acknowledged, and remembered having to clean the coach house stable. Poor chap, I hope he isn't blessed with a strong sense of smell.

Upon reaching Ardrishaig, I went to the Grey Gull Inn. Whenever I required lodgings, it served my purpose. Before entering, I removed my 21st century watch, and put it into my trouser pocket. I waited at reception for several minutes, then knocked three times on the wooden desk. A toilet was flushed and soon a woman wearing a high-collared cream blouse and long brown skirt appeared. "Sorry, to keep you waiting, sir."

"Do you have a spare room?"

The woman nodded. "Due to the war, most of our rooms are available."

Ah, it's a war year, but which one?

"Visitor numbers to the area are down this summer."

Because of conscription and lack of money, vacations became a novelty.

"How long will your stay be for, sir?"

"A week." If not less.

He has no luggage. "Please sign the register book." She dipped a black fountain pen into the reception desk inkwell, then carefully handed it to me.

Whilst signing the book, I looked at today's date, then laid the pen down. As she removed a brass key from the accommodation board, I noticed all other rooms were available.

"Do you require a deposit?" I took the key.

"Pay when you leave, sir, breakfast is at 7.30."

That's early.

"If you wish, it can be served thirty minutes earlier?"

"7.30 is fine." I observed a newspaper on the reception desk.

"Would you like to read it?"

I nodded. "Please."

The woman handed it to me. "Do you require an evening meal?"

"Yes, I do."

"What time would suit?"

"Between six and seven o'clock?"

"6.30?"

I nodded.

"We provide a laundry service." That's a strange shirt, there's no buttons to hold the collar on.

"Splendid." I'll have to visit to a local charity shop for clothes, especially a jacket.

"See you later." The woman smiled.

I walked up a flight of bare wooden stairs to my allocated room. Creaky staircases are not only confined to the coach house. The white emulsion walls had portraits of Loch Fyne, Ardrishaig's canal and the surrounding countryside. After entering, a sudden gust of wind slammed the door shut. Straight away, I turned around, staring at the door. I then cast my gaze around the spartan room, which comprised a wooden bed, scratched wardrobe and bedside cabinet. No en-suite bathroom this time, only a white ceramic sink with two large brass taps. After my return to the 21st century and modern bathroom amenities, once more, it is back to basics. I unfolded the Scottish Daily Express for 7th July 1916, with its headline, 'Slaughter on the Somme' in bold capitals. The article stated that on the first day in July, British casualties amounted to 57,000, and the carnage continues with no end in sight. Lord Kitchener's force of brave volunteers is being shot to pieces. Apparently, the bombardment of Germany's front line, before the battle commenced, had little impact. Sitting on my bed, I pondered. I had read history books about this battle, and watched countless documentaries on television. However, being in 1916 reading current news is surreal. Lord Kitchener's army of volunteers consisted of educated professionals and manual workers, plus sportsmen. Although military training would have been provided, they lacked skills in the art of war. The Somme conflict became one of the bloodiest battles in history, with more than a million casualties from either side. In future years, the term 'a lost generation' would describe soldiers who lost their lives during the First World War. Saddened, I put the newspaper aside.

Needing fresh air, I went downstairs to reception and left my key. After an hour of walking, I found a bench and sat down. I have now witnessed changes over three centuries, however, this timeline is distressing. The past two years have taken its toll on locals who fought. I've witnessed men and older teenagers with missing limbs, and no doubt, diminished self-respect. They walk dispirited on crutches, or wear a jacket with an empty sleeve. I've also seen facial bandages to cover a nasty head disfigurement, and with another two years of frantic fighting left, casualties will rise. A shameful aspect of the war will be failure to interpret 'shell shock' as an illness, and because soldiers flee the noise of battle, they are shot for cowardice. 1916 is not a good timeline in which to materialise. I got up, and several minutes later, approached a familiar main street location. Where the modern coffee shop stood in 2014, a quaint tearoom exists. When I entered, a bell rang. Certain characteristics never alter, however, it produced a faint smile. I looked around, even in 1916 the shop is popular, then, two women left their table. As with previous visits back in time, intriguing stares were directed at my unconventional clothes, however, I've now become used to them. The waitress with black attire and her hair tied in a bun came across and gave a curious look.

"Do you serve coffee?"

She shook her head. "Sorry, sir."

"A cup of tea, please."

After she left, I noticed only elderly customers. With able-bodied men conscripted to fight against Germany, women would fill their shoes in offices and factories. Also, drab brown stained walls and worn discoloured net curtains highlighted the austerity of war. With tables in close proximity, customer's conversations lacked discretion. A poignant piece of news related to Lady Beaumont's son and that he had been posted missing in action. Another customer had received a letter from her son serving in France, in which he mentioned being ordered to visit a dentist for the first time.

"Ordered?" said the woman's companion at the table.

"By his commanding officer."

"Why?"

"To ensure that George's teeth would be able to chew food in a proper manner, thus, adding enjoyment rather than discomfort."

"Mind you, it's known that an army marches better on a full stomach." The companion grinned.

"He wants to feel clean again."

"The trenches will be full of mud and vermin."

"He has stopped wearing the regimental kilt."

"Why?"

"Mustard gas burns bare legs."

"My goodness!" The woman's companion put a hand to her mouth.

A few minutes later, both women rose, went to the counter and paid for their cups of tea. A slim well-groomed young woman entered, looked around, then spotted the vacant table. She resembled Ann Anderson, however, her aura was that of a person very much alive. A patterned lilac dress, cream hat and jacket also lifted the tearoom's dull atmosphere. The waitress approached her table, and took an order. "Your day off?" she added.

"My employer is on holiday."

"Back soon."

A frail woman with a solemn expression walked in, and sat beside two acquaintances of similar age, then spoke to them. The waitress brought a white cup and saucer to the young woman and left. Lifting her cup, and about to take a sip, she stared at the three women. Customer's heads turned, and the young woman rushed out. Whilst picking up broken pieces of crockery, the waitress looked my way. "She overheard Lady Beaumont's son has been killed in action."

"Is her name Ann Anderson?"

The waitress nodded.

On a dull wet Sunday morning, the funeral of Edward Beaumont took place in Ardrishaig Cemetery. Mourners in sober black attire gathered to honour a local man killed during the Somme offensive. I met Edward in 1896 when he was a boy, and only two decades later, I say farewell. I observed a dignified tearful Lady Beaumont, and Ann Anderson flanked by her two brothers.

Following the funeral, relatives took Edward's widow, Rosalind, to a waiting black motor vehicle. She, and her infant daughter, Olivia, faced a difficult future. I sighed, this war has a lot to answer for.

I returned to the Grey Gull Inn saddened by what I had witnessed. Being a time traveller, you are aware of past events, but it does not deter grief. After entering the dining room, I sat down at a table set for Sunday lunch. The waitress appeared and I ordered a bowl of Scotch Broth. When it arrived, I stared. 1916 soup bowls are deeper than their future counterparts. With a near full stomach, I sat back, and waited for the main course. Hopefully, it won't fill the plate. A circular brass wall clock chimed, with the hands showing 12.34. I stared, that's a strange time. Then, I remembered what had been revealed to me about this fateful day. Ann Anderson returned to the cemetery, and committed suicide at the thirteenth hour. That's why I'm here! I rose from my chair, and brushed past the approaching waitress. Her head turned. "Your roast beef and potatoes, sir."

I made haste for the cemetery with quick steps to ensure a speedy arrival. Whilst walking, I went into the pocket of my jacket to check my watch, then took longer strides. That soup has given me a stitch. Upon entering the cemetery, I saw Ann Anderson at Edward's grave. Whilst approaching, I observed a knife in her hand with the blade poised to slash a bare wrist.

"Don't do it." I shouted.

She turned around.

Taking a deep breath, and holding my side, I faced her. "Why waste your life?"

She stared.

I took another deep breath. "Please, don't."

Her voice grew raspy. "I, I no longer have a life."

"What about your parents, and brothers?"

She sniffed.

"They will be heartbroken, as you are. Do you want them to suffer the same fate?"

"No, no, I don't." She lowered her head.

I moved closer, and held out my hand. "Give me the knife."

She looked at me, then the knife in her hand.

"Please."

Her grip loosened, and she handed me the knife. As I took it, Ann wiped a tear from her eye. "Why are you here?"

"It is a long story." I placed the knife in my jacket pocket.

"I saw you at Edward's funeral, you are not local."

I will be, although not for another century.

Sniffing, Ann lowered the sleeves of her dress to cover both wrists.

"Let us leave this place."

She nodded.

Reaching the gates, Ann stopped, and faced me. "What is your name?"

"James."

"Did you know Edward?"

"I met him when he was a boy, and envisaged him become a person of valour."

"Both of you have a special characteristic."

"As you have."

Ann nervously smiled, looked towards the cemetery, and paused. "I may leave my job."

"What will you do?"

"Join the war effort as a voluntary nurse." Ann paused. "That would have pleased Edward."

"Better to preserve life."

She took my hand, stared, then let go.

"Can I walk you to your parent's house?"

Ann looked along a gravel path leading to the cemetery. "Here comes my brother."

As a strapping man with a stern expression walked briskly to us, I turned to Ann.

"Goodbye."

She looked at me. "I will forever be in your debt."

Ann met her brother, spoke, and he comforted her. Knowing that my task had been completed, I headed in the opposite direction to Dochar. For discretion, I hope Docharnea is still uninhabited.

Glancing back at the stranger, Roy led his sister from the cemetery. Ann looked at her brother. "He knew Edward." And reminds me of someone.

I called into the inn to pay what money was owed, then headed for Docharnea. Upon my arrival, and with no one around, approached the coach house. I opened the door, walked upstairs, and stood in front of the mirror. Return me to 2014, I want to resume a normal life.

That evening, Ann sat in her room and read to take her

mind off recent events. Eventually, she put down the book, and thought about her encounter with a man called James. Ann recalled a boy two years earlier who had the same name, and sensed a connection. Moments later, she returned to her book.

CHAPTER 9

AWAKENING

Materialising from 1916, I felt drained of energy. When travelling through time, a side effect is normal, however, the latest trip has taken its toll. Perhaps my body can only withstand a certain amount of travel, but at least I returned to my timeline of 2014.

I switched on the kitchen radio for music relaxation, and thought about what Beth had revealed concerning Abbie. Being a father for the first time is a shock, especially in the manner I found out. I made myself a coffee, sat, and continued to ponder.

A short while later, I heard the postman and went to retrieve my mail. Returning to the kitchen, I opened each letter with apprehension. As suspected, one referred to debt that required urgent action, or I could suffer the consequences. Some diplomacy would be appreciated. Also, check your records energy supplier, with the night's drawing in, I made sure you received payment! I threw it aside, disposed of the junk mail, and reached for my mug of coffee. A song on the radio appeared relevant. Yes, I will now relax, though, Hollywood won't be my next destination. Smiling, I finished my coffee.

The mild sunny morning encouraged me to go for a walk, and clear my head. I observed many shiny vehicles whose owners had applied elbow grease at the weekend. Further on, the lady at work in her garden turned to face me with her usual warm smile. "Hello, again."

"Having a garden can be time-consuming."

She laughed. "This mild weather won't let me rest." She laid her trowel on the dyke. "I can't recall September being as mild."

"Long may it continue."

The lady nodded. "It will keep my heating costs down."

I echo her sentiment.

"The village?"

I shook my head. "Just out for a stroll."

"I used to see a lot of people out walking, however, the road traffic can be off-putting." The lady smiled. "As I'm a bit deaf, it doesn't bother me."

"Did Abigail Anderson walk much?"

"Oh, yes."

"On her own?"

"When her daughter visited, they often went for a walk."

"Recently?"

The lady shook her head. "The last time I saw them together must have been at least five or six years ago."

"Did Abigail visit her daughter?"

"Not that I'm aware off."

"What is her daughter's name?"

"April."

"Is she married?"

"You're inquisitive!"

I smiled. "I apologise, it's because I've been away from here for so long."

"I understand."

"See you later."

"Bye."

April? That could have been the month she was born. I walked at a slow pace, and passed a property whose garden required a helping hand. Whilst I write my book, maybe I could participate in garden maintenance to earn some cash. After all, my savings will only last for a limited period. I continued, and rather than head straight on to Ardrishaig, turned left along a remote narrow road. I spotted a wooden bench at the roadside, sat down, and began to reflect. A negative consequence of time travel is disappearing without warning, and relationships are severed in a callous manner. If I am the father of Abbie's daughter, a guilty conscience will ensue. In 1968, a single mother in rural Dochar would raise many an eyebrow. I must find out what became of April. A grey-haired woman and her black and white collie came down a hill onto the road. "Taking a breather," she shouted.

"Recharging my batteries!" I cried.

The woman approached, laughing.

"It's a grand day for a walk."

"September has been a friend to me." She glanced at collie at her side.

"Do you stay local?"

"With my husband, we've a small cottage."

"Have you lived there long?"

"Next year will be my fortieth anniversary."

Forty years ago, would she have known Abbie?

The woman looked at her dog. "He's coming up for fifteen, aren't you?"

The dog barked.

"Do many people use this road?"

"A few, you're new to the area?"

"I first came here fourteen years ago, travelled, and have returned for good."

"Far?"

I nodded. Back to 1896.

"Where do you stay?"

"Dochar."

"Oh yes, I know it."

"A fine walk to here."

"When I first walked these parts, I met a woman with a small child, and they came from Dochar."

"What was her name?"

"My memory isn't as sharp as it was." The woman smiled. "Let me think." She looked upwards. "Andrews? No, not Andrews."

"Anderson?"

"That's it! Abigail, Abigail Anderson, and her daughter

was called April."

"A neighbour of mine mentioned them."

"Since I last met Abigail, it has been many a year."

"And her daughter?"

The woman paused. "I'm sure Abigail said she had moved to Edinburgh."

Edinburgh! "Any particular reason?"

"To study."

"At what Institution?"

He's a curious one. "No idea." The woman looked at her dog, then at me. "Got to go, good to meet you."

"And you."

"Bye."

If April went to study in my home city, could she still be there? I got up, and continued walking for a short while, then turned back for home. Tomorrow will be a prominent day in Scotland's history with the Referendum taking place and tonight I'll watch political pundits and experts give their opinions and possible outcome. According to research polls, it will be close, and whatever the margin of victory or defeat, Nationalism in Scotland has grown at a dramatic pace.

I awoke at seven o'clock to my radio alarm going off, then the voice of Alex Salmond. Half awake, I listened to a magnanimous speech conceding defeat in Scotland's Referendum. I crawled out of bed, made myself respectable and then went downstairs to the kitchen. Whilst preparing breakfast, I listened to post-Referendum discussion on the radio. Nationalist supporters maintained the inevitable had only been postponed, and a second Referendum would secure Scotland's independence.

Following a light breakfast of coffee and toast, I went back upstairs, and into my office. Sitting down, I switched on the computer and clicked its dial-up connection. Bought new in 2000, it's now an ancient relic, especially, having noticed current computer design. I overheard customers in the coffee shop discuss various broadband providers. It appears that not only my computer has to get up to speed, also the user! When travelling back in time, acquired knowledge allows you to adapt, whereas ending up in the future brings insecurity. With all previous visits being in the past, I could cope, however, my current predicament frustrates me. My business philosophy states that you adapt to an ever-changing environment, thus, I will now have to practice what I once preached.

At mid-morning, I went to Ardrishaig in search of information for my book. As it will require a greater insight to this area, the local library should provide assistance. I approached the traditional stone building located next to the village hall, and stopped to reminisce. A boisterous crowd in 1938 gave the speaker pelters, and an egg was thrown. Smiling, I entered the library and walked up to its reception desk, where a petite redhead tapped her cell phone screen. Not wanting to disturb her frantic action, I stood still. Seconds later, she laid her phone on the desk and then turned round. "Oh!" She put a hand to her chest. "You should have knocked."

"I'm not in any rush."

"I was browsing Facebook, then sent a message through Twitter."

Phones have indeed progressed.

"How can I help you, sir?"

"I would like to research the local area."

"Do you have a particular location in mind?"

"Just in general."

The library employee's phone started to ring. "Excuse me, sir." She picked it up, and answered the call. "I'll get back to you later, Geoff, I'm busy right now." She ended the call, and placed her phone on a grey filing tray. "Sorry for the interruption."

"It's okay."

"You can use a computer which we provide for

members, or the traditional method." She smiled.

"Perhaps a bit of both."

"This way, sir."

The employee led me to a single desktop computer, reached for a nearby chair and placed it at the table. I sat down and stared at the screen. "Can I tell it what to do?"

She laughed. "Given our budget, not this model, maybe ten years from now."

I positioned myself in front of the screen.

"Do you know how to operate it?"

I frowned. Compared to mine, this is advanced.

The employee moved forward. "I'll give you a quick lesson."

She took me through a series of keyboard processes, and then I did my best to repeat them. "Information Technology is not one of my strengths."

"Got it?"

I nodded. "Thanks."

"Any problem, just ask."

After she left, I browsed through websites relating to Ardrishaig and neighbouring Lochgilphead on culture, history and travel. The latter site being conventional travel, and not the mode I experience, although, it is faster.

Going through an assortment of sites and reference books proved fruitless, therefore, I shut down the computer. When I returned to reception, no one was in attendance, so I waited. Minutes later, the employee emerged from a back room. "My apologies, I had to reply to an urgent text."

"I understand." The cell phone now dictates a person's routine.

"Find what you were looking for?"

"Do I have to register or sign a library document?"

She shook her head.

"Are mornings usually quiet?" I've had the place to myself.

"Thursday morning is not our busiest."

"Are you in charge of the library?"
The woman smiled. "I'm the librarian."
"Do locals use the library?" I looked at the deserted study area.
"There are regulars, though not many.
"How long have you worked here?"
"Next year will be my thirtieth anniversary."
I raised my eyebrows.
"Soon after starting, I recall a precocious teenager who came to the library on a regular basis for five years, then stopped."
"Perhaps her family relocated?"
"She gained a place at a city university and left the area."
"A city would be an eye-opener compared to Ardrishaig."
The woman laughed.
"What subject was she going to study?"
The librarian paused. "Accountancy, she wanted to become a Chartered Accountant."
"She must have been numerate."
"One of my relatives attended the same secondary school, and April excelled in arithmetic and accounts."
"April?"
"Did you know her?" He has the same eyes.
"A neighbour spoke of her mother."
"She passed away last year."
"Was there a good turnout?"
The librarian nodded. "April didn't look well."
With her mother having passed away, it's not a surprise.
"Thin and pale."
"Is she married?"
"I'm not sure." He is an inquisitive one.
A male visitor entered the library and then approached reception. I said goodbye to the librarian and as I walked home, my thoughts focused on April. At least I know she attained a place at university, and did she achieve her

professional goal? I should have asked what city.

Later that evening, I started my novel by formulating the all-important plot. It will involve an innocent bystander who becomes embroiled in espionage, witnesses a wrongful killing, and sent back in time to prevent it. I laid out a structure for the story, and after several hours, started to yawn. Being close to midnight, I saved my work, then had supper.

I lay in bed thinking about the introductory scene, and soon after, felt myself dropping off.

"James."

I opened my eyes.

"James, do not be afraid," a woman's voice whispered.

I lifted my head from the pillow, looked around my darkened bedroom, and pressed the bedside light switch. The room remained dark, and I peered at a shadowy figure in the corner.

"James, I am a friend."

As it was a warm calm voice, I did not feel intimidated, and listened.

"I have a message for you."

"From whom?"

"Go to Edinburgh, seek out April."

"Who are you?"

Finding courage, I got out of bed, and the shadow disappeared. I walked over to the corner, and scrutinised it. Returning to bed, I pressed the bedside switch, and this time the light came on. After switching it off, I lay back. Who was she?

After waking up, I looked at my alarm clock, and reflected on what had happened. I may not have been perturbed at the time, however, I am now. A spirit had appeared in my bedroom, spoke to me, and then vanished! Did it happen? Yes, it did. I lay and reflected on the surreal and sinister experience.

Throughout breakfast, my mind wouldn't rest, and even music from the radio wasn't a distraction. Could there be a connection to my spiritual experiences at the cemetery? By seeing only a shadow, her identity remains a mystery.

A short time later, I left Docharnea to visit the cemetery in the hope that I could find an answer. According to Beth, the workman is also a ghost, and may enlighten me. He struck me as a worthy chap. Prior to my own time travel exploits, if someone had suggested it was possible, I would have laughed. Since it's a reality, why not believe in ghosts?

I entered the cemetery, and observed only a silver-haired woman laying flowers in front of a headstone. I walked to Abbie's grave, faced the grey headstone and sighed. If I had not left in 1967, how would my life have turned out? A gust of wind blew in my direction and I felt a chill. The woman approached me. "She was a lovely person."

I nodded.

"We met often in the village, and chatted over a cup of tea." She smiled. "Are you a relative?"

"A friend."

He's too young to be a friend.

We departed Abbie's grave, and whilst heading towards the gates, I spotted Ann Anderson! As in previous visits, she wore black and stood at Edward Beaumont's place of rest. I stopped and stared.

"What's wrong?" The women stared.

"Over there, the young woman."

"A young woman!"

"Yes, in a long black dress and shawl." I pointed.

The woman looked, then turned to face me. "You're the only person here."

I looked at her, then Edward Beaumont's grave. She's gone.

"Cemeteries can play tricks on the mind, you know."

I headed for the main street, and its popular coffee shop.

Upon entering, I placed myself at one of the vacant tables. Looking around, it would appear Tuesday is not the most profitable day of the week. The shop assistant came across, and gave her usual smile. "A white coffee, sir?"

I nodded. "Do you have Danish pastries?"

"One or two?"

"Two, please." My cholesterol is in check.

"Back soon."

Noticing a newspaper on the next table, I reached over, then browsed through the 'Scottish Daily Mail' with interest. On my visits to the past, reading a newspaper resembled a history lesson, however, this time the news is topical. One of the main stories related to Alex Salmond. Following his defeat, he had relinquished control as leader of the Scottish Nationalist Party, and deputy leader Nicola Sturgeon would take charge. Also, due to internal party politics, Scottish Labour leader Joanne Lamont had quit. The political landscape in Scotland was indeed in a process of change. In terms of the Scottish economy, it had low inflation with unemployment falling. On the downside, 'zero employment' contracts which left workers vulnerable to pay restraints. Working as a coachman in 1896. I had a better deal. An intriguing article under the technology section revealed quantum computers had been introduced in Canada. One device could undertake the work of many current advanced computers. I should replace my 'dial-up' with a quantum device and then I'd be ahead of the pack rather than playing catch-up! What would the Victorians have thought about this article? An extract from HG Well's novel, 'The Time Machine'? The shop assistant returned with my order and I put down the newspaper. After she left, I continued reading with interest. The conflict between Russia and Ukraine, plus, a civil war in Syria, dominated the international section. Diminishing oil prices have affected the Russian economy, and sanctions from America plus Europe would not please Premiere Putin! As for Syria, British Nationals are heading there to fight. A similar situation existed in 1937 when men left Britain for Spain to fight in the country's civil war. I sipped my coffee, set the cup down its saucer, and turned to the sport section. Apart from Glasgow Ranger's financial predicament, golf's Ryder Cup at Gleneagles received good coverage. I put down the newspaper, and sampled the shop's pastries. A middle-aged woman came into the shop and then spoke to the assistant. Several moments later, the woman distributed leaflets to customers at a nearby table, then approached mine. "An event to honour Ardrishaig residents who died in the First World War is being held in our village hall." The woman handed me a leaflet. "A momentous anniversary."

I took the leaflet, and read it.

"Will you attend?"

I nodded.

"A commemorative plaque has been placed outside the village hall with a list of residents who received bravery awards, also those who sadly lost their lives."

I looked up. Admirable.

After the woman departed, I finished my coffee, went to the counter and paid the shop assistant. Before heading home, I stopped outside the village hall. I looked down the list of names printed in gold letters on a dark brown plaque for Edward Beaumont's name, which had Victoria Cross initials alongside. However, also on the list appeared the name of Ann Anderson, awarded the Military Medal, therefore, I had to investigate. Entering the village hall, I went to a reception area where a well-groomed woman looked up from her desk. "Yes, sir, can I help?"

"I have returned to Ardrishaig and a name on the plaque could be a distant relative."

"What is the person's name, sir?"

"Ann Anderson."

"You're in luck." The woman smiled. "My grandfather was a close friend of her youngest brother, therefore, I'm aware of her. In July 1916, she joined the Nursing Corps and moved to France seven months later, where she was based in a temporary hospital near the front line."

"Did she return to Ardrishaig?"

The woman shook her head. "Whilst Ann attended to a wounded soldier, a German shell exploded in the vicinity, and she was hit by shrapnel."

"She didn't survive?"

"Her wounds were fatal."

"Her family must have been saddened."

The woman nodded. "However, in caring for the sick, they were proud of her contribution to the war."

"Thanks for the information."

"You're welcome, sir, see you at the event."

I left with a feeling of sadness, but also happiness. Although Ann Anderson's life had been cut short, it is remembered as an honourable one.

After a visit to the florist, I arrived at the cemetery. The eerie atmosphere was no more, and birds could be heard. Approaching Ann's grave, I laid white carnations in front of the gravestone, and stood reflecting for several minutes. As I turned to leave, an elderly stocky man stood in front of me and tipped his grey cap. "I have a message for you, sir."

It's the cemetery worker.

"A young woman asked me to convey her gratitude."

I looked towards Ann's grave, then turned to face the workman. He had vanished.

CHAPTER 10

IN SEARCH OF APRIL

Following the revelation about Abbie having a daughter, and spiritual guidance, a trip to Edinburgh beckoned. The spirit's voice intrigued me, and I had heard it before, but where? Could it have been a relative, or perhaps Abbie herself? After all, April is her daughter, and I am now the guardian, albeit April will be in her forty-seventh year and older than me! I could treat the visit as a short break, although for the previous eighteen months, they have become routine. As opposed to my usual mode of travelling, I'll go to Edinburgh by conventional means. Checking the Internet, I discovered that at this late time of year, a coach from Ardrishaig to Glasgow is only twice daily. A contrast regarding trains from Glasgow to Edinburgh, with four every hour.

I packed a small suitcase, and walked the short distance to Dochar's solitary coach stop. The start of October had seen much rainfall, however, today remained dry. Already, dead leaves had fallen from surrounding trees onto the pavement and roadside. Then, the afternoon coach arrived, and I had my pick of seats. Sitting down, I recalled coming here in 2000, as the coach resembled a post-war relic. This version is comfortable, warm and clean, and according to an internal coach poster, it has wi-fi!

After forty minutes, the coach reached the small town of Inveraray, where three passengers departed, then two boarded. I checked my downloaded timetable, and Tarbet was the next stop. A short while later, the coach went around a sharp bend, and came to an abrupt halt. A woman in front reading a magazine looked up, whilst others stared straight ahead at rocks and earth which had tumbled down from a hill.

"This road is notorious for landslides!" said a fellow passenger.

Within several minutes, a queue of vehicles had formed on the narrow country road. Cars reversed and headed for a detour, however, as the coach did likewise, a loud noise came from its rear. The driver applied the brakes, and went outside to investigate. When he returned, a shake of the head followed, and he addressed the handful of passengers. "Sorry folks, it's a burst tyre."

"What about a replacement?" said a woman.

"What, change the tyre!" said the driver.

"A coach," replied the woman.

The driver once more shook his head. "One would have to come from our depot near Glasgow, and the road will be blocked for the foreseeable future."

"What now?" said a young woman, as she looked at other passengers.

Returning to his seat, the driver made a call on his cell phone, and moments later, faced the passengers. "As replacement transport will not be available until tomorrow morning, the company has agreed to pay for overnight accommodation."

"Where?" said another woman, "we're in the middle of nowhere!"

"The Tarbet Inn," said the driver, "it's five minutes to walk back that way." He pointed.

"Not with my corns!" said the same woman.

"Will there be enough rooms?" I said.

The driver nodded. "At this time of year, the place is dead."

I looked around the coach. Only four passengers.

"Can we go there now?" said the young woman.

The driver nodded. "I've spoken to our company representative, and he'll contact the Tarbet Inn. Show your coach ticket at reception."

Three women and I left our stationary coach, and walked

along the deserted road to the Tarbet Inn. On our arrival, we produced a ticket, signed the register book, and received room keys.

"Is dinner and breakfast included?" said the young woman.

"Breakfast only," said the male member of staff.

The young woman looked at her watch. "It's only just after five, surely dinner is included."

"What, no dinner?" said one of the other women.

"Do you serve bar snacks?" I said.

The member of staff nodded. "In the lounge bar, between seven and nine o'clock."

The young woman sighed. "It's better than nothing."

We went upstairs to our rooms, with mine being at the far end of a landing. I entered, closed the door, and laid my suitcase on a brown carpeted floor. Looking around, a modern en-suite bathroom and bedside radio pleased me. To ensure the radio worked, I switched it on, and smiled.

Just before eight o'clock, I made my way downstairs and met a fellow passenger returning to her room.

"Does your radio work?" the woman asked.

I nodded.

"Lucky you."

Upon entering an empty lounge bar, the male member of staff looked up from reading a newspaper. At the bar, he handed me a printed menu card. "Evening, sir."

"Thank you." I took it.

"Something to drink, sir?"

I looked at the three beer fonts. "A glass of lager, please."

He poured lager into a medium-size glass, then laid it on the polished wooden bar counter.

"Could I have steak pie and chips, please?"

"Certainly, sir, I'll inform my wife."

After he departed, I cast my gaze around the small but pleasant lounge bar. The teak wooden tables and chairs matched the flooring. Dark green curtains covered two windows and contrasted well with magnolia patterned wallpaper. The member of staff returned with a smile. "Be about ten minutes, sir."

"Do you have much passing trade?" I lifted my glass, and took a sip.

"Whenever a landslide occurs," he said laughing. "Our busy time is at the weekend."

"From the village?" I set my glass on the counter.

"Both villages, Arrochar, as well as Tarbet."

"Is it just yourself and your wife who work here?"

"We had a barman, but he's gone."

"A seasonal worker?"

"Cash went missing from the till."

"A regular problem with retail outlets."

"There is still one of your group to appear."

"The tall woman?"

He nodded. "The other two came down sharpish!"

"Perhaps hungry."

He smiled. "They did appear to have good appetites."

A woman walked into the bar and then ordered a glass of ginger beer. After paying, she sat down in the far corner, and took out a magazine from her bag. The owner's wife arrived with my food and looked at a table near the bar. "Is this okay, sir, or would you prefer to sit elsewhere?"

"There is fine."

As she left, I sat down with my drink, and tucked in, observing the woman sitting in the corner using a cell phone. Twenty minutes later, I finished my meal and also the lager. The third female coach passenger rushed in with an expression of shock and approached the bar. "A man has collapsed on the landing!"

"A man?" The owner frowned.

She nodded.

The owner and female passenger left the bar, and went upstairs. I observed the woman put her cell phone and magazine into her bag, then leave. A short time later, the owner's wife came into the bar with a worried look. "Sir, your room."

I stared.

"There has been an attempted theft!"

I dashed upstairs, and observed the owner with a police officer outside my room. When I approached, the owner frowned. "Mr Carsell-Brown, can you check that all your belongings are intact?"

"What's happened?" My room door is ajar.

"A thief, sir," said the police officer.

I sighed.

"My former barman," said the owner.

"He has been apprehended," said the police officer.

Holding my breath, I went into the room, and observed my open suitcase with items on the floor. I checked the contents, then returned to both men. "All my belongings are there."

"What about cash or credit cards, sir?" said the police officer.

"I keep them in my possession at all times."

The police officer grinned.

"Where is the thief?"

The owner pointed to a room. "In there with another police officer, and nursing an injury."

The other two women passengers emerged from their accommodation and stared in our direction, then at each other.

"Everything is okay, ladies," said the police officer.

"How did he receive an injury?" The owner must have thumped him.

"When in your room, he claimed a ghost appeared." The police officer stared at the entrance. "As it approached him, he fell back, and passed out."

"A ghost!" I looked at the owner. "Is the inn haunted?"

"Not to my knowledge."

Moments later, two police officers led the distraught

intruder away. I locked my door, and went downstairs to the bar for welcome refreshment. The owner's wife chatted to the young woman passenger, then looked my way and smiled. "A drink to calm the nerves, sir?"

"Yes, not to calm my nerves but to toast the ghost!"

The young woman laughed.

"A lager, sir?"

I nodded.

The owner's wife poured lager into a large glass, then filled a smaller one with white wine, and set them on the bar counter. "On the house."

"Thanks." I lifted mine. "To an admirable spirit." I took a sip.

"I'll drink to that." The young woman lifted her wine and did likewise.

I set my glass on the counter. "It has been an eventful day."

"Not the norm for here," said the owner's wife.

"I'll also drink to that," said the young woman. She took a swig, then put her empty glass down.

"Another?"

"Yes, thanks."

A glass of white wine came forthwith, and the young woman drank it, leaving a moderate quantity.

"Are you bound for Glasgow?" I said.

"Yes." She set her glass on the counter. "What about you?"

"Also, Glasgow and then a connection to Edinburgh."

"For business reasons?"

"Family reasons."

"I may be working there soon."

"Oh?"

"Tomorrow, I've a job interview with an agency in Sauchiehall Street, and if successful, I'll be based in Edinburgh."

Tall, slim and blonde, no doubt a model. "What type of

agency?"

"An escort agency."

I glanced at the owner's wife.

"They deal with clients who are in the city on business, and want female company."

The owner's wife raised her dark eyebrows.

"It pays well." The young woman smiled.

I'll bet.

"I believe a replacement coach will arrive here at 8.30," said the owner's wife, "what time is your interview?"

"One o'clock." She lifted her glass. "I intended to stay at a hotel in Glasgow tonight." She finished her wine, and placed the glass on the counter.

I finished my lager, and put the empty glass aside.

"Another?" said the owner's wife.

"I will retire."

The young woman looked at her. "I'm ready for another!"

I bid both women goodnight, went upstairs to my room, and as I opened my room door, entered with caution.

Lying in bed, I pondered over recent instances with the spirit world. Then, I smiled, this ghost did me a good turn.

As the sun shone with a slight nip in the air, my three fellow passengers and I boarded the replacement coach for Glasgow. Our driver told us that due to the landslide, a detour would be made, adding fifteen miles onto the journey. The young woman groaned, however, it may have been hangover-related. Looking weary here's hoping she'll give a good account of herself at the interview.

Shortly before ten o'clock, the coach arrived at Buchanan Street Bus Station, and as I got off, wished the young woman good luck.

"Thanks, I'm going for a strong black coffee!"

I walked via the Royal Concert Hall and then through a pedestrian shopping mall. Seven minutes later, I arrived at Glasgow's Queen Street Station for a train to Edinburgh

Waverley. After purchasing my ticket, I went to the designated platform, but just as I reached it, a train departed. A railway employee noticed my frustration and approached. "There will be another in twenty minutes, sir."

"Thanks."

"It's a busy service, hence, three per hour."

I won't have long to wait.

"During the Commonwealth Games, four trains left every hour."

On time, a train arrived and passengers got off, whilst those waiting, boarded. In my plush window seat awaiting departure, I recalled a similar trip to Edinburgh in 1940 by steam locomotive and carriages with hard seats. Although an uncomfortable excursion, the novelty of travelling by steam lingers, along with the distinctive smell. The luxurious powerful streamlined diesel multiple-unit sped to its first stop at Lenzie, then Falkirk High. Linlithgow and Haymarket followed, and the train emerged from a long tunnel into Waverley Station's multi-platform arena. When it stopped, doors sprung open, and passengers headed for the exit gates. Leaving the platform, I followed an exit sign, which guided me up an escalator to Princes Street. Since my visit in 1940, no taxi stands existed. I had to find accommodation for my stay in the Capital and spotted a Tourist Information Office on the opposite side of this busy historic street. After spending the first twenty-seven years of my life in Edinburgh, I've now become a visitor. I crossed at a pedestrian walkway, and soon reached the premises. Three tourist advisers with a presentable appearance sat and chatted to a member of the public. As one information-seeker departed, the adviser looked my way, and I approached the vacant chair.

"Please take a seat, sir."

I sat down, and laid my suitcase on the polished laminate floor.

The adviser smiled. "How can I be of assistance?"

"I require single accommodation."

"For how long, sir?"

"Perhaps a week."

"Is it a room with an en-suite bathroom you require?"

I nodded.

"Any particular location within the city?"

"Central, if possible." It will be easier to travel around the city.

The adviser's nimble red painted fingernails tapped the desktop keyboard, and she stared at her screen. "Unfortunately, most city centre hotels and guest houses are fully booked." She glanced at me. "There is accommodation at a hotel not far from here, at £85 per night."

I'll skip that.

"Do you have a preference for the type of accommodation?" The adviser plucked a blonde hair from her dark blue blouse.

"No preference, a comfortable bed will suffice."

"What is your budget?"

"Within reason."

She smiled. "It has to be central?"

"If possible."

The adviser tapped her keyboard several times, stared at the screen and then me.

"There is a room available in the Royal Mile."

"Terrific!"

She glanced at the screen. "It's a shared bathroom with another occupant, however, a reasonable price."

I pondered. "What part of the Royal Mile?"

"Bottom of the High Street."

I stayed there in my time as a student.

"The World's End Close."

"I'll take it." That's a coincidence.

After finalising details, I walked up North Bridge, then down the Royal Mile with its assortment of shops, cafes and bars. Since my student years, the area has become more commercial, and with it, less studying for local under-graduates!

I arrived at the World's End Close, walked through a passageway and approached a brown wooden door with an intercom next to it. Realising the adviser had not given me a name, I pressed one of six buzzers and waited.

"Yes?" said an authoritative male voice.

I moved closer to the voice transmitter. "I'm here about the room for rent."

"Wrong buzzer, next one up - Hendrie."

"Thanks, sorry to disturb you."

"Don't mention it."

I pressed the appropriate buzzer, however, no response came. I hope the person is in! As I was about to try again, I heard a voice.

"Yes?"

"I have come about the vacant room."

The door opened automatically, and I faced a grey concrete winding flight of steps with brown walls. I entered, closed the door, and walked up two flights. The landing had maroon carpet tiles, and in keeping with the property's ambience, pictures of Edinburgh's Royal Mile hung on walls. A woman stood outside the entrance door, and held out her hand. "Andrea Hendrie."

I shook it. "James Carsell-Brown."

She drew her hand away. "It's cold!"

I smiled. "Warm heart."

She laughed. "Come in."

I entered, and Andrea closed the door. The bright narrow hallway had paintings of Edinburgh's ancient Canongate and Grassmarket, which caught my attention.

"Are you interested in art, do you paint?"

I laid my suitcase on the dark wooden flooring. "A distant acquaintance specialised in landscapes, but I don't have that talent."

"What is it you do?"

"Business consultant." And time traveller.

"Are you kept busy?"

"Most of the time."

"Have you come to Edinburgh on business?"

"Family business."

"I detect a slight Edinburgh accent, are you originally from the Capital?"

"After my studies at Edinburgh University, I moved to Aberdeen, then Nice."

"How did you find living in Nice?"

"I enjoyed it." Apart from being kidnapped.

"Me too."

"Can I see the room?"

"Certainly, this way."

Picking up my suitcase, I followed Andrea along the hall, then was shown a room. As the saying goes, you can't swing a cat, however, it appeared spotless and cosy. My host smiled. "It's not the most spacious of rooms, but warm, and I make a delicious breakfast."

I turned to Andrea. "You've got me hooked."

She pointed. "The bathroom is down the hall."

"Do you stay in the property?"

"Some of the time, I have a cottage in Stow, and commute between there and here. I own a bookshop in Galashiels, and another in Rose Street."

"What type of books do you stock?"

"Crime, historical fiction, romance and horror."

"Time travel?"

Andrea shook her head.

"You're handy for Rose Street."

"It's only a fifteen-minute walk."

"You'll soon be able to take a train to Galashiels."

She nodded. "The Borders line from Edinburgh will soon reopen, and Waverley Station is just around the corner."

Her property is indeed an ideal central location.

"I'll let you settle into your room, let me know if you

want to discuss any issue."

"Thanks."

Whilst unpacking, I thought about April, and where do I begin my search to find her?

As she may have attended Edinburgh University, I could contact them for a last-known address. No doubt I would be made aware of a certain 'Database Protection Act' that the institution adheres to. The local police station may assist, then again, April is not a missing person, and if I'm asked details about myself, it will be difficult to explain where I've been for the past fourteen years. I will ponder and consider options over an evening meal in one of the local establishments.

Following a good night's sleep, and Andrea's breakfasts, I called Edinburgh University from my room. As the number was engaged, I tried again, and a well-spoken gentleman answered. "Edinburgh University, can I be of assistance?"

"I am a former student and want to trace a past acquaintance."

"An acquaintance you say?"

"Yes, a former student."

"What is your name?"

"James Carsell-Brown. I graduated in July 1981 in an arts discipline."

"Hold on, please."

I sat upright on my wicker chair, and could hear a computer keyboard clicking. I moved the cell phone to my better ear.

"Found you, although, the current details we have is that you are based in Aberdeen."

"I now stay near Ardrishaig. When I return, an update of my personal details will be forwarded to the university."

"Where are you now?"

"In Edinburgh, hence, my urgency to contact this person."

"We do not give out information on former students."

"It is important."

"What is the name?"

"April Anderson, she studied Accountancy, and would have graduated in 1989." He's quick on the keyboard.

"She graduated in 1990, however, I cannot give you her address. Also, she may have moved, similar to yourself."

"If you could give an indication of her last-known district, it would be a starting point." I gripped my phone. "You wouldn't be revealing her address."

The operator paused. "Very well, the district is Granton."

"Thank you, I'm grateful."

"Goodbye, and good luck."

I left my accommodation, and caught a bus from North Bridge to Granton. A good place to start would be the local church, and even if April isn't an attendee, I may receive information of her whereabouts.

Twenty-five minutes later, the bus reached my destination. The driver let me off near a church, and upon entering the grounds, a woman with short white hair walked towards me. As she approached, an inquisitive expression ensued. "Are you lookin' for someone?"

"The minister."

"You're out of luck, he's no' in the church."

I sighed. "That's a pity."

"Is it aboot the forthcomin' Halloween event?"

"I'm looking for someone in the district."

"Whit's their name?"

"April Anderson."

The woman paused. "I lose track of names nowadays, people do not stay in one place for long."

Me included.

"Why not try the local newsagent?" She pointed. "In that row of shops."

"I'll do that."

I accompanied the woman out of the grounds, and as we

departed, she wished me well. I arrived at a newsagent, and was greeted by the male shop assistant.

"Yes, sir?"

"I wish to know if a certain person still lives around here."

"People who come in here usually wish for a lottery win!"

I laughed.

"What's their name, sir?"

"Anderson, April Anderson."

A customer who browsed through magazines on a metal rack looked my way. "A family of that name stay in Granton Crescent."

"Granton Crescent?" I said.

"Aye," said the older teenager, "it's no' far frae here."

The shop assistant shook his head. "There's nobody called April in the 'Crescent', let alone Anderson!"

A middle-aged woman appeared at the counter. "April Anderson moved to Trinity."

I turned around to face her. "Recently?"

The woman shook her head. "Years ago."

"Thanks."

"Are you a relative?" said the woman.

"Yes, I am."

She smiled. "I thought so, you have her eyes."

"You can catch a bus part of the way, sir," said the shop assistant, "from outside the church."

"Much obliged."

Having been brought up near Trinity, it's uncanny that April lived there. I departed the newsagent, and minutes later, arrived at a bus stop. In front of me stood two men with frustrated expressions.

"I remember when this stop wiz a terminus," said the tallest.

"Aye, there wiz always a bus parked here, sometimes two!"

"Now ye have tae wait ages fur one."

"Nothin' is the same any mare."

The tall man looked at the row of shops. "Apart fae that newsagent, they've all changed over the years."

"And whit they sell!"

"The chemist, draper, confectioner and grocer have gone."

"Don't forget the barber."

"Since 1963, I've tried tae!"

His companion laughed. "Did ye get one o' his 'specials' tae?"

The tall man nodded his shaven head.

"Mind you, that style is trendy noo, shaved around the sides and full on tap."

"The barber wiz aheid o' his time!"

As both men laughed, a bus arrived, and after the two locals boarded, I followed. I paid the standard fare of £1.50, and took a seat. I'll wager both men had more humorous tales to tell about local shop traders.

A short while later, the bus reached Trinity, and soon I came across another newsagent. I entered the compact shop, and joined a small queue, which soon diminished.

"Yes, sir," said the female assistant.

"I'm trying to find a relative who may stay within the district."

"What is their name?"

"April Anderson, she will be about my age?"

"Doesn't ring a bell, sir, you could ask in the Starbank Inn."

I went down a steep road, turned left and there it was. The pub rekindled memories of my visit in 1940 with drab public and 'snug' bars along with rickety scraped furniture. Entering, I observed only one bar, with plush brown leather upholstery and polished oak furniture. The female bar person wearing a tight black top and trousers came forward. "Yes, sir, what can I get you?"

"I'm trying to trace someone."

"Are you a private investigator?" The voluptuous auburn-haired individual smiled.

"No, I'm a relative."

I've heard that one before. "What is the person's name, sir?"

"April Anderson."

A male customer standing at the bar looked over, then approached. Tall, well-built and with a broken nose, he also had a stern look. "Did you say April Anderson?"

I nodded.

"Are you her brother?"

I shook my head.

"Who are you?"

"A distant cousin."

He looked at the bar person.

She stared.

"Why do you ask?"

"I did maintenance work on her flat." He blinked like an owl. "She left the property without paying me!"

"How long ago?"

"Thirteen years."

The bar person smiled. "Unlucky for you, Steve."

He looked at her. "£350!" He blinked.

"Was this the property in Granton?"

"In York Road."

"Where is that?"

"Not far from here," said the bar person.

"Could you lend me a tenner?" said the man, "I'm skint."

I shook my head. "I'll ask her to send you a cheque."

"You'll have to find her first!" He finished his pint of beer, and left the bar.

I looked at the bar person. "Perhaps a neighbour has an idea of where she moved to."

"Do you know where York Road is?"

"I have a rough idea."

The bar person came out from behind the counter, I followed her outside, and she pointed. "Turn right, walk up the road and then turn right again. York Road is first on the right."

"Thanks, I will keep turning right!"

She laughed.

Reaching the top of a steep road, I turned right, and entered a narrow cul-de-sac. On the right stood five large detached villas with high boundary walls, and opposite, a row of terraced houses with less privacy. I approached one of them, walked up a narrow gravel path, and pressed the doorbell. I stood for a few moments, looked around, and pressed it again. A woman came out of the next property, and stared. "She's at work, and won't be home until later."

I turned to face the neighbour. "Does April Anderson stay here?"

"Are you a detective?"

"No, a relative."

"She once stayed in the next property to me."

"Do you know where April has moved to?"

"Jersey."

"Jersey?"

"Yes, to work in a bank."

April isn't a home bird.

"She left without paying a number of bills, are you here to settle them?"

"The creditors should contact her employer in Jersey."

The woman smiled. "I believe they tried, but without success."

"Thanks for your help."

"Good luck."

I walked in the direction of Ferry Road, and caught a bus back to the Royal Mile. Why are people wishing me good luck? Also, leaving without paying bills isn't what I wanted to hear. Perhaps problems occurred in April's life, which contributed, and she moved to Jersey for a fresh start.

For an evening meal, Andrea suggested a place in the Canongate. The 39 Steps theme bar and restaurant had become one of Edinburgh city centre's popular hotspots. Outside the establishment, a tall male in a black evening suit with an authoritative stance guarded the entrance. When I approached, he gave me an icy stare, nodded his approval and opened a glass door. The restaurant was straight ahead and a spiral staircase led to the downstairs bar.

After a quick bite to eat, I paid my bill and left hoping that the bar would provide atmosphere, thus reviving my expectations of this establishment. Walking down the grey metal staircase, I counted thirty-nine steps, then went into the bar. Whilst standing in a queue, I cast my gaze around the vicinity. Dark stained-glass tables, black leather chairs and patterned burgundy wallpaper caught my eye, as did a full-size wax figure in each corner. Dashing Richard Hannay, patriotic Colonel Scudder, knowledgeable Mr Memory and the evil Professor Logan made representation. Behind the bar, three individuals with jet-black hair, dark waistcoats and a white top, didn't stand still. When served, and due to no seats, I stood at one side of the bar sipping my chilled bottle of beer to background music from 1935, 1959 and 1978. Two women with long platinum hair and trim waistlines, stood next to me. "Are you here for the quiz?" said the hottest.

"Quiz?"

"It's hosted by Mr Memory," said her partner.

"Each midweek evening, a particular year is chosen."

"Do people know the year in advance?"

Both women nodded.

"What year is it tonight?"

"1967!" both said.

Fifteen minutes later, the background music stopped, and people having a conversation could be heard. The 'bouncy' music hall tune synonymous with Mr Memory in the 1935 film began. Taking a central position in the bar, customers applauded Mr Memory's arrival. When the applause stopped, he smiled. "Tonight, ladies and gentlemen, I will answer any question you wish to ask on the year 1967." He coughed. "A momentous year for many reasons, therefore, I am sure you will have an abundance of questions." He looked around the bar. "Who would like to ask the first question?"

"What song by the Monkees went to number one in the charts?" said a man standing at the bar.

"I'm A Believer, and hope you are too, sir."

I grinned, and the audience laughed.

A woman raised her hand.

"Yes, madam?" said Mr Memory.

"Who did Frank Sinatra duet with on his chart-topping record?"

"His oldest daughter, Nancy. You and she have the same colour of hair, madam."

The woman smiled. "Correct."

"Which Tamla Motown artists visited Glasgow in the summer?" I asked.

"The Four Tops, Stevie Wonder, The Supremes. Plus Martha Reeves and the Vandellas."

I raised my glass.

Whilst sipping my drink, I spotted a young woman discreetly move towards a table and lift another woman's handbag lying next to a chair. I alerted a male member of staff, pointed, and he left the bar. Seeing him, she dropped the handbag and dashed upstairs. I observed two men in the vicinity stare my way and then leave. The unsuspecting customer was given her handbag, and a look of astonishment followed. I finished my drink, went upstairs to the exit, and a steward opened the door. Being early evening, I walked up a deserted Canongate, passing a close with two men standing inside the entrance.

"Excuse me," said one of them.

I looked at him.

He approached with a piece of paper in his hand. "Where is this place?" He showed it to me.

I looked at it.

From his black jerkin, he produced a knife, ushering me inside the narrow close. I recognised both men from the bar.

"You ruined our night, money in the bag was for our fix!"

"We'll take what money you have instead," said the accomplice.

"I only have a few pound coins on me."

"Then we'll take your credit card." He held up the knife.

"I don't have one with me, it's at my property."

"Where do you stay?"

"Ardrishaig."

"Don't get smart! I'm not afraid to use this." He pressed the sharp tip against my stomach.

The accomplice nudged his partner. "Jack!"

"What?"

"Look!" The accomplice stared into the close.

The other man turned his head sideways, screamed, and both thugs ran off. I turned round, and looked into the close. What did they see? Composing myself, I walked up an empty Canongate to Andrea's flat, went straight to my room, and reflected on a close shave. Before feeling drowsy, an hour had passed.

When I awoke, the anxiety of what happened last night had not diminished. I sat up, and stared at the pair of dark green curtain which covered the daylight. I heard the apartment buzzer, then Andrea's voice. Not long after, she knocked on my door. "James."

"Yes?"

"Two police officers are on the way upstairs."

"Police officers!" That's all I need.

"They want to speak with you."

I jumped out of bed, dressed in double-quick time, and checked my appearance in the mirror. Opening my room door, I observed two dark blue uniformed gentlemen with Andrea in the hallway. Walking towards them, I felt lousy, and no doubt looked it. Both officers and Andrea stared.

"We would like a word, sir," said the senior officer.

I cleared my throat.

"It is about last night."

"Last night?" I want to forget about it.

"An incident which took place in the Canongate?"

I nodded.

Andrea looked at both officers. "You can use my lounge."

She headed for the kitchen, and I followed both officers into the bright lounge. Late October sunshine engulfed the room, however, it did not lift my spirits. The two officers sat on a couch and I opposite on a chair.

"Did you suffer any injury, sir?" said the senior officer.

I shook my head. "Just a bit shaken."

"Can you tell us what happened?"

"Whilst in the 39 Steps theme bar, I witnessed an attempted theft. After leaving the premises, I was confronted by two men standing at Pirrie's Close."

"Did you recognise them, sir?"

I nodded. "From the bar."

"Did they take any valuables from you?"

I shook my head. "How did you find out?"

"Fellow officers on patrol spotted two men running from the Cannongate, and one dropped a knife. As he picked it up and ran off, officers pursued both men. After they caught up with them, they were searched, and each had a knife. When questioned about being in possession of a weapon, they stated it was to defend themselves."

"From me!"

"Not from you, sir, but a ghost."

I raised my eyebrows.

"Both men also maintained they heard you scream, and went to your assistance."

I grinned.

"After intense questioning, they admitted confronting you."

"How did you know where to find me?"

"This is our beat, sir, there isn't much what goes on that we don't know!"

The second officer smiled. "We have heard many tales in our time, that one is up there with the best."

"Mind you," I said, "there are only a few days until Halloween."

Both officers laughed, stood up, and departed the apartment. Andrea came into the lounge, sat down, and I revealed what had happened last night.

"They saw a ghost!"

"That's what they told police officers."

"I hope they received the fright of their lives." Andrea smiled. "It must have been a lost soul from the haunted trail that runs underneath the Royal Mile."

I laughed.

"Breakfast?"

I sighed. "Please."

As Andrea walked into the kitchen, I sat and reflected. Again, a ghost has been my saviour.

Walking down St Mary Street, the senior officer glanced at his colleague. "That's the first sighting in Pirrie's Close."

"It's always Gullan's Close."

CHAPTER 11

INDEPENDENT LADY

I said farewell to Andrea, complimented her cooking, and went to catch a tram bound for Edinburgh Airport. Andrea had tried to trace April through social media, however, no joy, and banks in Jersey stated they did not give out staff details. As a consequence, I will have to find April through a conventional method.

I boarded a tram at St Andrew Square and paid my £5 single fare to the airport. Given the limited number of seats available, interest for this new mode of Edinburgh transport remains high. I sat next to a male passenger wearing a smart grey hat, scarf and overcoat. Due to the tram's bright interior, his black shoes gleamed.

"Are you off to a warmer climate?" he said.

"Jersey."

"New York?"

I smiled. "The Channel Islands."

He looked at my suitcase. "A short break?"

I nodded.

The man adjusted his hat, revealing white hair.

"Do you use the tram much?"

"Back in the 1950's, I travelled on the original trams!"

Did he see the Famous Five in action?

"Apart from a Sunday, I used it every day." He coughed. "I stayed in Great Junction Street, and commuted to the top of Leith Street and back."

"Did you attend any games at Easter Road?"

The man shook his head. "Saturday was our busiest day, and we didn't get time off." He grinned. "Besides, I'm a Hearts fan."

"What did you work as?"

"A tailor."

"All of your working life?"

He nodded. "I worked for Hepworth, and then moved to Jackson." Once more, he coughed. "In my day, men had their suits made to measure." He cleared his throat.

"Similar to the current tram design, things change."

The man laughed. "The original trams could only take seventy passengers - this can hold a lot more!"

I looked upwards. And now trams have CCTV. "It's a pity Edinburgh City Council discarded the original trams and track."

He sighed. "It would have saved a lot of taxpayers money and upheaval."

"At least the trams are now here to stay."

"Let's hope so!"

I laughed.

The man stood up. "Murrayfield Stadium, this is my stop."

I looked at my watch - 1.15pm. "Is the rugby on today?"

He shook his head. "I'm off to meet several old colleagues for a reunion in the Murrayfield Bar."

"Have a good time."

"I always do, and end up with a hangover." He laughed, then walked to the exit door.

When the jovial individual got off, he walked past my window, and waved. A number of passengers boarded, then the tram continued along Corstorphine Road to the terminus at Edinburgh Airport. I had been fortunate to acquire a late booking on a 'no frills' airline to Jersey, via Southampton Airport.

Having time to kill after checking in, I headed for a lounge, which had two separate licensed bars. As I entered, a lady leaving brushed past me without apologising. Maybe she has sampled too much hospitality.

Just over an hour later, I boarded the sky blue and white aircraft. Its distinctive logo would ensure brand awareness for any passing high-flying angel. Looking for an empty double-seat, I spotted one further along the aisle, but someone beat me to it. I sat down on the outside, and unbuttoned my jacket.

"You made it in one piece, then?"

I looked to my right, and smiled. "Just about."

"I intended to only have a couple."

"How many did you have?"

"Four."

"That's not too drastic."

The lady smiled. "They were doubles."

That could be drastic.

"Are you bound for Southampton?"

"No, Jersey."

"Business?"

I shook my head. "Personal."

"Your first time in Jersey?"

"I've visited the island on a previous occasion for a short break."

"Did you enjoy it?"

I nodded. "Are you on a business trip?" Her sober white blouse, navy blue pinstripe jacket and skirt suggests so.

"Hic!"

Maybe not so sober.

"I was in Edinburgh on business, and now returning home."

"With its vibrant economy, Edinburgh is an ideal place for business."

She nodded, then glanced at her trim silver watch. "This flight should have taken off by now."

"What is it you do?"

"I represent a Jersey chain of hotels."

"I'm booked into the Hotel de France, in St Helier."

"Dinner, bed and breakfast?"

I nodded.

"It's not one of ours." She smiled. "Pity, I could have arranged a good discount."

A pity, indeed.

"Why not cancel?"

"I booked online with my credit card, they have my money!"

"How long are you staying in Jersey?"

"Three days."

The lady took a card out of her jacket pocket, and leaned forward, revealing her cleavage. "If you're unhappy with the hotel, contact me and I will arrange alternative accommodation in one of ours." She brushed a blonde hair off her lapel. "Damn!"

I read the burgundy-coloured card with italic gold letters. 'Diana Bray, Director of Sale, Stylon Hotels'.

"The card allows you to access our website." She pointed to the gold insignia logo. "You can book accommodation, a variety of function suites, or even a meal in one of our hotel's fine restaurants."

"Splendid."

"What is it you do?" I don't get this guy.

"Business consultant."

"What sector?" The lady's blue eyes flickered.

"Most sectors, I suppose you could describe me as a general consultant."

She yawned.

I should have said time traveller.

The lady looked up. "Here comes the boring safety demonstration, a waste of time."

I fastened my seat belt, and paid attention to the presentable uniformed air hostess.

After the demonstration, my window seat passenger had her eyes closed. I took out a magazine from the seat pocket in front, and started to read. Minutes later, the aircraft took off, and a head of long blonde hair rested on my shoulder.

I collected my suitcase from baggage control, and walked to the exit gate for a taxi. Whilst waiting at the stance, my fellow passenger appeared. "Can I give you a lift into town?"

I smiled. "You certainly can."

"This way." She pointed. "My car is in that direction."

I glanced at her suitcase. "Let me take that for you."

"I can manage."

Arriving at a shiny black BMW Convertible, Diana Bray opened the boot, and we deposited our luggage. I eased into a black leather passenger seat, and the BMW took off.

"A lovely car."

"I have to watch my speed." She glanced at me.

"Did you get caught?"

"Last August, on my way to the airport. The authorities maintained I was doing 72mph."

"And were you?"

"I'm sure it was closer to 80!"

I laughed. "Late for your flight?"

"Why, yes!" Once more, she glanced my way.

"You won't be able to achieve the car's potential within Jersey."

"I would like to."

I laughed.

It wasn't long before we reached Jersey and then the Hotel de France. I collected my suitcase, and as I stood at the passenger door, the window slid down. "Hope you don't like your accommodation."

"If not, you will receive a call."

"What are your plans for this evening?"

"Dinner in the hotel, then an early night."

"That sounds dull!"

"Any other suggestions?"

"Meet you for a drink in Minosas at nine o'clock."

The car moved off, and I walked up several steps, then entered the hotel. A large foyer with magnolia-coloured walls and brown leather couches greeted me. Approaching the reception desk, my footsteps could be heard on the marble floor. A grey-suited male member of staff came forward. "Good afternoon, sir."

"Good afternoon." I laid my suitcase on the floor.

"Do you have a reservation?"

"Yes, I do."

"Your name, sir?"

"Mr Carsell-Brown."

The member of staff checked a black register book. "Ah, yes, a late booking." He turned around, removed a key from a numbered hook, and put it on the desk. "Second floor, sir, please sign the register." He turned the book around, and handed me a pen.

I wrote my name and address, then picked up my room key. The member of staff turned the book around, and looked at my details. Lifting my suitcase, I started to walk, then realised I had put his pen in my inside jacket pocket. When I gave it back, he smiled. "Thank you, sir."

"My apologies, I have a similar pen at home."

"You almost had two!"

I laughed. "What time is dinner served?"

"Between 7-9pm, sir."

I took a lift to the appropriate floor, and upon entering my room, observed a modern spacious habitat. I unpacked, then put the contents into one of two wooden wardrobes. From the bowl of fruit, which lay on a table, I picked up an orange, and peeled it. As dinner isn't for several hours, now would be an ideal time to catch a couple of hours sleep. After finishing the orange, I removed my shoes, and lay back on the comfortable bed. As I became drowsy, the bedside telephone rang and stretched my arm towards it.

"James?"

"Yes." It's Diana.

"How is the room?"

"It appears okay."

"Just okay?"

"It's suitable."

"Do you want me to book you into one of our hotels?"

"I'll stay here."

"Are you sure?"

"Positive, see you tonight."

"Bye."

I replaced the black handset into its matching cradle, then lay back. No additional business for Stylon Hotels on this occasion, then my thoughts turned to April and why I am in Jersey. Being a small island, finding a forty-six-year-old bank employee from Edinburgh shouldn't be difficult, and with St Helier having the majority of Jersey's population, I'll start here.

Following dinner, I went to the reception desk, and handed in my room key. Smiling, the female member of staff took it.

"What's the quickest way to Minosas?"

"After leaving the hotel, turn right, go straight on for a hundred yards and then second left." The receptionist pondered. "No, it is third left."

"Thanks."

"Have a good evening."

I departed the hotel, and adhered to the given directions. After entering a street with no bar in sight, I retraced my steps, took a second left, and came across the establishment. Two solemn suited male stewards, full of muscle, stood outside barring any access. When I approached, they let me in and gave a courteous nod. Given the sophisticated lighting and decor, my first impression was positive. Looking around, I observed a downstairs and an upstairs bar, then a slim young woman in a revealing dress came up to me. Her long dark auburn hair rested upon her bare shoulders. "Are you looking for the night club?"

"Night club?"

She pointed. "It's upstairs, along with the piano bar."

I glanced upwards, then at her. "No, I'm looking for an

acquaintance."

"Male or female?"

"Female."

The young woman stared behind me.

I turned around. "Good evening."

The young woman departed.

Diana smiled. "I nabbed you just in time."

"A hooker?"

"No, a predator!"

I turned around, and saw the young woman approach a well-dressed man standing at the bar. Acknowledging her, she then put an arm around his waist and other men nearby looked on with envious expressions.

"Let's have a seat," said Diana.

She led me into a busy dimly lit lounge with black leather couches and white cushions. We found a vacant couch, and Diana sat down.

"What would you like to drink?"

"A glass of Chardonnay, large."

I made my way through a crowd of people to the bar, and whilst there, noticed the young woman conversing with a younger man. She glanced at me, then continued to chat with her new acquaintance. The cut of his suit and youthful looks no doubt assisted in gaining the young woman's attention.

"Yes, sir?" said a male bar person.

"A glass of Chardonnay and a lager, please."

"Large, sir?"

"Yes, a pint."

"I meant the glass of wine, sir." He smiled.

I nodded.

The bar person stood at the Stella Artois font, pouring into a pint glass. He set it in front of me and then filled a glass of wine. "£16.65, please, sir."

£16.65! I handed him two £10 notes. In future, hopefully, I'll end up back in time.

After examining both notes, he put them in a till, then handed me a bundle of coins. I put them into my jacket pocket, lifted both drinks, and headed back. When I eventually reached there, a man stood beside Diana. She introduced him as a business acquaintance within the Hospitality sector, and then he left. As soon as I set our drinks on the table, Diana picked up her glass, and took a swig. I lifted mine, and took a sip, whilst she finished hers.

"Another?" She stood.

"I'll get it."

"What do you want?"

"Just a half of lager."

After she left, I lifted up my glass and then took a swig. Keeping pace with this lady may prove difficult. I took a second swig, laid my glass on the table, and cast my gaze around the popular location. For women of all ages and sizes, black appears the popular colour - including Diana. Male attendees wore suits, or similar to me, a casual jacket and trousers. I perceived the atmosphere as cordial, therefore, a plausible reason for its popularity. Diana returned with my lager and a large glass of wine, then set them down.

"Are denims allowed?"

Diana lifted her glass, took a swig and then shook her head.

"A strict dress code exists?"

"Since it opened, that has been the case." She took a sip.

"I can't imagine trouble occurring."

"Only on one occasion that I'm aware of."

"What happened?" I lifted my pint glass, and took a swig." She doesn't believe in half measures.

"The person I introduced you to has a brother, and a political firebrand. A discussion with another guy on migrants became heated, several punches were thrown and then a fracas erupted between two groups of men."

"Has the owner banned political debates?"

Diana nodded. "Due to the recent Referendum, there must have been much discussion around Scotland?"

"Indeed, one member of a political party had eggs thrown at him by opposition supporters!" I grinned. "However, no brawls."

She laughed, drank her wine, and set the empty glass down.

I took another swig. "Another?"

"Please, hic!"

I put my glass on the table, rose, and went to the bar. Waiting for service, I spotted the voluptuous young woman in the company of another man, and drinking out of a champagne glass.

"Yes, sir?" said the male bar person.

"A large glass of Chardonnay, please."

"And for yourself, sir?"

"Just the glass of Chardonnay, thanks." I don't want a hangover.

I observed the young woman finish her drink, and from a bottle of Bollinger in an ice bucket, her gentleman friend filled her glass. Given the bubbles, no doubt an expensive brand.

"Two large glasses of Chardonnay, sir." The bar person laid them on the counter.

I raised my eyebrows. "Two?"

"Did you only want the one, sir?"

I nodded.

I paid for one drink, returned to the lounge and as I sat down, noticed a lipstick stain on my glass of lager.

Diana smiled.

"Did you enjoy it?" I gave her the glass of Chardonnay.

She took it. "Your lager tasted terrible."

I turned the glass around.

"What type of food do you enjoy?" She took a swig, and put her glass firmly on the table.

"Indian, however, my stomach doesn't."

She laughed. "Pity, there's an excellent Indian restaurant not far from here."

"What type of cuisine does the local restaurants specialise in?"

"Most types, but mainly seafood."

"I'm sure we'll find somewhere suitable."

Diana smiled, picked up her glass, and drank the remaining wine.

After a light breakfast, I left the hotel dining room, and before reaching the lift, a male member of staff at reception raised his arm. "Mr Carsell-Brown."

I looked round, and walked up to the desk.

"I have something for you."

He reached under the desk and then placed a watch in front of me. Smiling, I lifted it.

"Thank you."

"A woman handed it into reception." He looked behind to view the circular wall clock. "Almost an hour ago."

"Did she have long blonde hair?"

"Average build, height, and mid to late thirties."

Observant. "Did she leave a message?"

"No, sir."

I entered the lift, pressed the designated floor button, and put on my watch. When the doors opened, I walked along the bright corridor, which didn't help my fragile eyes.

Beginning my search in St Helier, this morning I will attempt to contact April. I put on my jacket, collected loose cash, and locked the room door. Upon entering the lift, a chambermaid stood, and when we both stepped out, she smiled. As I handed in my key, the member of staff took it. "Have a good day, sir."

"Thanks."

Drinking orange juice and coffee at breakfast didn't cure a dry throat. Two large beers, plus three glasses of wine with a meal last night have taken their toll. I spotted a coffee outlet across the street, and when I entered, a loud bell rang. Of all the mornings, not this one! A tall slender woman laid out cakes and biscuits onto a glass display. She turned around. "Just take a seat, sir, I'll be over soon to take your order." She flicked back her long dark hair.

I sat down beside a window, and gazed at people passing by. What does April look like? I'm aware of her age, however, not much else.

"Yes, sir." The shop assistant paused. "Sir!"

I looked away from the window. "Apologies, my mind was elsewhere."

She smiled. "What would you like?"

"Just a white coffee, please."

The shop assistant returned to the counter.

As I turned towards the window, a well-groomed lady walked past, and acknowledged me. Returning the compliment, it struck me that she would be of a similar age to April. It is still difficult to comprehend that I have a daughter, and she is older than I am.

"Your coffee, sir."

I looked up. "Thanks."

She set the white cup and saucer on the wooden table, and left.

I lifted the cup, and took a sip - that is strong. Perhaps she thought I needed a jolt. Whilst sipping, I contemplated the next move. In St Helier, there must be a place in which to trace family members. On finding it, I will pass myself off as a cousin who has travelled all the way from Ardrishaig, where April's family comes from. Glad I have my travel receipts on me as proof. I finished my coffee, and as the shop assistant attended to other customers, waited at the counter. Returning, she handed me a receipt.

"£3.25, please, sir."

I gave her three £1 coins and silver 50p piece.

"Thanks, sir."

"I'm trying to trace a relative who travelled here some

time ago."

"To St Helier?"

"Maybe."

"A Scottish woman?"

I nodded. "She'll be about my age."

"It's not much to go on, sir."

"At some point she may work or have worked in a local bank."

The shop assistant shook her head. "Sorry, sir, can't help."

"Thanks, anyway."

"Try the Register Office."

"I will do."

"Bye."

I left to the sound of that bell, however, since my cup of coffee, it's not as prominent. Then, I heard a woman's voice behind me. "Excuse me!"

I stopped, turned around and a woman came towards me. She stopped, took a deep breath, and looked up. "I overheard you speaking to the shop assistant." She took another deep breath. "There's a guest house in the centre of St Helier owned by a Scottish woman."

"About my age?"

She nodded. "But not as tall."

"Do you know her name?"

"I think it may be Avril."

"April?"

"Yes, that's it!"

"Does her guest house have a name?"

"The Fyne Guest House. Fyne has a 'y' instead of an 'i' letter."

"Thank you."

The woman walked slowly back to the coffee shop, and I continued on my way. The Fyne Guest House is appropriate for an owner born and raised in the vicinity of Loch Fyne.

I arrived at the centre of St Helier, and soon found the

guest house. Situated in a narrow side street, I observed the sign above a dark green entrance door in bold white letters. With it being closed, I contemplated whether the guest house remained open for business. I pulled a traditional brass bell handle, but no answer came. Trying again, the door opened, and a woman smiled. "Can I help you?"

As this woman looks in her mid-thirties, it can't be April.

"Are you looking for somewhere to stay, sir?"

"I've come to pay April a visit."

"Are you a relative?" He resembles April.

"I knew her mother, I'm James."

"I'm afraid April is not here."

"I can call back."

The woman frowned. "April is in hospital."

"Hospital!" I stared.

"Please come in." The woman fully opened the door.

After I entered, she closed the door, and led me into a room with seven tables and sets of chairs. I took this to be the dining room, although, the tables had not been set.

"I'm Julie, please, have a seat."

"Thanks."

"Would you care for a coffee?"

"Yes, please." I'm still thirsty.

"Be right back."

As Julie left, I cast my gaze around the compact tidy and tastefully decorated room. Dark wooden furniture blended in with the polished wooden floor. The magnolia-coloured walls complemented a white ceiling and dark green curtains, but why no guests? Julie returned with a tray containing a cup of coffee, small jug of cream, plus a bowl of brown sugar. "I'll just be a minute."

I poured cream into my coffee, lifted the white cup, and took a sip. A few minutes later, Julie reappeared, and sat opposite me. "April has been unwell for some time."

I set my cup on the saucer.

Julie sighed. "It is serious."

"Can you tell me what the illness is?"

"Malignant meningioma."

A brain tumour.

"Early this year, April was diagnosed with the condition."

"She has had medical treatment?"

Julie nodded. "Nothing else can be done."

I stared at my cup.

"She is a patient at the nearby hospital."

"Can I visit her?"

"The hospital is located in Gloucester Street, a short distance from here."

I stood up. "Thank you."

Solemn-faced Julie accompanied me to the door, then opened it. I stepped outside, looked at the sign, then at Julie.

"Now that the summer season has finished, business is non-existent."

"Thanks for the coffee."

"Bye." She closed the door.

Walking along the street, I had forgotten to ask directions for the hospital. April must feel isolated in Jersey, however, as she is my daughter, an independent streak may exist.

Fifteen minutes after receiving accurate directions, I arrived. I entered the grey stone building, and approached a reception desk.

"Can I help you, sir?" said a well-groomed woman.

"I have come to visit a patient, an April Anderson." I cleared my throat. "Can you tell me what ward she is in?"

From her computer keyboard, the receptionist entered information, then looked at the screen. "She is in a private ward, C4."

"Where is it located?"

A sturdy female nurse, who appeared at the reception desk, leaned towards me. "I'm heading that way, I'll take you there." She handed a white folder to the receptionist, then looked at me. "This way, sir."

After following the blue and white uniformed nurse along a series of corridors, she stopped and faced me. "When did you last see April?"

I hesitated. "Not for a while."

"A long while?"

I nodded.

"Are you a relative?" There is a familiarity.

"I've been on my travels and after returning home, discovered April's condition." Once more, I cleared my throat. "I've journeyed down from Edinburgh."

"You are aware of her condition?"

"Yes."

"Her vision is severely impaired."

I sighed.

"You'll appear as a blur, therefore, I'll take you into her ward, and introduce you."

"Thanks."

"What is your name?"

"James."

The nurse led me along another corridor and then into a room where I would meet my daughter for the first time. Before entering, my heart was pounding, then I observed a woman with cropped hair sitting up in her bed. She looked at the nurse, then me, and removed her earphones.

"April, this is James," said the nurse in a calm voice.

"James?" She looked in my direction.

"I knew your mother." April has my eyes.

"Have you come all the way from Scotland?"

The nurse looked my way.

"I was in London on business, it's a quick flight."

"Please, have a seat."

"If you require anything, April, press the buzzer."

"Thanks, nurse." April looked at me. "How did you find me?"

"I met a woman who works at your guest house."

"Julie Beck?"

"Yes." Nervous, I took a deep breath.

"Did you rush to get here?"

"I walk fast."

I sat down on a firm chair close to April's bed. Given her condition, she did not look her forty-seven years.

"Where are you staying?"

"The Hotel de France."

"It's not far from my guest house."

I coughed.

"Were you a friend of my mother?"

"Yes." I cleared my throat.

"Where in Scotland do you come from? You have an East Coast accent."

"Edinburgh."

"My daughter, Victoria, stays there."

April has a daughter!

"Which part are you from?"

"Originally Newhaven, then I moved to the city centre."

"Victoria lives a short distance from Newhaven."

"With her father?"

April shook her head. "Every fortnight, she catches a flight from Edinburgh, and stays for the weekend."

"At your guest house?"

April smiled. "At least there's one guest."

"What is it she works as?" Once more, I cleared my throat.

"Would you like a glass of water?"

"I'm fine." Not really.

"An Account Manager with an advertising agency."

Similar to what I did in Nice. "She must be creative."

"And demanding."

Another family trait.

"What is it you do, James?"

"I'm self-employed, as a consultant."

"A medical consultant?"

"Business."

"After retiring, why did you continue to work?"

Retired? Off course, being a friend of her mother, April will perceive me as an elderly individual and her impaired vision won't reveal my age. "I wasn't ready to retire."

"You voice is that of a younger person." April yawned.

"Do you want me to leave?"

"I get tired easily." Her eyes flickered.

"If you wish, I will return tomorrow."

She nodded.

As April closed her eyes, I stood up, and quietly left. She resembles Abigail in appearance and manner, however, during my visit, I'm glad she couldn't see my strained expression. My goodness, I am also a grandfather! Now is a good time to ensure my assets are bequeathed.

Returning in a daze to the hotel, I collected my room key, got into the lift, and pressed a button for my floor. Time travel did not prepare me for this. As I left the lift, a chambermaid came out of a room and looked my way.

"Hello." It's the chambermaid I saw earlier.

"Did you enjoy last night?"

Last night?

"At Minosas."

"Yes, thanks." I can't remember this person.

She smiled. "You spoke to my friend."

I hesitated.

"She wore a revealing dress."

I grinned. "Yes, I remember."

"You had a lucky escape."

I laughed.

As she departed, I entered my room, and closed the door. My room had been cleaned, and also a white printed card had been placed on the bedside cabinet. I picked it up, Volcanos, St. Helier's Hottest Nightspot. That's interesting, Minosas has a rival. The chambermaid no doubt receives a commission, however, this evening will be an early one.

Then, the telephone rang, and I picked up the receiver.

"Mr Carsell-Brown, there are two gentleman who wish to speak with you," said the receptionist.

"Oh?"

"From the local police station."

"I'll be right down." What's up now? I replaced the receiver.

I left my room, locked the door, and went downstairs. Leaving the lift, I observed two stocky men in plain clothes standing in a conspicuous manner and upon reaching reception, both turned around.

"Mr Carsell-Brown?" said the oldest.

"Yes."

"I am Detective Sergeant Albright, and this is Detective Constable Bennett." He produced an ID from his inside overcoat pocket.

I looked at it. In 1938, I met a police officer with that unusual surname.

"Can we have a word?"

I nodded. "Certainly."

We went to the far corner of a lounge, and sat on its brown leather couches. Facing them, they appeared within my age group, however, their hair had turned premature grey.

"How can I be of assistance, gentlemen?"

"What is your connection to April Anderson?" said Detective Sergeant Albright.

"I was a friend of her late mother."

"How well do you know April Anderson?"

"Yesterday, I met her for the first time."

"You travelled all the way from Edinburgh to see her?"

"I returned from abroad, and found out that April had moved to Jersey."

"You came to Jersey just to pay your respects?"

I nodded. "Upon my arrival, I went to her guest house and learned of her condition." I looked at both officers.

"What is this about?"

"We believe she has received threats over the past eighteen months."

"Why?"

"Relating to her guest house."

"In what way?"

"Competition, Mr Carsell-Brown. St Helier is a small place, therefore, intense rivalry between businesses exists. Also, April Anderson is not from Jersey, and this can cause resentment."

"I've been told that the guest house is not busy, with little or no custom."

"It wasn't always in that situation," said Detective Constable Bennett. He coughed. "In fact, the guest house was St Helier's busiest."

"What happened?"

"We believe someone had been in collaboration with a competitor to discourage customers," said Detective Sergeant Albright

"There is a woman in charge, and she appears genuine."

"Julie Beck?"

I nodded.

"She is a new start," said Detective Constable Bennett, "her predecessor left."

This situation probably contributed to April's illness.

Detective Sergeant Albright gave a wry smile. "We wanted to make sure that you had not arrived in Jersey to extract revenge on certain individuals."

I smiled. "No, just to visit April."

"How is she?"

"Not good."

"Sorry to hear that." He stood up. "We won't take up any more of your time, Mr Carsell-Brown."

Detective Constable Bennett also got to his feet, as I did, and walked with both officers to reception. Detective Sergeant Albright faced me. "Incidentally, my grandfather is from Scotland."

"Oh?"

"He worked as a police officer in Glasgow, then in 1946 he transferred to Jersey."

"A more amiable climate."

Detective Sergeant Albright grinned. "And environment."

His colleague nodded.

After they left the hotel, I returned to the lounge, and pondered over what they had revealed. Soon, a waitress came across and asked if I wanted anything to drink.

"A coffee, please."

"White?"

"Strong."

"Be right back."

I sat back and thought about the situation concerning April's guest house. To build up her business would have taken time, energy, plus expense, and now it's all to no avail. Even though the guest house is presentable and has a reliable person in charge, to revive it would be difficult, but perhaps a recent acquaintance could assist. As Diana Bray works in the accommodation sector, I will attempt to 'pick her brains' and obtain knowledge as well as contacts.

On my way to the hospital, I popped into a florist and bought flowers. Not long after, I arrived at reception and a woman advised, "in future, sir, just go direct to April's ward."

I thanked her, and upon my arrival, April was sitting up with headphones on. Then, she looked in my direction, and removed them.

"Hello." She should recognise my voice.

"Hi." April sniffed the air.

"I brought flowers." I gripped the white wrapping paper.

"Flowers!"

"Yes."

"Just lay them on the window ledge, a nurse will put them in water."

I placed them on the ledge.

"You walked all the way from the flower shop?"

"It's not far."

"Please, James, have a seat."

I sat down opposite April. "How are you today?"

"Same as yesterday." She looked at the window. "How is the weather outside?"

"There's a slight nip in the air, then again, it is late October."

"When do you depart?"

"Tomorrow, late morning."

"Why don't you extend your stay in Jersey? You can stay at the guest house."

I could, and more time to meet with Diana.

"Unless, you have to return home."

"No, I can stay for another few days." I'll rearrange my flight home.

April smiled. "Yesterday evening, Julie visited, and we spoke about the business."

"With the summer season over, hotels and guest houses will have less trade."

"We must try and recover what we lost in custom."

"Do not worry, your health is more important."

"Have you enjoyed Jersey?"

"Yes, I've noticed a French influence."

"I considered going to France."

"To live and work?"

April nodded.

"Did you have a specific location in mind?"

"Nice."

That's a coincidence! "Why that particular city?"

"Comparable in size to Edinburgh, and its commercial heritage."

At that moment, a nurse entered, and spotted the bunch

of flowers. She lifted them off the window ledge. "I'll put them into a vase of water."

As the nurse departed, I noticed April's eyelids flicker, then she covered her mouth and yawned.

"I lived and worked in Nice."

"Oh, when?"

"I went there twenty-five years ago."

"You must have enjoyed Nice, that's a long time."

"I only stayed for ten years."

"Why did you leave?"

"I was left a property in Scotland, and made the decision to return."

"Where about?"

"Dochar, near Ardrishaig." She knows the place well.

"I was raised there by my mother and grandmother." April paused. "My father died before I was born."

He disappeared, and couldn't prevent it.

"Is it still as picturesque?" Once more, April yawned.

"Very much so."

Just as April started to feel drowsy, the nurse returned with flowers in a vase, and placed it on the window ledge.

I stood up, and whispered to the nurse. "Time to go."

She looked at April, and nodded.

After leaving the hospital, I visited Julie, and mentioned what April had suggested. Courtesy of the owner, this would be my new residence for several days.

"Good, we now have a guest." Julie clasped her hands.

After a coffee, I returned to the hotel and collected my room key. Whilst waiting for the lift, a young woman emerged from a nearby staff room, then came up to me. "Hello, again."

"Hello." It's the chambermaid in casual attire.

"That's me finished for the day."

"Lucky you."

She smiled. "Are you going out tonight?"

I shook my head. "An early start tomorrow morning."

"You're leaving tomorrow?"

"I'm leaving the hotel, but will be staying at a local guest house."

"What's wrong with the hotel?"

"I know the guest house's owner and she made me an offer I couldn't refuse."

The young woman laughed.

"Are you clubbing tonight?"

She shook her head. "I also have an early start tomorrow."

"Work prevails."

The young woman stared. "At Minosas, I noticed you with Diana Bray."

"Do you know her?"

"I know of her!"

She now has a serious expression.

"Bye." The young woman departed.

The lift arrived, I entered, and pressed a button for my floor. That reminds me, I have to contact Diana, however, the chambermaid didn't appear complimentary. In a small location, jealousy will no doubt exist, especially, when the focus is an attractive successful woman.

CHAPTER 12

SCANDAL

Opening my heavy eyelids, I lifted a tired head to check the time. Since daylight had not broken, I let my head drop onto the soft white pillow and then stretched my arms. I lay for a short while, threw back the single duvet cover, and struggled out of bed. Entering the bathroom, I shaved, and then took a shower. After making myself presentable, I headed downstairs for breakfast, where a smiling Julie greeted me. Being the sole guest, I had my pick of the tables and chose one beside a window.

Following a full breakfast, Julie joined me for coffee, and revealed several truths about local business rivalry.

"In the accommodation sector?" I set my white cup on its matching saucer.

Julie nodded. "Within St Helier, competition between hotels and guest houses is fierce."

"I met a woman on my flight to Jersey who represented a chain of hotels within the island."

"What was her name?"

"Diana Bray."

Julie sat back.

"Do you know her?"

"I know of her."

That's the second time I've heard this phrase in as many days.

"She became involved with a local politician, and I believe they've now parted."

At Minosas, Diana mentioned a politician.

"When Diana met him, he was married."

"Was she aware of this?"

"Oh, yes." Julie nodded. "Diana Bray and the politician's wife had been best friends for many years."

My goodness.

"After Diana got what she wanted, the relationship ended."

I looked at Julie.

"Being a politician, he had influence on the Jersey Licensing Board. One hotel in St Helier had been due to lose its license, however, the decision was reversed."

"A hotel Diana represented?"

Julie nodded.

"And the politician?"

"I heard he tried to save the marriage, but his wife told him to sod off!"

I laughed.

"Quite right, too." Julie smiled. "Got what he deserved."

No doubt.

Julie frowned. "April and I believe the woman who worked here, had been planted by Diana to cause problems."

"Problems?"

"Deter people from staying."

As Detective Albright stated.

"When a person called to enquire about accommodation, April discovered they had been told someone would call them back."

"I take it that nobody did."

"Correct."

"How did April find out?"

"She took a call enquiring why nobody from the guest house had called back, and when it happened again, she confronted the woman."

"And?"

"The woman pleaded her innocence. Next day she didn't turn up."

"A plant."

"Devised by Diana Bray."

"Is the accommodation sector that cut-throat?"

"Oh yes, I could reveal more, but it's too early."

I looked at my watch.

"Any plans for today?"

"I'll visit April, then head into the town centre for a look round."

"The festivities for Halloween will be underway, therefore, don't be alarmed by people dressed as a ghoul, ghost or witch."

"In the morning?"

"Three days prior to Halloween, wearing a costume in the city centre is commonplace, it's a tradition which dates back to the Millennium."

I lifted my cup, and took a sip.

"Do you believe in spirits?"

"No, only time travellers."

Julie smiled. "I've heard of people seeing a ghost, but no time traveller."

There's always a first time."

Julie laughed, then lifted a tray. "There is something else about Diana Bray."

I set my cup on the saucer.

"She organises fund-raising events for the Channel Island's handicapped children to visit Euro-Disney in Paris."

I raised my eyebrows. Admirable.

As Julie took a tray of dishes and crockery into the kitchen, I went up to my room, and made ready for my hospital visit.

Fifteen minutes later, I left the guest house, and walked to the hospital. Although it was late October, the climate in this southerly part of Britain remained mild, thus, my jacket will be sufficient for now. Then, dark clouds and rain replaced a crisp sunny morning. My steps got quicker, and I managed to reach the hospital entrance without getting soaked. Walking to April's ward, I spotted the nurse from my previous visit, and she approached with a solemn expression. "I am afraid you cannot visit April today, sir."

"Why not?"

"She had a rough night, and is now fast asleep."

"Can I come back tomorrow?"

"It would be advisable to call the hospital tomorrow morning."

"I'll do that."

I retraced my steps to the exit, and was relieved that the rain had stopped, although I could smell it. Feeling colder, once more, I quickened my step towards St Helier's city centre, and a warm drink.

Puffing and panting, I arrived at the coffee shop, and upon entering, warm air hit me. Not long after I took a seat, the same shop assistant appeared. "Hello, again."

"A white coffee, please."

"Be right back."

After she left, I noticed a leaflet on the next table, and stretched across. It advertised a Halloween dance at Minosas this coming Friday evening, and emphasised a late license until 1.30am. The assistant returned with my cup of coffee, laid it on the table and glanced at the leaflet. "Will you go on Friday?"

"I'm not sure."

"It's the latest I've known for a drinks extension in Jersey."

"The bar owner must have a good friend on the Licensing Board."

The assistant smiled, then departed.

I took a sip of the piping hot coffee and then set my cup on the saucer. An approaching car's roar disturbed the street's peaceful atmosphere and a black convertible sped past. Seconds later, the assistant returned with a plate of bourbon biscuits. "On the house."

"Thanks." I smiled.

She looked towards the window. "She's been caught twice for speeding, and got off on both occasions."

"Lucky her."

"It's not luck." The assistant departed.

On Thursday morning I called the hospital, and since April's condition had improved, I could pay her a visit. On this occasion, I bought flowers at a recently opened florist beside the hospital.

When I arrived at April's private ward, she was sitting up awaiting my arrival. "I thought it was you."

"How?"

"By your footsteps."

Her hearing is not impaired.

"I can smell flowers!" April sniffed. "A sweet scent."

I moved closer.

She gently touched them. "Tulips."

"Pink ones."

"Thank you."

"My pleasure."

With perfect timing, a nurse appeared and noticed the bouquet of flowers, smiled at April, then me. "Would you like me to put them in water?"

I nodded. "Please."

Moments later, she returned with a glass vase, took the flowers, and laid the vase on a table near April's bed. "Perfect," said the nurse as she smiled and then left.

"Have a seat, James."

I sat on the chair close to April's bed.

"Are you enjoying your stay at the guest house?"

I nodded.

"You don't like it?"

Dash! April can't see me clearly. "Yes."

"Good."

"Last night I slept like a log."

"That's good to hear."

"Also, the food is excellent - especially the cooked breakfast."

"Oh?"

"I never have a cooked breakfast."

"Why not?"

"I don't cook."

April laughed. "You will appreciate Julie, she's an excellent cook."

"If business at the guest house improves, Julie's cooking would entice customers to return."

"I'm certain of it, however, enticing people to book is the problem."

True.

April paused, then stared in my direction. "As you were a friend of my mother, did you meet my father?"

I had a suspicion this question would come my way.

"You didn't meet him?"

"Only on a couple of occasions."

"What was he like?"

"About my height, 5ft 10, and of medium build."

"That's not what I meant, James, what was he like as a person?"

"He was fond of your mother and spoke about her a lot. He cared for things which meant a lot to him." I smiled. "He was hard to please, at times."

"Then why did he suddenly leave my mother?"

"Perhaps he could not prevent it."

"Prevent it!"

"I'm unsure as to why he left, there must have been a valid reason." This is complicated.

April's voice grew raspy. "Not once did he get in touch." She wiped a tear from her eye.

I feel terrible.

She coughed repeatedly.

"Would you like a glass of water?"

She nodded.

I rose, and poured water from a jug on the bedside table into a glass. Handing it to her, she took several sips, and gave the glass back to me.

"I don't feel well."

I placed the glass on the bedside table, went into the corridor, and spotted a nurse. When I raised my arm, she looked my way and then approached.

"Is it April?"

"Yes."

I followed her into the ward, she examined April, then looked at me with a sad expression.

I whispered, "I'll come back tomorrow."

The nurse nodded.

Leaving the hospital, I was at loggerheads with myself. A shift in time during the summer of 1967 had caused heartache for two loving individuals, but in my defence, I couldn't prevent it.

Solemn-faced, I walked back to the town centre, and for a distraction, browsed around an array of shops. I came across a male boutique with suits, shirts and ties displayed in the large front window. After entering, bright ceiling spotlights caught my eye, as well as the male sales assistant reading a book behind the counter.

He looked up. "Hello, can I help you, sir?" He put his book under the counter.

"Just in to have a look around."

"No problem, if you need assistance, let me know."

"Thanks."

"Your welcome."

Coming across a pale blue shirt, which would match my jacket, I glanced at the price tag, and shook my head. I noticed price tags for suits were not displayed, and perhaps an indication of their value. Before leaving, I acknowledged the sales assistant and he put down his book. "Since we're introducing new stock for Christmas, there's a sale on next week."

With my current financial restraints, the sale price may also be out of reach. "I may come back."

"See you next week, sir."

I doubt it.

"Bye." The sales assistant returned to his book.

I departed the boutique, which went by the name of Beau Brummel, and walked back to the guest house. With the attire I have at my disposal, it will suffice for tomorrow evening's Halloween event. How I miss my previous timeline of 1930 and its price tags.

On the final evening of my stay, I ventured to Minosas, for their publicised Halloween event. When I arrived, a queue had formed, which stretched for thirty yards. With my conventional dark jacket and trousers, plus, a casual shirt, I stood out from locals wearing an assortment of costumes. A pirate, witch and skeleton queued in front of me, however, I didn't spot a coachman. As the queue moved forward, I could see two tall doormen in black formal suits and bow-ties. When I approached, both surveyed my inappropriate Halloween appearance.

"The costume did not arrive in time."

"Pity you aren't a time traveller!" said the broadest steward, "you could have gone back in time and ordered it earlier."

"I'm off duty."

His colleague laughed. "Have a good evening, sir."

After entering, I faced a woman dressed in a red with horns sticking out of her head sitting behind a desk. "£8, please."

£8 to enter a bar! If I argue, she may blow fire in my direction. I handed her eight £1 coins.

"Thanks." She put them in a large metal box, and handed me a ticket. "Have a good evening, sir."

I took the ticket. Here's hoping.

She smiled. What a square.

I manoeuvred through a packed floor to eventually reach the bar, where staff dressed for the occasion. The two male members had black pointed wizard hats, whilst both female members had decided on wide brimmed witches headwear. I will wager the males have conjured up scary drink prices. After ten patient minutes, a witch came forward. "Yes, sir?"

"A lager, please."

She poured into a shiny glass, and set it in front of me. "£7, please."

I handed the witch a £10 note.

She took it, gave me three coins and stared.

Moving away from the bar, a man wearing a formal suit brushed past me, and walked on. I recognised him as the person Diana Bray introduced me to on a previous visit. This time he appears the worse for wear. With the 'Monster Mash' by Bobby 'Boris' Picket playing, I looked around the vicinity. The majority of entrants wore costumes, plus make-up to enhance their disguise. A distinctive bronzed Roman Centurion stood drinking a pint of beer with a woman dressed as a yellow and black pumpkin. As she finished her glass of red wine, a passing waitress with jet-black hair in a vampire outfit took it. A werewolf put his empty pint glass on her silver tray, and in return, she gave him a polite smile through prominent blood-red lips. A person, who resembled an extra-terrestrial, edged past me and stared.

"Which planet are you from?" I said.

"Originally, Glasgow," said a male voice, "what about you?"

"Edinburgh."

"Then you are also an alien!" He departed.

Smiling, I sipped my drink, and a woman with blonde hair dressed as a Greek goddess approached. I recognised her as one of the staff at my previous hotel accommodation.

"Hello, I'm looking for Zeus."

"He's with Poseidon in the upstairs lounge."

She laughed.

"They were having a heated discussion."

"Poseidon could receive a nasty thunderbolt!"

I laughed. "Are you Aphrodite?"

"No, I'm Gemma."

I grinned.

She looked towards the bar. "I've spotted my friend, see you later."

The goddess departed and walked up to a woman dressed as Medusa. No moving snakes on her headwear, however, a terrific imitation. Amidst all those costumes, don't I feel like a party-pooper. I finished my lager, and with 'Ghostbusters' playing loudly, struggled back to the bar. The four bar staff served customers in a frantic manner, with one male wiping his brow. I could smell a pleasant jasmine fragrance, and glanced sideways.

"Meow."

Catwoman! "I don't speak your language."

"If you did, it could be to your advantage." She licked her lips.

I laughed.

"You're Scottish?"

"Yes, I am."

"I trust you haven't come all this way just for the Halloween event?"

I shook my head. "To visit someone, I leave tomorrow."

She smiled. "I'm not into one-night stands."

I raised my eyebrows. "Nor me."

"Then you won't fit in around here."

No comment.

"My name is Caitlin." She held out her black leather glove.

I shook it.

"Did your outfit not arrive in time?"

I shook my head.

"What were you coming as?"

"A time traveller."

"What is it you do?"

"A business professional trying to become a writer."

"Me too! How many words have you written?"

"About a hundred."

Catwoman smiled. "I have written one hundred thousand.

A female bar person approached. "Yes, madam?"

"Two vodka and lemonades, please."

The bar person removed her witch's hat, put it behind the counter and then poured two drinks.

"How much?"

"£14.60."

Catwoman handed over two notes. "Keep the change." She leaned towards me. "That barmaid should have dressed up as the 'Joker' tonight, these prices are a scream!"

As she left, I waited patiently for service. Due to being worked off their feet, all bar staff had discarded headwear. I caught one's eye.

"A lager, please."

"Is that all?"

I nodded.

"Coming up."

A minute later, the bar person came back with an expression of sympathy. "The lager barrel is being changed, you'll have to wait."

"How long?"

"It would be quicker going to the upstairs bar."

Whilst leaving the bar, I spotted Diana with a group of people laughing and drinking. Losing her balance, she bumped into a ghoul, and drink splashed onto him resulting in a shake of the head. As I walked upstairs, the Righteous Brothers rendition of 'Ghost' echoed. In a corner of the bar, I observed the person who had earlier brushed against me having a heated discussion with another man. I ordered a lager, and waited. When both men's voices grew louder, customers stopped talking, and one man stormed off. Moments later, music began playing and conversations resumed. Then, he reappeared with a grim expression, approached the other man, and pulled out a gun from his jacket pocket. As a woman screamed, two shots were fired, and the victim slumped onto the floor. Whilst everyone stared in disbelief, the shooter ran off. A woman at the bar shouted. "Someone call an ambulance."

The bar person picked up a handset, and as he spoke, the woman attended to the victim.

"She's a doctor," said a man next to me.

Two stewards rushed into the bar, and stared at the wounded individual whose blood seeped through his suit. A steward spoke to the bar person, who then ushered customers down the staircase.

Within minutes, an ambulance crew arrived, and soon left with the wounded man. Police officers also appeared, and took statements from witnesses. The scary event had a gruesome finale.

As evening became morning, subdued partygoers departed the establishment. I spotted Diana Bray in the foyer with two police officers, and going by her body language, the conversation wasn't cordial. A woman who stood beside me looking on remarked. "She's done it this time!"

I walked back to the guest house with the recent shooting fresh in my mind. As I shivered, was it because of the incident or chilly November? Whatever, my pace quickened.

Opening the door with a passkey, I went quietly upstairs to my room. Glancing at the bedside clock, it read 12.55, and given that my flight leaves in less than nine hours, glad I didn't overindulge.

I arrived fresh at the breakfast table earlier than my normal time. After sitting down, Julie came into the dining room. "Good morning, how are you feeling?"

"I didn't have too late a night, and left Minosas not long after midnight."

"Any particular reason?" said Julie with a wry smile.

"The evening came to an abrupt halt."

"It's all over Twitter, and since one o'clock, tweets have been going to and fro from people who attended the event."

I sat back on my chair. "Technology rules."

"Did you tweet anyone?"

I shook my head.

"News before it's printed or heard on radio."

"The tabloids may eventually disappear!"

Julie laughed. "What would you like for breakfast?"

"Scrambled egg on toast, please."

"And the usual white coffee?"

I nodded. "Is April's daughter arriving today?"

"Last night she contacted me to say it would be tomorrow."

Pity, I would have met her.

As Julie departed, I thought about Victoria, and that her age will be comparable to a daughter. Julie returned. "Since you don't use twitter, here is a traditional medium." She laid a newspaper on the table and left.

I picked up the Daily Mail, and browsed through it. Politics, celebrity gossip, sport and international affairs received coverage, but no earth-shattering articles. Julie appeared with a wooden tray. "Any interesting news?"

I put down the newspaper. "Maybe I should go onto twitter!"

She laughed. "It would reveal an interesting love triangle concerning a certain Diana Bray."

"When I left Minosas, she was being questioned by two police officers."

"Oh?" Julie laid my plate of scrambled eggs, a small white pot and a jug of milk onto the table.

"What did Twitter have to say?"

"When her affair with a married politician ended, she dated a work colleague, however, it appears she was seeing both men."

I shook my head, whilst pouring coffee into a cup.

"If you ask me, she is trouble, with a capital T!"

I lifted my cup, then sipped some coffee.

"Is the coffee warm enough?"

I nodded. "Yes, thanks."

"I'm going to check Twitter, there may be a Diana Bray update."

I smiled, then set my cup on the saucer.

"Be back in a short while."

I devoured my delicious, scrambled eggs, complete with toasted bread, prepared and then served. When I return home, normal service will have to resume, but given my laborious primitive experiences of 1896 and 1912, my grievances will be minimal.

Since a Diana update did not transpire, I left the dining room, and went upstairs to pack. A short while later, I came downstairs, and Julie emerged from the kitchen.

"I've enjoyed my stay."

She smiled. "What time is your flight?"

I looked at my watch. "In just under three hours. I'll call into the hospital and say goodbye to April."

"Have a safe journey home."

At least it will be by a conventional method rather than time travel.

Julie walked me to the door, and after opening it, a gust of wind blew the door fully open.

"My goodness!" she cried.

I stepped out of the doorway, and looked up to the dull grey sky. "It could be a

rocky flight home."

She nodded.

I frowned.

"Bye."

Against a strong wind, and carrying my case, I walked to the hospital. Out of breath, I entered the nearby florist shop, and a sales assistant behind the counter looked my way. "If it's fresh flowers you want, sir, the delivery van hasn't arrived."

"That's a pity."

"I was told by the delivery firm that the van broke down." The woman shook her head.

"Thanks, anyway."

"Have a good day."

I entered the hospital, and whilst walking to April's ward, a senior nurse called to me. "Excuse me, sir."

I stopped, and looked round.

"Have you come to visit April?"

"Yes, I have."

"She had an uneasy night, and is now fast asleep."

"I'm leaving Jersey at lunchtime, therefore, wanted to see her."

"Due to a strong sedative, April will be asleep for several hours."

I sighed.

"I will let her know that you called in."

"Thank you."

The white-uniformed sister walked on, and I made for the hospital exit. Once outside, I spotted a couple getting out of a black taxi, and approached the driver's window. "Are you for hire?"

"Yes, sir."

I got into the vehicle, shut the rear door, and sat on the black leather seat. I laid my suitcase on the floor, then unbuttoned my jacket.

"The airport, sir?"

"Yes."

"Are you in a rush to catch a flight, sir?"

I looked at my watch. "No, I'm in good time."

The grey-haired driver looked in his mirror at me, and gave a faint grin. "Good, I won't have to break the speed limit."

I laughed. "Do you have to at times?"

He nodded. "Frequently, sir."

The taxi moved off, exited Jersey's hospital grounds, and

headed for the airport at an appropriate speed.

"Enjoy your stay, sir?"

"Yes, I came to visit a relative."

"Did you take in any of the sights?" The driver looked in the mirror. "The German hospital built by them when they occupied us is a popular attraction."

I shook my head. "Didn't get round to visiting it."

"Confrontations were non-existent." He laughed. "The natives bided their time till the Germans left."

"Whilst here, I did witness a confrontation – last night at Minosas!"

The driver nodded. "I heard about it."

"On Twitter?"

He shook his head. "Passengers in my taxi who had been there."

"Gossip is the quickest form of communication."

"There has been an abundance of it surrounding a particular blonde on this island."

No doubt, a certain blonde.

"Have you heard of Diana Bray?"

"I overheard a conversation about her."

"And that's not the first time she's been involved in a scandal." The driver shook his head.

I looked out of the window. She certainly has acquired a reputation. This, being a small island, won't help. Ah, here we are.

"It could be a bumpy flight home, sir."

I nodded. "Windy November, indeed."

The driver found a vacant parking space outside the airport terminal, and drove into it. He applied the handbrake, and turned round. "£12.50, sir."

"There's £13, keep the change."

"Thank you, sir."

I picked up my suitcase, opened the rear door, and it flew wide open. After firmly closing it, the driver drove off, and several blustery minutes later, I entered the calm building.

Phew! A group of people stood at the check-in desk, however, I soon handed over my return ticket.

"Are you aware that there is a stop at East Midlands, sir?" said the airline representative.

I nodded. "Yes."

The representative asked a series of standard baggage questions and then I placed my suitcase on a metal compartment. She stamped my ticket, handed it to me and smiled. Leaving the queue, I glanced at my watch, and had over an hour to kill. I observed a coffee shop, and headed for it. Inside, empty tables were in short supply, then, one became available. I went to the counter, ordered a white coffee and shortbread biscuit. After paying, I sat down. These chairs aren't comfortable. A woman sitting at the next table stood up, and departed, leaving a newspaper. I reached over, and looked at the date - yesterday's Jersey Evening Post. No doubt tonight's edition will highlight the incident on Halloween at a prestigious venue in St Helier. Whilst browsing through the newspaper, I became aware of customers with a hand-held device. Two tables from me, a young woman moved her nimble finger to and fro on the screen - the content must be interesting. Before long, only one other person and myself were reading a newspaper! A waitress approached the next table, lifted cups and saucers onto her tray, and looked over. "The airport shop doesn't sell many newspapers nowadays."

"I've noticed."

"People prefer to read a book from their Kindle or iPad."

After she left, I continued to read the newspaper, conscious of my traditional method of passing time. In the 14 years I have been away, it's still difficult to grasp how technology has advanced. I put down the newspaper, then added a sachet of brown sugar to my coffee. Stirring the cup with a cheap plastic spoon, I spotted Diana Bray enter. To cover my face, I picked up the newspaper, and pretended to read it. I slowly lowered it, and saw Diana sit at a table occupied by a well-dressed middle-aged gent. I sipped my coffee, thinking Kindles and iPads can't make you discreet in the manner a newspaper can.

As the flight left Jersey, I noticed a lot of passengers had started reading from their personal devices, however, I'll settle for the standard airline magazine. I removed one from the seat pocket in front, and started to read, and soon after, a steward went up and down the aisle with refreshments. Given the turbulence, having a drink could result in a stained jacket and trousers, therefore, I'll pass.

After an hour and a bit, the flight arrived at East Midlands Airport, and I left the aircraft for a connection to Glasgow. I collected my suitcase, then walked to the lounge alongside a couple. Before reaching there, two Customs Officers in standard black suits, white shirts and dark ties, stopped us.

"We would like to check your belongings," said one officer.

They took us to a nearby table, where a further two officers stood with stern expressions. The couple laid their suitcases on the table, and I waited my turn. After the man and woman opened their cases, an officer scrutinised them. During this process, the couple looked at each other, then the officer signalled to a colleague, and he came over. After examining a particular item, he looked at the woman. "Please come this way."

Two officers led her into a room, and closed the door. The woman's companion glanced at me, then at the other officers.

"Thank you, sir," said the officer who had examined his suitcase, "you can close it."

"What about my wife?"

"She is being questioned, we will advise you of the outcome."

The man closed his suitcase, lifted it off the table and then stood aside. I put mine on the table, opened it, and the officer examined its contents, then smiled.

"Thank you, sir."

I closed my suitcase, lifted it off the table, and whilst walking away, noticed the man being taken away.

Passengers from the Jersey flight congregated in the lounge to await information on their connection, including a woman sitting next to me, who leaned forward. "It's not Diana's weekend," she whispered.

I looked at her. "Were you at Minosas?"

She nodded. "The woman taken by Customs Officers is her sister."

I raised my eyebrows. "A weekend Diana will want to forget."

The woman smiled. "And a few others too."

"Do you know Diana?"

"I thought I did until she stole my husband."

I looked at the forty-something dark-haired woman. "Was your husband a politician?"

The woman shook her head. "That was another affair she had."

My goodness.

"I saw her at the airport and kept my distance."

Then, a female voice came over the tannoy to announce my flight departure, and I said goodbye to the woman.

After boarding, I sat at a window seat, and looked out. With the wind still prevalent, let's hope a traumatic flight doesn't ensue. Glancing at my watch told me there were ten minutes until take-off, and I would be in Glasgow around one o'clock. Several minutes later, a well-spoken composed male voice came over the intercom. "Ladies and gentlemen, this is the pilot. There has been a terrorist alert at Glasgow Airport, and as no flights are being allowed to land, we have been diverted to Edinburgh Airport. Also, our departure has been delayed and, apologies for any inconvenience."

Groans came from several aisles, and the three

stewardesses wore brave smiles. I sat back and considered a new travel plan to get home. I'll journey from Edinburgh to Glasgow by train, then catch a coach to Dochar, but due to a winter timetable, it leaves Buchanan Street Bus Station around mid-day. If I am to get that coach, there will be no margin for any more delays. Damn terrorists!

Forty minutes later, the now Edinburgh-bound service departed, and I looked at my watch. No way will I make Glasgow in time for a coach to Dochar, therefore, an overnight stay in the Capital beckons.

With my seatbelt on, the aircraft touched down without a hitch at Edinburgh International Airport. For an overnight stay, a stewardess advised I try the nearby Holiday Express Inn. When I approached reception, a tall dark-suited gentleman with combed-back hair came forward. "Can I help you, sir?"

I lay my suitcase on the polished floor. "Do you have a room for tonight?"

"Single or double, sir?"

"Single with en-suite, please."

The member of staff checked his computer, looked at me, and analysed the screen. "One is available, sir. £57, including breakfast."

"I'll take it."

"Do you wish to pay now?"

"When I leave."

"Fine, sir."

I received a key, lifted my suitcase, and went in search of the room. As the hotel had a selection of formal and informal dining amenities, and my limited funds, an evening meal in the 'pub lounge' will suffice. I found my room on the first floor, entered and then closed the door. After unpacking some essentials, I lay on the soft comfortable bed and closed my eyes.

I woke up, looked at my watch, and discovered several

hours had passed. Since breakfast, I had not eaten, and my stomach now called out. I made myself respectable, and went downstairs to the lounge bar for an informal bite to eat. Due to only a handful of customers, I had a choice of tables. I picked up a menu and as I read it, a woman approached with a writing pad and pen. "Ready to order, sir?"

"Chilli and rice, please."

She wrote on the white pad. "And to drink?"

"A lager, please."

"Stella or Tennents?"

"The latter."

"Thank you, sir."

After she departed, I surveyed the traditional-style lounge with dark wooden furniture and a polished wooden floor.

Following my bar meal, I sat back and sipped my glass of lager. The quick efficient service and quality of food impressed me, plus, used plates and cutlery had been quickly taken away. Laying my half-empty glass on the table, I noticed a tall slim young woman in a black coat enter the bar. When she looked around, then at me, I recognised her as one of the passengers who along with me got stranded. She spoke to the bar person, received a drink and then came across to where I sat. "Can I join you?"

"Be my guest."

The young woman sat down, laid her drink on the table, and unbuttoned her coat to reveal a low-cut black dress. "It's a small world!" She lifted her glass, took a sip, then frowned. "Not enough gin, too much tonic."

I grinned. "How is the escort business?"

"Tonight, I'm meeting someone in this lounge." She laid her drink on the table, and glanced at a stylish gold watch.

"Is he late?"

"No, ten minutes, yet."

"Are you kept busy?"

She plucked a blonde hair from her coat. "Yes."

"Who is your market?" Her answer could be interesting.

"Businessmen and politicians." She lifted her glass. "Have you ever been out with an escort?"

"No, I lead a sheltered life."

She laughed lifter her glass, and took a sip. "Men tell me intimate details."

I raised my eyebrows.

She put her glass down. "A politician once told me he was being blackmailed by a former partner."

"A woman?"

"She threatened to ruin his career and family life."

"Murky business."

"Apparently, this person tends to target politicians."

"In Scotland?"

"Jersey."

Surely not.

"I believe this woman is connected to the hospitality sector."

"This person does not sound hospitable."

The young woman glanced at the entrance. "Here's my date." She stood, and smiled. "Bye."

"Good luck." Where have I seen him before?

As the voluptuous individual met her evening date, I picked up my drink, and finished it. A male bar person came across, and lifted both glasses.

"Another drink, sir?"

I shook my head. "Do I pay for my meal and drink now, or at reception when I leave?"

"Either, sir." He departed.

I went to the bar, and the person who had earlier served me, handed over a receipt. Looking at it, I noticed an additional drink. "I only had a lager."

"The young woman who joined you asked me to put her drink on your bill."

I grinned.

"Is that okay, sir?"

"Yes."

After breakfast, I went to my room and made ready for departure. At the reception desk, another articulate male member of staff was on duty. When I handed over my room key, he smiled. "Did you enjoy your stay, sir?" He took the key.

"Yes, thanks." I laid my suitcase on the floor.

He handed me a bill, which I checked, and paid. Lifting my suitcase and bidding him farewell, I headed to the exit swing door. Upon reaching it, a young woman came through it.

"You're in demand!" I quipped.

She stopped, and looked at me. "I lost my purse last night."

"In the hotel?"

"Yes."

As she walked on, I went to catch a tram into the centre of Edinburgh, where I could take a train from Haymarket Station to Glasgow Queen Street Station. Approaching the nearby tram stop, one had just arrived, and people boarded. I paid my fare, and took a seat for the start of a five-hour trek to Dochar. On the tram, I was the only person not dressed for the start of winter. Oh, to get home and be warm in my own habitat.

The single-decker white-livery mode of transport hurtled along Corstorphine Road and soon reached Haymarket. I got off at a stop on Haymarket Terrace, opposite the station. When I arrived at a pedestrian crossing, a young woman and teenage boy waited. Winter sun shone down, therefore, I put a hand above my eyes to see the proceed signal. When safe, the teenage boy and young woman moved off, and I followed. Then, I heard a motorbike engine and a police vehicle siren. As the motor bile sped towards the young woman and boy, I rushed forward and pushed them out of its path.

CHAPTER 13

A NEW DAWN

Arriving within minutes, two officers got out of a police car. The area was then cordoned off, and traffic in both directions opposite Haymarket Station diverted. Whilst onlookers comforted the ashen-faced young woman and teenage boy, a second police car drew up, followed by an ambulance. A medical crew rushed out, carefully lifted the injured man onto a stretcher, and took him into the ambulance. After it sped off, a female police officer approached the young woman who began to sob. The officer gave her a paper handkerchief, and she wiped her eyes. "I couldn't move." Her voice grew raspy. "The motorbike was heading for me."

The young woman looked at the boy holding his arm as a consequence of falling onto the pavement being spoken to by another police officer. A well-dressed lady came up to the young woman. "Are you hurt?"

She sniffed, and shook her head.

"Don't blame yourself, it was that clown driving the bike." She gently touched the young woman's arm.

Once more, she sniffed.

"A brave man." The lady looked at where the accident occurred.

The young woman nodded.

"He didn't have time to avoid the bike," said a male onlooker.

The lady sighed.

As police officers questioned onlookers, the young woman stared at them, and the female police officer returned. "We would like a statement from you at some point."

The young woman nodded.

"What is your name?"

"Victoria, Victoria Anderson."

"When you feel better, Victoria, call into your nearest police station."

"What about the man who saved me?"

"At present, his condition is not known."

The police officer departed, and the well-dressed lady returned, then stared at a small suitcase.

"I was on my way to Jersey." The young woman sighed. "Now, I don't feel like going."

"A vacation?"

"To visit my mother, she isn't well." The young woman looked at her watch. "I will miss my flight."

The lady went across to the female police officer taking a statement, and after a short conversation, both returned to the young woman.

"When is your flight?" said the officer.

The young woman glanced at her watch. "I should have been at the airport by now."

"The other police car will give you a lift to Edinburgh Airport."

The lady smiled.

"At the check-in desk, explain what has happened, and if you have any problem, ask them to contact Torphichen Police Station."

"Thanks, and when I return, I'll call into my local police station."

"Fine." The police officer smiled.

The young woman lifted her suitcase, walked towards the police car, which had arrived following the incident. The well-dressed lady looked towards the young woman. "To witness what has happened and then visit a sick mother."

"She shows composure."

The well-dressed lady stared at the area cordoned off with investigative police officers going about their business. "Motorbikes." She shook her head.

As soon as the young woman got into the police car, it sped off. Due to a distinctive appearance, the vehicle eased through busy traffic, and soon arrived at the airport. After thanking both officers, the young woman rushed into the main building and then to her flight check-in desk. Glancing at the time, she reached the desk where an airline representative had a pensive look on her face.

"Sorry I'm late. I witnessed an accident." The young woman put down her suitcase, and took a deep breath.

The well-groomed female representative looked towards a wall clock. "The flight to Jersey will soon depart."

"You can contact Torphichen Street Police Station to verify my story." The young woman held an airline ticket in her hand.

"You will have to rush."

She handed her ticket to the representative.

The representative took it, and moments later, the young woman went into a departure lounge, found a vacant seat, and unbuttoned her raincoat. Whilst she pondered over the recent traumatic event, a man sitting beside her sneezed several times, then blew his nose. The young woman glanced at the man with cropped silver hair wearing a dark overcoat.

"When November arrives, so does my cold!"

"It's that time of year."

The man looked upwards to the departure screen. "Ah, at last."

Passengers for Jersey left their seats, and headed towards the respective departure Terminal. Keeping her distance from the man, the young woman could hear a fit of sneezing behind her.

The flight left as scheduled, and after releasing her seat belt, the young woman leaned forward to lift out a catalogue from the seat pocket in front. Following an uninteresting browse, she replaced the catalogue, and leaned back. Hearing someone sneeze several rows in front, she popped her head up, and observed the silver-haired man blow his nose. A forty-something gentleman in a camel coat sitting next to the young woman reading a paperback, put it down, and looked forward. "Thank goodness that chap is not in this row!"

The young woman nodded, then glanced at the well-spoken gentleman's paperback cover.

"I purchased it at the airport."

"Is it a good read?"

"Ask me later, a business colleague recommended it to me."

"A male colleague?"

"Female." The gentleman gave a faint grin. "She believes it will improve our relationship."

He has the correct shade of hair.

As the gentleman returned to his book, the young woman closed her eyes and made herself comfortable. She thought of her mother's condition, hoping there had been an improvement, however little. As her mother hated being confined to a particular place, the young woman longed for the day she would be discharged from hospital. A sudden jolt broke her train of thought, and her fellow passenger shook his head. "Glad it happened now and not when drinking a coffee."

The young woman looked behind. "Here comes your coffee."

A dark blue uniformed stewardess served drinks on both sided of the aisle, then once more, the aircraft jolted and liquid spilled onto the unfortunate gentleman. A stifled curse followed, and when the stewardess looked towards the young woman, she declined. The airline employee handed the gentleman a white paper napkin, and he dabbed his coat.

"Would you like a drink sir?" She took the damp napkin from him.

"A white coffee, please."

He put the book aside, and after receiving his drink, placed it on a black tray attached to the seat in front.

The stewardess smiled. "On the house."

Again, the young woman lay back and closed her eyes. A short time later, she fell asleep, however, soon woke up.

"Are you alright?" The gentleman stared.

The young woman blinked.

"You are as white as a ghost!"

"I had a flashback."

"A bad occurrence?"

The young woman nodded.

"You were murmuring."

"Before arriving at the airport, I was almost hit by a motorbike, but I was pushed out of its path." The young woman paused. "He was hit by the bike."

"How is he?"

"An ambulance took him to hospital." The young woman stared out of the small circular window.

One chilly dark November evening, a male and female police officer arrived at a first-floor tenement flat in Lorne Street, Leith. Soon after pressing the doorbell, a young woman with long blonde hair and casually dressed, answered.

"Victoria Anderson?" said the male officer.

"Yes."

"We are here concerning the man hit by a motorbike, opposite Haymarket Station."

The young woman looked at both officers. "Come in." She opened the door wide.

As both officers stepped into a narrow hallway, the young woman closed the door, and led them into a small bright lounge. The female officer glanced at the tastefully decorated room.

"Please, have a seat."

The officers sat down on a brown leather two-seater

couch, and their host opposite on a single matching chair. "How is he?"

"I am afraid he died from his injuries," said the male officer.

The young woman sighed. "A local man?"

"His name was James Carsell-Brown, and from personal documents, we have discovered that last month he visited St Helier, in Jersey, and left on 1 November."

The young woman paused. "A man called James stayed at my mother's guest house in St Helier." She put a hand to her mouth. "Oh, no!"

"We can't trace any family to inform them of his death," said the female officer, "are you aware of anyone?"

The young woman shook her head.

"His address is a property in Dochar, near Ardrishaig," said the male officer.

"My mother was born and brought up in Dochar."

The male officer looked at his colleague, then the young woman.

"When growing up, they must have known each other," said the young woman.

"Would your mother know of his family?" said the male officer.

"She is in hospital and very ill." The young woman sighed. "Her memory is impaired."

"Mr Carsell-Brown's funeral will be held at Warriston Crematorium."

"Why in Edinburgh if he lived near Ardrishaig?"

"He wanted it that way," said the female officer.

Both officers got up, and accompanied to the door. After they had left, the young woman returned to the living room, and stared at a painting on the wall given to her mother many years ago.

The two officers entered their police car, parked outside the block of flats. The female officer looked at her colleague, then he nodded. "An uncanny resemblance in that painting to our mystery deceased person."

"A nineteenth century coachman!" The female officer adjusted her hat.

When the male officer turned the ignition key, a stocky middle-aged man staggered out of a nearby public house, and spotted the white, yellow and blue vehicle. Straightening up, he passed it, and took a deep breath. After the police car moved off, he bumped against a recycle bin and as it fell sideways, rubbish emptied onto the pavement. Hearing a dog bark, the man made himself scarce.

Following a short private service at Warriston Crematorium, the minister approached Victoria with a warm smile. His white thinning hair was a distinctive contrast to dark sober attire. "Thank you for attending the service."

"His bravery saved me from serious injury, if not death."

"In his Will, James had a special request."

Victoria paused.

"He wanted his ashes scattered around Docharnea, his property in a place called Dochar, near Ardrishaig."

"Docharnea?"

"The name of James's property. Would you carry out his final wish?"

Victoria nodded. "It will be my pleasure."

"Are you aware of the location?"

"Yes, my mother came from there."

The minister raised his white eyebrows. "What an extraordinary coincidence."

Victoria smiled.

"On the day you travel, call into the Crematorium, and I will give you his ashes."

"I will do."

"Splendid." The minister shook Victoria's hand.

As Victoria left the Crematorium, she reflected on recent events. A man who saved her life, and as a consequence, ended his. If she had caught her scheduled Friday flight, this man may still be alive.

"Excuse me, miss, do you have a light?" said a male passer-by.

Victoria hesitated.

The man held up his cigarette.

"Sorry, I don't smoke."

The man walked on and Victoria headed for a nearby bus stop where she boarded a bus to Leith Walk. After paying her fare, Victoria sat at a downstairs window seat and then the heavens opened. Whilst people ran for cover, the fortunate ones had an umbrella to protect themselves from being drenched. Before Victoria got off, the rain stopped, and whilst walking, she could smell it. Entering the flat, Victoria wiped her damp shoes on a mat, and closed the door. Whilst removing her dark coat, the handset on a small wooden table started to ring, and she picked it up. "Hello?" Victoria paused. "Hello?"

She replaced the handset, went into the kitchen, and whilst preparing a cup of coffee, the handset rang. Returning to the hall, Victoria grabbed the handset. "Yes," she shouted.

"Can I speak to Victoria Anderson, please?"

"Speaking." Victoria coughed.

"My name is Jane Mackay of Macmillan Mackay Solicitors, in Ardrishaig. Is it a bad time, would you prefer I called back at a convenient time?"

"Did you say Ardrishaig?"

"Yes, we are located in the main street."

"Why are you calling?"

"A client of ours who sadly passed away, has left his property to you."

"Me!"

"We sent you a letter."

"I didn't receive it."

"Our client was a Mr James Carsell-Brown."

My goodness.

"The property is located near Ardrishaig."

"How did you trace me?"

"Mr Carsell-Brown supplied us with your details. We require your signature for documents relating to the transfer of ownership, therefore, I will forward them to you."

"No need, I am travelling to Ardrishaig within the next couple of days."

"Perfect! Call into our office, and either myself or Mr Macmillan, will go through the process with you."

"Thanks."

"My pleasure, Miss Anderson."

"Did you try to contact me earlier?"

"This is the first time I have called."

"Bye."

"Goodbye, Miss Anderson."

Victoria replaced the handset into the cradle. A property! Why me?

She returned to the kitchen, and later sipped a cup of coffee, whilst pondering over her recent call. Then, as she heard ringing, Victoria rushed into the hall, and picked up the handset. "Hello?"

No voice could be heard, only a crackle, and several seconds later, it stopped.

Victoria collected James Carsell-Brown's ashes from the Crematorium, and began the journey to Dochar, in rural Argyll. She caught a bus to Waverley Station, then boarded the train bound for Glasgow Queen Street Station.

Forty-five minutes later, the sleek, multiple-unit, with blue and white livery, entered the Glasgow terminal. With a small case, Victoria walked the short distance to Buchanan Street Bus Station for her Dochar connection.

When she arrived at the designated coach stance, a large queue had formed for the twice-daily service. A petite woman turned to face Victoria and her deep wrinkles suggested a long existence. "At least I'll get a seat this time."

Victoria looked at her.

"On my previous journey, I had to stand!"

"Did no gentleman give up his seat?"

The woman shook her head. "Chance would be a fine thing."

After all passengers had boarded, the coach departed for a two and a half-hour scenic journey via Loch Lomond, Arrochar and Inveraray. Victoria would be travelling back to where her mother lived until leaving for university, therefore, the trip was also sentimental.

As the coach travelled through lush green fields and hills, Victoria gazed out of the window, and given that it was December, mild weather persisted. The once freezing snow-filled countryside now fell victim to an abundance of rain, resulting in road closures through landslides.

After Inveraray, Victoria glanced at her watch, and in forty minutes, she would arrive in Dochar. As a child, hearing stories about this quaint remote hamlet from her mother, Victoria became intrigued. Extreme in contrast to bustling vibrant Edinburgh, Dochar conjured up tales of fantasy.

When a particular road sign appeared, Victoria's apprehension grew. After the coach departed, she laid her case on the pavement, and looked around the location, then across to Loch Fyne. Its banks on the waterfront and green hills above were stunning. Victoria shivered, however, not due to the scenic beauty, but the inclement unsheltered stop. Turning up the collar of her coat, and wishing for a scarf, Victoria walked along the narrow pavement. Approaching a row of large distinctive properties, she stopped and put down her case. A green wreath with red ribbons had been placed upright against one of the cream-coloured gateposts. As Victoria bent down to read a message attached to the wreath, a sudden gust of wind blew into her face, and also scattered a pile of nearby brown leaves. She flicked back her long blonde hair, picked up the case and wreath, then walked up Docharnea's driveway. Upon reaching the villa's main door, Victoria put down her case, and laid the wreath against the door. Opening her case, she took out a small grey casket containing James's ashes and then a gust of wind blew dead leaves away from the entrance. Victoria hesitated, then scattered the casket's contents over Docharnea's lawn. When finished, she closed the casket, and laid it next to the wreath. Being curious, Victoria walked round the property, then back down its driveway. With Ardrishaig a half-mile away, her tight black shoes would be a hindrance, then, a white Porsche drew up alongside. As she looked round, a well-dressed gent stepped out the driver's side. "Victoria Anderson?"

Who's he?

"I am John Macmillan, a partner at Macmillan Mackay Solicitors." He smiled. "I'll give you lift to our office, it's easier on the feet."

Victoria looked at the shiny white car, then its driver, who got back into his seat. After he opened the passenger door, Victoria stepped inside, and laid her case on the floor. As the car moved off, John Macmillan handed his passenger a business card, which she took and read.

"My father is looking forward to meeting you."

"Your timing was perfect." Victoria turned down her collar.

"It helps to know the coach times, fortunately, it ran as scheduled."

Thank goodness.

"We'll be at the office in a jiffy."

The sleek Porsche soon reached Ardrishaig's main street, and as it parked outside Macmillan Mackay Solicitor's office, Victoria looked at the facade.

"Just go inside, my father will see you shortly."

"Thanks for the lift."

"My pleasure."

Victoria got out, retrieved her case, and closed the door.

As John Macmillan drove off, she entered the premises, and a woman looked up from her desk. Victoria closed the door, and approached a reception area with chairs, plus a circular table.

"Just take a seat, Miss Anderson."

"Thanks." Victoria sat down, and laid her case on the laminate floor.

"Would you care for a coffee, or tea?"

"Do you have sparkling mineral water?"

The woman shook her head. "Sorry." She resumed typing on her desktop computer.

Victoria browsed through the pile of business-related magazines, sighed, then looked out of a window facing the street. Passers-by were well equipped for winter with hats, coats and scarves. She was glad that the office heating was working. Several minutes later, a tall shaven-head dark-suited man came out of an office, and walked towards Victoria. "Hello, Miss Anderson, I am Alistair Macmillan." He held out his hand.

Victoria stood up, and shook it.

"Come this way, please."

Victoria lifted her case, and followed Mr Macmillan into a room with a wooden desk, grey metal filing cabinet and two black leather chairs.

"Have a seat, Miss Anderson."

As Victoria sat down, she glanced at the top of the filing cabinet. Mr Macmillan closed the door, and sat behind his desk. "We've booked a single room for you at a nearby establishment."

"Oh?"

"Due to Ardrishaig's rural location, the last coach to Glasgow has departed."

Victoria smiled.

"It's called The Grey Gull Inn, and not far from our office."

"I intended to stay overnight, thanks."

Mr Macmillan coughed. "Fourteen years ago, Mr Carsell-Brown sat where you are, his great-aunt left Docharnea to him." Mr Macmillan looked sideways towards a small window, then at Victoria. "Even though our paths barely crossed, his death was a shock."

"Did he not frequent the village?"

"Shortly after moving into Docharnea, he apparently travelled abroad, and only recently returned."

"It's a long time to be away."

"He left suddenly, and told nobody of his intentions." Mr Macmillan sighed. "His electricity, gas and water supply were cut off for non-payment of bills."

"If he wasn't there, he wouldn't require them."

Mr Macmillan smiled. "However, when he came back, the debts were settled."

"The property is now habitable?"

Mr Macmillan nodded. "Every aspect is in order - even the adjoining coach house."

"What is it used for?"

"At present, nothing."

"I may convert it into a holiday chalet for visitors to the area."

Mr Macmillan raised his grey eyebrows. "A splendid idea, the scenery in this area is superb." He lifted a file from his desk, and brought out several forms. "If you would care to read these and sign them, please, Miss Anderson." He laid the forms in front of Victoria.

She read each form.

"Please sign your name on the appropriate line." Mr Macmillan handed Victoria a pen.

After signing the forms, Victoria handed them back to Mr Macmillan, and he put them to one side of his desk.

"Is that it?"

Mr Macmillan rose from his chair, and walked towards her. "Congratulations, Miss Anderson, you are the new owner of Docharnea." He held out his hand.

Victoria stood up and shook it. "When do I receive the keys?"

"You can collect them tomorrow morning."

Victoria lifted her case, Mr Macmillan opened the office door, and accompanied her to the exit. "See you tomorrow, Miss Anderson."

"What time?"

"After nine o'clock." Mr Macmillan pointed. "The Grey Gull is on this side of the street, and further down."

"Thanks."

Mr Macmillan opened the door. "Bye for now."

"Bye." Victoria left the premises with a smile.

Mr Macmillan watched Victoria for several seconds, closed the door, then walked up to his secretary.

"Is Miss Anderson the youngest owner of Docharnea?"

"And the prettiest!"

"A lucky young lady to have been left that property." The computer fell silent.

"No reason was given."

"I believe her late grandmother once worked at the Grey Gull."

"When?"

"During the sixties."

"I was living in Glasgow, what age would she have been?"

"Around thirty-five, and, also pretty."

Mr Macmillan smiled.

"She had an illegitimate child."

Mr Macmillan raised his eyebrows.

"The father's identity remains a mystery."

"In this village, that is unusual!"

The secretary laughed.

Mr Macmillan returned to his office, and looked at the filing cabinet. Damn! Forgot to hide the bottle. He brought out a glass from his desk drawer.

Victoria approached the Grey Gull Inn, and entered

through its glass doorway. She walked up to the reception desk, laid her case on the brown carpeted floor, and looked around the vicinity. Two green leather sofas matched magnolia walls, which had framed pictures of Loch Fyne and its surrounding countryside. One in particular, caught Victoria's attention, therefore, she moved closer.

"It's by an artist who once lived in the area."

As Victoria turned around, a slim casually dressed middle-aged man, walked behind the reception desk. "Sorry, to keep you, I was attending to a customer in the lounge bar."

"A room has been reserved for me."

The man opened a black register book, and turned to a page. "Miss Anderson?" He looked up.

Victoria nodded.

The man turned around, lifted a key off its hook, and walked towards his female guest. "I'll give you a hand." He lifted Victoria's case. "This way, Miss Anderson."

Victoria followed him up two flights of carpeted stairs and then he unlocked a door. After entering, the man pressed a light switch, then laid Victoria's case on the floor. "Any problems, just let me know, I'll be serving in the bar."

Victoria smiled. "A multitasker."

The man nodded. "Since the no-smoking ban and banking crisis, business has fallen away, and I now do a variety of roles." When departing, he gave Victoria the key, and closed the door behind him.

She took off her coat, put it on a hanger inside the wooden wardrobe, then unpacked her case. After walking across the room, she went to the window and observed Ardrishaig's well-lit main street. It would not be long until decorative Christmas lights enhanced the main thoroughfare along with festive snow, which had as yet, declined tradition.

Victoria sat back on her chair, and looked around the

lounge bar. A male bar person removed her empty plate, and gave her a warm smile. "Was my recommendation to your taste, miss?"

"Yes, the fish dinner was delicious."

As he departed, Victoria sipped her glass of white wine, and watched an elevated television set. A weather presenter spoke of more heavy downpours for Argyll, which was followed by a loud groan from the only other customer. Standing at the bar, he shook his bald head and then looked at the white shirted bar person. "Given the recent weather, your black tie is appropriate!"

The bar person grinned. "At least, there is no snow."

"I've lived in this area for nearly seventy years, give me a proper winter anytime."

"What about the snowdrifts we once endured?"

The customer took a swig his whisky. "The road to Glasgow has been closed more in the last ten years through downpours than the previous sixty!" He put his glass on the bar top. "This constant ruddy rain is a menace."

"Another whisky?" The bar person cleaned a small glass.

"Naw, no just now." The customer looked towards Victoria. "Are you a visitor, hen?"

Victoria looked at him, and nodded.

The bar person whispered to the man.

He stared at Victoria. "You're the new owner of Docharnea?"

Victoria nodded.

"It's haunted!"

"That's only a rumour," said the bar person.

The man looked at him and then shook his head. "My grandfather worked at Lochgilphead Hospital durin' the depression and told me aboot a porter who called into Docharnea to pick up furniture for the hospital charity." He looked at Victoria. "After enterin' the coach house, he was never seen again!"

"He just vanished?" said Victoria.

The man nodded. "Aye, never to be seen again."

"There was a rumour that the previous owner had vanished," said the bar person, "but he returned."

"And now dead!" The man looked at Victoria. "I'm tellin' ye, young lady, watch yerself."

The man drank the remainder of his whisky, then walked unsteadily out an exit door. The bar person wiped his bar, grinning at Victoria. "He's well-known for telling tales."

"And, in a convincing manner."

"It's the whisky."

Victoria smiled.

"Mind you, the property has had its share of controversy." The bar person put his damp cloth under the counter.

Victoria stared.

"Older people in the village maintain a coachman haunted the property." He grinned. "However, that was almost a century ago."

"Perhaps he has no reason to haunt it anymore?"

"It would appear so."

Victoria lifted her glass, and finished her drink.

"Can I get you another?"

"No, thanks."

After watching television for a short while, Victoria rose, and went to the bar. She gave her empty glass to the bar person and he bid her goodnight.

The following morning, a taxi brought Victoria to her new residency, and as she got out, tipped the driver. She approached the main door, stopped, and cast her gaze around an idyllic setting. As trees surrounding the property were bare due to autumn's passing, Victoria had an unrestricted view of Loch Fyne. She took out a key from her coat pocket, opened one of the double-doors, and entered. Once inside, she closed the door, then laid her suitcase and a carrier bag on the grey stone reception floor. After walking through a bright hallway, Victoria peeked into each room, and upon noticing a spider's web, she removed it with a piece of tissue paper. Of the five upstairs bedrooms, one in particular looked onto the courtyard and traditional coach house. The two-storey white-walled building, with shiny black doors and window frames captivated her. She walked down a painted white staircase, through the hallway and then into a spacious modern kitchen. On a shelf, lay a set of large keys with a tab marked 'Coach House'. From the property's rear brown varnished door, Victoria stepped into a courtyard covered with small grey chipping stones and faced the distinctive coach house. Since being built in 1896, what mysteries did it hold? A gust of wind blew across the courtyard and Victoria shivered. After closing the door, Victoria turned on the central heating and fortunately it was in working order. Returning to the reception room, she picked up her case and carrier bag, and went into the kitchen. Food purchased from a local supermarket was taken out of the bag and stored. Feeling tired and beginning to warm up, Victoria headed for the living room and a comfy couch.

Waking up in a darkened room, Victoria looked at the luminous dial of her watch - six hours had passed. She rose, switched on the lights, and went into the kitchen to prepare her first meal.

On the evening of a full moon, Victoria sat at the kitchen table with her chicken and mushroom risotto, plus a glass of Chardonnay. She thought of her mother, and what her reaction would be when told about James's passing. She enjoyed his visits, and looked forward to seeing him again.

A couple of glasses later, Victoria sat back on the pine chair and reflected on her special day. Sitting in a large property in acres of ground was surreal compared to a one-bedroom city tenement flat. She had a picturesque view of Loch Fyne, whereas in Leith, it was a tenement block. The burning question she asked herself was why me? Victoria put down her empty glass, and checked that both exit doors were secure. After switching off the downstairs lights, Victoria walked upstairs to her chosen bedroom for a welcome night's sleep. Then, a thud came from outside, and after pulling back a curtain, she stared into the courtyard. One of the coach house doors was ajar, therefore, she went downstairs, and lifted a set of keys. Unlocking the back door, an owl's hoot echoed from a nearby tree. Victoria approached the coach house, fumbled to find the correct key, and locked the door. Returning to her bedroom, she made ready for bed. Whilst doing so, Victoria recalled that when walking round the property yesterday, all coach house doors appeared secure. She lay pondering for a short while, then started to feel drowsy.

Victoria woke up, and heard a cry come from the courtyard. She got out of bed, pulled back the curtain, and peered out. As the gusty wind had blown itself away, the owl's hoot broke the night silence.

Victoria yawned. Must have been a fox.

She remained at the window for several moments, returned to her warm cosy bed, and fell fast asleep.

Victoria went into the living room, pulled back the curtains and admired the view of Loch Fyne. The damp Argyll weather did not diminish a morning scene to savour. Victoria stood motionless for several minutes, then went through to the kitchen. Whilst preparing breakfast, she pictured her compact tenement kitchen and its clutter. Inviting a friend over for dinner was only possible if the fridge and tumble dryer had been vacated. Docharnea not only had a kitchen with a dining area, also its own dining room! For breakfast, she would settle for one thin slice of brown toasted bread with marmalade, and a cup of white coffee, which suited her trim waistline.

A short time later, Victoria went upstairs to make ready for her journey back to Edinburgh. After closing her small case, she put on her coat, and looked in the mirror. Victoria went over to the window, looked at the coach house, and pondered.

What should I do? The property is too big, also, far from Edinburgh, however, it's beautiful.

Hearing the doorbell, Victoria went downstairs, and opened the main door. A sturdy middle-aged man wearing a yellow jerkin and black trousers smiled. "Good mornin', miss."

"Good morning."

"My name is Alex, I'm the local gardener."

"What can I do for you?"

"It's what I can do for you!"

"Oh?" Victoria raised her blonde eyebrows.

"My family has served the occupants of this property for well over a century, and as you are the new owner, I would like to offer my garden expertise. "

"How do you know I'm the new owner?"

"This is a small community, miss." He gave a wry smile.

Victoria stepped outside, and looked around the vicinity. "The garden appears tidy."

"When the January storms come, miss, the garden will need attention." He pointed. "Them trees have branches about to break off."

"What if there is no storm?"

"There will be, miss, I can assure you!"

Victoria smiled.

The man looked up at the grey slated roof. "Your gutters need to be cleared of leaves and muck."

Victoria looked up.

Alex gave Victoria a small white printed card. "Call me, if and when, you want work carried out."

Victoria took the card. "I will, and thank you."

The gardener departed, entered his white van parked outside the front entrance, and drove off. Then, Victoria heard footsteps coming up the driveway and a postman approached. "Morning." He laid his red bag on the ground.

"Good morning."

He took out a letter, and handed it to Victoria.

"For me?"

"You are Victoria Anderson?"

Victoria nodded.

"It's for this address."

She looked at the letter.

"Bye, miss." The postman lifted the bag, put it over his shoulder, and walked back down the driveway.

Victoria stepped inside, closed the door, and locked it. Returning to the kitchen, she opened her letter, which contained a hand-written note. After reading it, Victoria picked up a set of keys, exited the rear door, and headed for the coach house. She unlocked the main door, and whilst walking up a creaky staircase, the door slammed shut. Victoria looked back, gripping the set of keys. Upon reaching the top, she entered a room, which smelled of flowers. Observing the mirror hanging on a wall. Victoria approached it, and stared.

CHAPTER 14

REUNITED

James found himself in a large green field, which bordered onto a loch. He looked up to a blue cloudless sky, and shaded his eyes from the warm sun. Birds sang in the nearby trees, several rabbits ate grass, however, no other person was in sight. A white dove hovered above, then into the distance. As James pondered on this pleasant traditional rural summer day, his last memory was that of a cold morning in Edinburgh's city centre! He examined his clothes, and after being hit by a speeding motorbike, why did they look new? Also, the pain he endured for days lying in a hospital had gone. James shook his head. "This is surreal, where am I, and how did I get here?" He cast his gaze around the calm countryside with curiosity. It appeared familiar, however, he could not recollect the location. Whilst deep in thought, James walked towards the loch, and upon reaching it, the white dove reappeared. Shading his eyes once more, he looked upwards. As the dove flew off, James's stare focused on the loch. A young woman with long raven hair, wearing a white dress, stood on the opposite side. After several moments, she vanished. A warm gust of wind blew into James's face, and he closed his eyes. When he opened them, a past acquaintance was standing next to him. James stared at her dark blonde flowing hair complimented by an appropriate summer dress. Glad to see him, the lady held out her bare arms. After they embraced, the lady stood back and smiled.

"Since we last met, you look exactly the same."

James took her hand.

"That is because this is how you remember me."

"Have I travelled back in time?"

"In a certain manner, but not as in previous occasions."

James hesitated.

"You have passed from a previous existence to another."

"Abbie, where or what is this place?" James glanced around the vicinity.

"For you, it's the supreme sanctuary."

"A sanctuary?"

"That is not precisely true, this is a halfway house."

James stared.

"Where you can say goodbye to loved ones."

"This could also be your halfway house."

Abbie nodded. "For both of us."

"Why was the young woman here?"

"She became your Guardian Angel."

"Watching over me."

"She was grateful for preventing her suicide many years ago, and as a consequence, her parents and brothers did not have to grieve and suffer."

"I discovered her suicide resulted in ill-health for her parents."

"Thanks to you, that didn't happen."

"She prevented me from certain injury on at least two occasions." James paused. "Abbie, I'm sorry for disappearing." He looked into her blue eyes. "I did try to get back."

"But not quick enough, I died of old age!"

"You don't look old."

"My 1967 appearance is for you." Abbie touched hair above James's ear. "Only a few grey hairs have appeared."

"Given my experiences, I am fortunate."

Abbie laughed. "Come, let's have a seat." She pointed. "Over there."

The reunited couple walked in a casual manner to a nearby location, which had a wooden bench. James took off his jacket, and as the couple sat down, put it aside.

"Did you ensure that the weather would be perfect?"

"Of course."

"After the warm summer of 1967, I arrived in a freezing cold and austere 1930."

"I know you did."

James raised his eyebrows. "How?"

"In 1970, a woman who worked in the local coffee shop retired, and at her party, it was revealed that in 1930, a stranger came into the shop wearing unusual clothes."

"In 1930, the shop was a tearoom."

"She kept the coins that you left, which had been made in the early 1960s!" Abbie moved closer to James. "I suspected it could only be a certain time travelling individual."

James put his arm around Abbie's slim waist.

She looked at him. "And you're now a grandfather."

James sighed. "And as a parent, I wasn't around."

"It's not your fault, James."

He looked at Abbie.

"At least you have met April, and also, Victoria."

"I didn't meet Victoria."

"You saved her life."

James stared.

"The young woman with blonde hair."

"My goodness!"

Abbie gripped James's hand. "You prevented her from serious injury, if not death itself."

James paused. "It must have been fate."

"It was fate that brought us together."

James smiled.

"Would you have altered any part of your life?"

James shook his head, then looked up to the sky. "Is that the same dove I have seen several times?"

"Yes, it is."

He looked at Abbie. "The young woman with raven hair?"

She nodded.

At that moment, a solitary sparrow landed on the grass,

close to where Abbie and James sat. He stared at the small bird.

"Another spirit," said Abbie, "of someone that you have met."

"Who?"

"A gentle and kind person."

James looked at the sparrow, then Abbie. "Who?"

"A girl from your schooldays."

Jenny. "Her life was taken at a young age."

The sparrow flew up into the air, circled, and flew off. James looked at Abbie, then to the sky.

"Are you pondering over what you will become?"

"Not a bird, Abbie, I can't stand heights."

She laughed.

"A field mouse would suffice."

"In what way?"

"I could sneak into the coach house, find a discreet cubby hole, and still remain a resident of Docharnea."

Abbie laughed.

"That coach house has a lot to answer for!" James stared. "Was it your voice I heard in my bedroom?"

"Yes."

As the couple reflected on past events, a robin landed close to where James sat. He stared at the bird, and seconds later, it flew off. James turned to Abbie. "I've not seen a robin in summertime."

"It's the sign of a new beginning."

"Appropriate."

Abbie rose. "Let's walk."

Whilst they reminisced, James and Abbie strolled along the loch's bank, and still no other person had been seen.

"Why are we the only people here, Abbie?"

"This is our final time, together."

"If there had been a coach house, I could have travelled back in time."

"You may have gone to a hostile period in time."

"I did, shortly before and during the Second World War!"

Abbie smiled.

"Although, that is when we first met."

"And I was a young girl who spotted someone dressed as a coachman."

"A legend about a ghostly coachman began, and it still exists."

"Blame your grandfather and his brother – they started the rumour."

"How do you know?"

"They told me.

"But they are dead."

"So are you!"

James grinned. "This situation will take a lot of getting used to."

"When I spoke to your grandfather and great-uncle, they did not believe that you were a time traveller, but your great-aunt convinced them."

James pondered.

"Yes?"

"April and Victoria."

"One day, Victoria may discover your true identity."

James stopped walking. "How?"

"She has your genes."

"And April?"

Abbie shook her head.

"Why not?"

"Fate."

"I was not born a time traveller."

"No, you became one."

"And, not until the age of forty-two."

He does not recollect going back in time as an eight-year-old.

James sighed. "It was sad to see April in her present

condition."

"She is strong, and can cope." Abbie faced James, and held his arm. "Do you regret what happened?"

"With us?"

"No, your adventures through time."

Then, the white dove flew above, circled and disappeared into the distance. Abbie looked at James. "Someone has no regrets."

"That was a rewarding aspect of my travels through time, also, meeting my distant relatives, and preventing them from suffering trauma."

"You will soon be reunited."

"Has a welcome party been arranged?"

"This isn't Docharnea, James!"

"I trust no beer is allowed here?"

Abbie laughed. "Or food, you won't require either."

The couple continued to walk along the bank, then sat down on a dry patch of grass. James loosened his tie, and looked at Abbie. "Are you aware of all past occurrences?"

"When it concerns family and close friends."

"What became of Charles and Mary Carsell-Brown?"

"They moved to Africa, and remained there, until passing on."

"I will be reunited with them, too?"

"All your past family."

"Does that include Michelle Duvallier? I discovered that a family connection existed."

"Your great-uncle William can enlighten you on her. I've been told she's having an interesting life."

"Of that, I've no doubt."

Abbie smiled.

"Have my past family members aged?"

"They will appear as you last saw them." Abbie stared at James. "You haven't asked me about your parents?"

James sighed. "Not long after we visited my great-aunt, they were killed in a car accident."

"Is it a painful memory, James?"

He nodded.

"They are waiting for you."

"They will be younger than I am!"

"However, you can be together again."

"Mother will no doubt have many questions."

"How it feels being a grandfather?"

"It was only a short time ago that I found out a daughter existed."

Abbie pointed. "Look!"

"What is it?"

"The rabbits have returned."

James turned his head. "Another sign?"

"Did you ever keep rabbits?"

"My grandfather bought me a hutch suitable for two." James paused. "After I vanished, what did you think?"

"That you had gone to another timeline for a particular reason." Abbie flicked back her hair. "Remember, I was aware of your ability."

James nodded.

"I returned to the coach house for a clue as to what had happened."

"I didn't have a chance to leave any."

"It must be frustrating, and painful for people you have known."

James held Abbie's hand. "Especially, when you reappear, and discover that changes have taken place."

"Nancy?"

"She wasn't pleased."

"Because you left without saying goodbye?"

"No, she had grey hair, whereas, I hadn't."

Abbie laughed.

"Upon meeting Nancy in 1896, I was older, however, on the final time our paths crossed, I was much younger."

Abbie shook her head. "The grief you bring."

"Don't blame me, Abbie, that damn coach house is at

fault."

Abbie put a forefinger to her mouth. "Where you are going, cursing and bad language is not permitted."

James glanced around the vicinity. "There is only us, nobody else can hear."

Soon, a loud thunderclap echoed around the tranquil scene. James looked at Abbie, and acknowledged the warning with a grin.

"One more, and you won't be in such a picturesque setting."

"Extreme heat and darkness?"

Abbie nodded. "Full of fire and fury."

James looked up to the sky. "My apologies, sir."

"Why, sir?"

"Is the Supreme Being a woman?"

"You'll find out later." Abbie paused. "Someone wishes to meet you."

"Who?"

Abbie looked behind James.

He looked round, and got up. A short, sturdy woman with grey hair tied back in a neat bun and wearing a long black dress faced him.

"You're as I remember in 1912."

The woman gave a hearty laugh. "That's when you vanished for a second time." She glanced at Abbie. "He still needs a good meal!"

The two former acquaintances hugged each other, and then the woman wiped a tear from her eye.

"I did return many years later, Nancy."

"When I was about to pop my clogs!"

Abbie laughed.

"I knew you would return, James." Nancy touched James's arm. "I told William and Geoffrey that one day we would see you again."

James smiled.

Once more, Nancy hugged James, looked towards Abbie

and then at James. Another tear was wiped from her eye. "It's good to see you again."

"And you too, Nancy."

"It's not fair." She glanced at Abbie.

Abbie nodded.

James looked at Abbie.

"You don't age!" cried Abbie.

Nancy laughed, then paused. "I have to leave now, James, but we'll meet again."

"I'm glad it's here, and not in a lower domain."

Nancy laughed.

As James laughed, Nancy's image slowly disappeared. He looked at Abbie, and she put her hand on the grass. "What do you remember most about your parents?"

"My mother dragging me to school every day and father driving us to seaside locations."

"Didn't you enjoy school?"

"Not at first, but as I got older, loved it." James stared. "When they were killed, if not for being ill, I would have been in the car."

"Where did the accident happen?"

"Ardrishaig, another visit to my great-aunt. I stayed with my grandparents in Newhaven, and can still recall how upset they were at having to explain what had happened."

Abbie held James's hand.

"On their previous visit in 1967, I met my great-aunt for the first time."

"And, other occasions followed."

"Our paths crossed on several occasions. Each time she wasn't aware of my true identity."

"Was there not a temptation to tell her?"

James shook his head. "It may have resulted in my life being more complicated!"

Abbie laughed, then looked behind James.

"It was also complicated for me."

James turned his head, then stood up.

A slim attractive middle-aged lady with dark greying hair in a 1960's black polka dot dress smiled. "Hello, James."

James hesitated.

"Not as young as when our paths crossed in 1930, or 1940." Olivia moved forward, hugged her great-nephew, and stepped back.

"Did you recognise me at the hospital in 1930?"

Olivia shook her head. "Not until another ten years, when you brought William safely home."

"He required a helping hand."

"You saved his life, and because of your intervention, we had many more years together."

"Where is William?"

"You'll meet him later, along with your parents and grandparents."

"When we met the following day, I felt uncomfortable."

"I was aware of that." Olivia glanced at Abbie. "He's a quick drinker!"

Abbie laughed.

"As an adult, I came to visit you three decades later."

"My housekeeper told me you had visited, but soon departed."

"She scared me off!"

Once more, Olivia glanced at Abbie. "If Pearl hadn't, you may not have met with a certain lady."

James looked at Abbie, then his great-aunt. "At least you received the letter I left."

"And I carried out your instructions."

"It meant a young woman didn't have to lose her life."

"Did she survive?"

James hesitated. "I presume so."

"She survived," said Abbie.

Olivia hugged James, stepped back and her image faded.

James stared into the space his great-aunt had occupied, and sat down. "At Lochgilphead Hospital in 1930, I remember not only a young teenage Olivia, also, a teenage

William."

"Oh?"

"Charlotte, his mother, brought him to the hospital."

"For what reason?"

"William had injured his leg."

"Why were you at the hospital?"

"I thought you were aware of what happened in the past?"

"Not everything!" She raised her thin fair eyebrows.

"I worked there as a porter. When I arrived in October 1929, the coach house was freezing, and if I had lit a fire, smoke from its chimney would have drawn attention."

"True."

"The hospital was ideal."

"Food and accommodation."

James nodded.

"Lucky you."

"And in the midst of a depression, however, I had to start work at six o'clock in the morning."

"Outside, it would have been pitch black."

"I hated those dark austere times."

Abbie looked up to the blue cloudless sky and bright sun, then at James. "No more dark nights or difficult times."

"Promise?"

Abbie nodded. "Also, there is no cash requirement."

"What happens if you break a promise?"

She sighed. "You don't want to know."

James looked towards the calm waters of the loch. "In 1938, I met a woman in Glasgow, and found out she worked for the French Secret Service." James glanced at Abbie. "What became of her?"

"I'm uncertain of that person, but I'll find out." Abbie stared at James. "That is if she came here."

James laughed.

"When did you meet Philip and Charlotte?"

"In 1929 and 1938, but they didn't remember me from

1929."

"Why not, you don't age?"

"In that timeline, I sported a beard."

"How long were you in that timeline?"

"A slow four months." James sighed. "When you are used to modern comforts, and travel back to a period with little technology, it's frustrating."

"Did you long for an electric razor?"

"Oh, yes."

"Anything else?"

"A television, however, since it hadn't yet been invented, I listened to a radio."

"Experiencing past historical events as they happen must have been fascinating."

"When the Wall Street Crash unfolded, hospital staff were 'glued' to a radio in the rest room."

"On your travels, were you ever tempted to reveal forthcoming events?"

"I told you in 1967 about the Beatles splitting up in 1970."

"I should have put a bet on how long they would last."

James smiled.

Abbie glanced sideways.

James looked at Abbie, turned round, and a middle-aged couple stood smiling. The man wore a grey suit and the woman a long pink dress, which touched the grass.

"Hello, James," said the woman.

"I trust you remember us?" said the man, as he removed his horn-rimmed spectacles.

The woman looked at the man. "Philip!"

He glanced at the woman.

"You cannot see without them." She looked at James, and smiled. "Philip's vanity does not diminish, no matter how many decades pass."

Abbie laughed.

James got up, approached the couple and the woman

gave him a warm hug. As she stepped back, the man shook James's hand.

"Why did you not tell us about your identity at Nancy's funeral?" said the woman, "you're part of our family."

"Would you have believed me?"

"The woman glanced sideways. "Abbie did."

"After meeting me on two previous occasions, she twigged." James glanced at Abbie.

Abbie looked at the woman. "Mind you Charlotte, it took me twenty-seven years!"

Charlotte laughed. "As someone once said."

"Better late than never," added Philip.

James looked at Charlotte. "Did you recognise me in 1929, at the hospital?"

"In Lochgilphead?"

"You were with William, and approached me seeking a nurse."

"I do now." Charlotte looked at Abbie. "He didn't suit the beard, it made him look scruffy."

Abbie laughed.

Charlotte moved closer to James, stared at his eyes, then looked at Philip. As her voice grew raspy, she wiped a tear from an eye. "I saw the resemblance with James and Geoffrey all those years ago."

Philip put his arm around Charlotte, and looked at James. "Your grandfather and great-uncle await your arrival."

Charlotte took hold of James's hand. "Thank you for preventing serious injury to my sons."

Whilst Charlotte let go of James's hand, Philip replaced his horn-rimmed spectacles and straightened his necktie, then their image started to fade.

"Maya sends her best wishes, James," cried Charlotte.

Seconds later, James's great grandfather and grandmother were gone, and he sat down.

"You appear drained."

"It's meeting people from the distant past again." James

sighed. "Even in death, it can be overwhelming."

"There is someone else who wishes to thank you."

James took a deep breath.

"You saved her life a century ago."

"Elizabeth?"

Abbie nodded.

"For me, it is less than two years."

Sensing someone behind him, James turned round and saw a well-groomed lady with bobbed blonde hair in a medium-length dress.

"Hello, James."

He rose.

"Lovely to see you."

"Your appearance is as when we first met." James approached Elizabeth.

Elizabeth glanced at Abbie. "He never struck me as being a coachman."

"His hands are smooth."

James glanced at Abbie, then at Elizabeth. "But you still hired me."

"Because I liked your manner and how you conducted yourself." Elizabeth looked at Abbie. "The other coachman made a pass at me!"

Abbie laughed.

"In 1930, you were not receptive."

Elizabeth touched James's arm. "I did not know it was you, and you don't suit a beard!"

"Fortunately, when you painted my portrait, I didn't have one."

"If you had, there may not have been a portrait!"

James laughed.

"Your namesake sends his best wishes."

"Pass on mine to your husband."

"Which one?" Elizabeth smiled. "I have been married twice."

Abbie laughed.

James snapped his fingers. "Of course, Adam."

"He also sends his best wishes."

"I prefer your Scottish dialect."

"As do I. New York took its toll." Elizabeth stared at Abbie. "It almost killed me."

"Killed you, how?"

"It is a long story, James, and when we next meet, one that I will tell you in full."

Seconds later, Elizabeth's image disappeared, and James resumed his place next to Abbie. "My intuition tells me that if Elizabeth had been single?"

"When I first met her, she was fifteen years younger than me."

"In 1912, it was not uncommon for men to court women many years younger than themselves."

"Perhaps, but I'm from an age where the couple tend to be of a similar age."

Abbie watched a butterfly land nearby.

James studied it. "Is this of some significance?"

"No, just the warm climate."

James grinned.

After the butterfly took off, James cast his gaze around the area and then looked upwards.

"What's up, James?"

"It's too perfect, Abbie."

"You're hard to please!" Abbie took James's hand. "The problem is that you have not yet transcended."

"Therefore, after my graduation ceremony, I will feel different?"

"You will qualify to become part of a Supreme Order for all time, similar to the people you have met."

"They are good people."

"And each of them care for you, as I do."

James put his arm around Abbie, and the small sparrow returned. It circled above and then flew off.

"There is another person who is looking forward to

greeting you."

"Who?"

"Someone you helped in 1896."

"The first occasion I travelled back in time."

"This person was undisciplined, plus he had a wife and baby son to support."

"As I recall, he also had an addiction to alcohol."

"However, he mended his ways, and started a company that still exists to this day."

James sighed. "Angus."

"You also met his son?"

James nodded. "Andrew, in 1912, when he was working in his father's business premises." James paused. "Sixteen years had passed in moments."

"No ill effects?"

"Some initial dizziness, however, it soon disappeared."

"Similar to you leaving me in 1967."

James laughed. "I couldn't avoid my exit."

Abbie smiled.

"Is Andrew with his father?"

"He lived to a good age, and did a lot of work within the local community." Abbie stared at James. "He became aware that you were a time traveller, but never revealed it to anyone."

"How did Andrew find out?" James snapped his fingers. "At Nancy's funeral, Andrew would see that I had not aged from 1912." James touched his chin. "Mind you, just because I hadn't aged, that doesn't make me a time traveller."

"The alternative is that you are born lucky!"

James laughed.

"In the early twentieth century, people aged rapidly."

James nodded. "Two wars and a depression would take its toll on society."

"Many people died before their time."

"Including me, I'm in my mid-forties."

"Think of the experiences you had."

James remained silent.

Abbie nudged him. "Be grateful."

"Is that allowed?"

"I will soon find out."

James laughed, looked upwards and then at Abbie.

"You must have deserved it."

He stared at Abbie.

"What's up?"

"It couldn't have been easy for you."

"Because I had to bring up April, without a father?"

"Yes."

"I had my mother to support me."

James sighed.

"Don't blame yourself, James, it's who you are."

"You mean, what I became."

"If you had led a normal life, we wouldn't have met."

James gripped Abbie's hand. "An unmarried mother in 1968 would have raised eyebrows."

"It's not as if I was a teenager."

"Then, you only looked thirty instead of thirty-seven."

Abbie kissed James on the cheek. "The people in Dochar were still receptive."

"Maybe they were coming to terms with the permissive age."

"And the retail resurgence of Ardrishaig's main street."

James glanced at Abbie.

"Many businesses owed you a debt of gratitude, I discovered how it all came about."

"A consequence of my arrival in 1938."

"Philip embraced the concept of marketing, then advised Ardrishaig's business community."

"However, fruition took almost thirty years."

"Better late?"

James nodded.

"It's a pity the retail revolution stalled."

"What happened."

"The people who ran successful businesses were lured to Glasgow by large companies, and the main street never recaptured those vibrant times."

James looked at Abbie. "Ardrishaig's retail prowess won't be of consequence to us anymore."

She laughed, then pondered.

"What's on your mind?"

"You never had the opportunity to spend time at Docharnea."

"I was there in 1896, that's well over a century ago."

Abbie laughed.

James pondered.

"The past?"

"When I came to in 1896, the coachman's quarters looked similar, and only after leaving it, realised something was wrong."

"Wasn't it just!"

"No trees, bushes or hedges!"

"What did you do next?"

"I went down the driveway, and at the bottom, discovered a muddy dirt track instead of a road."

"My mother's property would not be there."

"Only two properties existed."

"Did you panic?"

James shook his head. "I walked along the track for about fifteen minutes, then a horse and cart approached."

"That must have been a strange sight."

"The driver stopped, and asked if I wanted a lift."

"That was a kind gesture."

"As I sat next to him, he stared at my wrist."

Abbie put a hand over her mouth. "Oh no, your digital watch."

"Eight decades before its time."

"Did the driver enquire about it?"

"I explained that it was a gift from an American relative – a clock watch."

"Did he buy it?"

James stared at Abbie. "I wasn't going to sell it."

"Did he believe you?"

James frowned. "I think he did."

"I trust, later, you took the watch off."

"Yes, I kept it concealed in my pocket at all times."

"Your watch no doubt raised the driver's eyebrows."

"As did wearing a coachman's outfit."

"Why were you dressed as a coachman?"

"Before passing out, I came across a closet, which contained the outfit, and being curious, tried it on."

"Did it fit?"

"Yes, perfectly."

"Prior to going outside, why did you not take off the outfit?"

"The clothes I had been wearing were gone."

"Did the cart driver take you into Ardrishaig?"

"Coincidentally, he was making a delivery to Docharnea."

"To whom?"

"The original owner."

"So, home-delivery took place in the nineteenth century!"

James laughed.

"What happened next?"

"A tall, well-built woman stood at the driveway entrance and when the cart stopped, she looked at me."

"And?"

"She presumed I had hitched a lift to Docharnea, and had come for an interview."

"For a coachman's position?"

"Yes."

"That was indeed a coincidence."

"It's not as if I could tell Mary Carsell-Brown I was the current owner of her property."

"But you were."

"Yes, over a century later."

Abbie laughed. "What was she like?"

James hesitated. "Bossy, but fair."

"What did her husband do?"

"Manager of a local bank."

"Dressed in a conservative manner?"

James nodded. "A regular coachman duty was to take him to Ardrishaig and back six days per week."

"And to clean out the horses' stable."

"I can still smell it!" Abbie laughed.

"Speaking to Charles, I got the impression he longed for an adventure, and Africa certainly fulfilled his ambition."

"A stark contrast from working in a bank."

"Indeed."

Abbie caressed James's hand. "Had it not been for your intervention, Charles would not have achieved that dream. Furthermore, he would have lost his life in a coach accident, with Mary later dying from injuries she sustained. Because you spotted a faulty axle, no crash occurred."

"Also, working as a coachman in 1896, allowed me to meet Olivia's grandmother, and her father. Then, Edward was a young teenager."

"And, during the First World War, became a war hero."

James sighed. "But died not long after Olivia was born."

"The reason why Olivia's husband didn't want to fight in WW2?"

James nodded. "William felt he could not live up to his father-in-law's reputation, and would disgrace the family name."

"You prevented his motor accident, which resulted in Olivia and William being together for another twenty years. Charlotte spoke of her other son, your grandfather."

"In 1940, a British agent asked me to act as an observer at Leith Docks."

"Why?"

"He was convinced a German agent worked there, and

required an outsider to infiltrate."

"Did you have a choice?"

"He offered me money, I needed it."

"Did you uncover anything?"

"I spotted a person acting in a suspicious manner near a ship and alerted security personnel, who discovered a bomb on the ship timed to go off whilst at sea."

"Terrible."

"My grandfather was a member of the crew."

"All of us owe much to you."

"The credit should be directed at the coach house."

Abbie laughed, then wiped a tear from her eye.

James stood up. "Let's walk."

She rose.

The couple strolled across the lush green field close to where rabbits had gathered to eat grass.

"They're not afraid," whispered James.

"Why should they be?" Abbie looked at James.

"In the grounds around Docharnea, even at the sight of someone they run off."

"This is not Docharnea. Here, there is nobody they fear."

James looked into the distance. "How far does this stretch?"

"Stretch?"

"Is it a landscape?"

"It can be what you desire."

James pondered.

"During your travels through time, you must have witnessed wondrous sights."

"I was going to write a book."

"It would not have been fiction."

"Complete authenticity."

Abbie laughed.

James grinned.

"What was your favourite era?"

"1967?"

"Apart from when we met."

"All of the eras were interesting." James paused. "I think viewing Docharnea as it changed became fascinating."

"In what way?"

Decor, furniture and how fast trees grow!"

Abbie smiled.

"Those initial coachman duties came as a shock to the system."

"Hard labour?"

"That plus the smell of the stable."

Abbie laughed.

"With technology in its infancy, and no cars or buses, life would have been simple and uncomplicated."

"More walking."

"Less people with weight problems."

"You would have been the first, and last coachman of Docharnea."

"After I left in 1896, another coachman was hired, however, he had an injury and I replaced him."

"And you were on hand to push Elizabeth out of the runaway horse's path."

"After being hit by the horse, I ended up in the local hospital."

"How long were you there for, James?"

"Between two and three weeks and then I returned to Docharnea."

"Did you resume your coachman duties?"

"I couldn't, the coach and two horses had been made redundant – replaced by an automobile."

Abbie laughed.

"Technology began to affect Docharnea."

"You then met Charlotte and Philip."

"When I met them in 1930, the depression started to bite."

"Dire times."

"But a spirit amongst local people ensued and whilst

working as a porter in Lochgilphead Hospital, I witnessed it at first hand."

"In what way?"

"Patients not only had their family as visitors, also, other families."

"A community spirit."

"After visiting time ended, it became difficult to usher them out."

Abbie laughed.

"Nobody wanted to leave!"

Abbie gripped James's hand. "It was in 1938, we first met."

"I had left the coach house."

"And dressed as a coachman."

"1967 was a strange year."

"In what way?"

"Being there as an adult, and as a child."

"How could that be?"

James shrugged his shoulders.

"Time travel is bizarre."

"I don't give it much thought, and if I did, a headache would ensue."

Abbie smiled.

"An advantage of going back in time was being able to attend that concert at the Glasgow Apollo in 1967."

"The pop concert?"

"Most of the Tamla Motown stars appeared."

"Tamla Motown?"

James stared at Abbie. "Stevie Wonder, the Supremes and the Four Tops?"

"That concert is a distant memory for me!"

"When my parents and I visited Olivia in June of that year, I still recall feeling sick in father's car."

"Too much chocolate on the journey?"

"That and the strong smell of leather upholstery in father's new car."

"Don't make excuses, James, you love chocolate."

James paused. "Strange."

Abbie looked at him.

"I don't remember much about that visit."

"Being at Docharnea?"

"I recall arriving there, meeting Olivia, and leaving to go home." James stared at Abbie. "That's about it."

"Your long-term memory is similar to mine."

James sat with Abbie, and continued to reflect on enthralling experiences gained travelling back in time. His physical form had ended, and a spiritual existence about to begin.

CHAPTER 15

RE-ENACTMENT

Victoria blinked, felt light-headed and then steadied herself. Looking into a Gothic mirror, which faced her, she saw the reflection of a figure encompassed in brightness. Victoria shrieked, turned around, and stared at the mysterious apparition several yards in front of her.

"Do not be afraid," said a calm voice.

Victoria stepped back. "Who, who are you? What are you?"

"I have a connection with your family."

Victoria paused. "Why, why are you here?"

"I will explain, Victoria."

Victoria cleared her throat. "How do you know my name?"

The apparition moved forward, and Victoria stepped back. As the apparition stopped, Victoria stared at its head, however, the face was a blur.

"I am not going to harm you."

Victoria clenched both hands tight. "What do you want with me?"

"I require your assistance."

"Me!"

"Yes."

"In what way?"

"There has been an error in the timeline, and I require you to put right the wrong."

"A timeline?"

"It involves James."

"James?"

"Yes, Victoria, James Carsell-Brown."

"He's dead!"

"Not as you perceive him to be."

"Are you an angel?"

"That is one title I have been referred to as."

"Why can't you reveal yourself?"

"It would complicate matters, you have to trust me."

"In this current situation, it's difficult."

"That is what James would say."

Victoria gave a faint smile.

The apparition pointed. "Please, take a seat, Victoria."

She looked at a wooden chair. "Where did that come from?" Victoria touched it.

"When I entered the room, there was no chair."

"I have a startling revelation for you."

Whilst gazing at the apparition, Victoria slowly sat down, and it pointed to the window.

Victoria turned her head. "Have I been out cold for a long time?"

"No."

"Why is there daylight?" Victoria stared at the apparition. "When I came into the coach house, it was dusk." She looked at her watch. "It's stopped."

"For you, Victoria, a new dawn has started."

Victoria stared at the apparition. "What do you mean?"

"You have received the power to travel through time."

"That is for the writers of fiction, not me."

"You have travelled back to June 1914."

Victoria frowned. "1914!"

"Does the room not appear different from when you entered?"

Victoria looked around. "It's warmer." She unbuttoned her coat.

"When you go outside, do not be alarmed."

"What will I find?"

"A different landscape."

Victoria rose, walked to the window, and looked out. The trees are smaller. "What about the villa?"

"That has also changed, a family stay there."

"A family?"
"However, they are at present on vacation."
Victoria carefully walked down the staircase, opened the door, and stepped out. The villa's exterior was grey instead of cream, no rear extension existed, and grass had replaced the courtyard's gravel surface. She looked upwards at the deep blue cloudless sky and warm sun. Victoria went back upstairs, and stood opposite the apparition.
"Are you convinced?"
"What now?" She took a deep breath.
"First of all, you have to find an eight year old James, who has also travelled back in time."
"How did he get here?"
"Please, make yourself comfortable."
Victoria removed her coat, folded it over an arm, and sat down.
"I would like you to rectify two separate instances."
"In 1914?"
"The first is in this current year."
"And the other?"
"In the present." The apparition paused. "Listen carefully, this is what you must do."

After leaving the coach house, Victoria walked down the driveway, and being a pleasant day, she did not require a coat. Turning left at the driveway's end, Victoria headed towards Ardrishaig. Whilst walking, she heard an unfamiliar sound from behind, and turned around. As the slow-moving vintage vehicle went by, Victoria watched in amazement. Twenty yards on, it came to a halt, and the driver looked round. "Want a lift?" he shouted.
Victoria walked hesitantly to the vehicle, stared at its chassis, then looked at the driver. He lifted up his driving goggles, and grinned. "No charge."
She smiled.
"Where are you off to?"

"The village."

The driver leaned over, pushed down a handle, and the door flew open. Victoria got in, and surveyed her surroundings. After the driver replaced his goggles, and the vehicle moved off, Victoria continued to look with interest. The driver glanced at his passenger. "Lost something?"

"I have not been in a car like this, where's the seatbelt?"

"A car, what's that?"

"What do you refer to this vehicle as?"

"An automobile." The driver glanced at Victoria. "You're not from around here, are you?"

"I'm from Edinburgh." Victoria stared at the driver. Retro gear indeed.

"Are you on holiday?"

"Visiting relatives." This is surreal, it's like being in an old film.

"That is the second time in recent days I have heard that."

"Visiting, or relatives?"

The driver laughed. "No, car."

"What other person mentioned it?"

"A boy." The driver glanced at Victoria. "He also came from Edinburgh, are you related by any chance?"

"A distant cousin." Victoria looked at the driver. "Do you know where he is?"

"My wife and I took him to the police station, located in the village."

"Will he still be there?"

"I'm not sure, I'll take you there."

"Thanks." Victoria looked at her watch.

The driver stared at it. "What's that?"

Oh, shit! "It's, it's a gift I received, from an aunt in America." It's working again.

"As far as devices go, they are one step ahead."

Victoria put a hand over her watch.

As she admired rural surroundings, the Rover reached

Ardrishaig and headed for its local police station. "Would you like a cup of tea, first?"

Victoria nodded. "Yes, please." Something stronger would be better.

"There's a tearoom nearby."

The shiny maroon vehicle drew up outside a small quaint establishment, came to a halt, and the driver removed his goggles. As they were about to enter the tearoom, Victoria looked behind, then at the driver. "Don't you lock your vehicle?"

The driver frowned. "Lock my vehicle?"

"The doors."

The driver grinned. "Nobody else can drive around here."

Victoria smiled.

"By the way, what is your name?"

"Victoria."

Upon entering, the driver took off his cap, and led Victoria to a woman with bobbed dark hair reading a book. As they approached her table, the woman looked up.

"Rosalind, this is Victoria, she is related to the young boy we found."

The woman closed her book. "Please, have a seat."

Victoria sat opposite her.

The driver looked at Victoria. "I have business to take care of, my wife will give you directions to the police station."

"It's not far," said Rosalind.

"Thanks for the lift."

"My pleasure." The driver departed.

Victoria looked at Rosalind. "I was glad of a lift."

"Edward is always the gentleman." Rosalind glanced at Victoria's narrow shoes.

"Cool."

Rosalind stared. "A cup of tea will help." Rosalind looked towards the counter.

"What does your husband do?"
"He is an officer in the army." Rosalind looked at Victoria's top. "Are you warm enough?"
Victoria nodded. "Is he on leave?"
Rosalind nodded. "Unfortunately, he has to report back within the next three days."
A waitress in an ankle-length black dress appeared, and Victoria stared at her hair tied in a bun. The waitress smiled at Victoria. "Afternoon, what can I get you?"
"A white coffee, please."
"Coffee?" said the waitress, "this is a tearoom."
"A cup of tea, please."
"Would you care for some of our home-made shortbread?"
Victoria nodded.
"Another glass of water for me, please" said Rosalind as she looked at the waitress.
"Certainly, Mrs Beaumont."
When the waitress departed, Victoria put both hands under the white tablecloth, removed her watch, and put it into her denim jeans pocket.
"The young boy wore unusual clothes, are you also from Edinburgh?"
"Yes."
"Once my baby is born, and I feel up to it, I must visit the city." Rosalind smiled. "I want to view the latest fashions."
"There are many boutiques."
"Boutiques?"
"Another name for a shop selling clothes."
Rosalind smiled. "Ah, I see."
A man came into the tearoom and then approached two middle-aged women sitting near the shop counter. The waitress returned with a glass of water, cup of tea, plus a plate of shortbread fingers.
"Thanks," said Victoria.
The waitress stared at Rosalind. "I overheard a customer

say that the Archduke of Austria and his wife have been assassinated."

"Assassinated!" said Rosalind, "surely, not in Vienna."

The waitress nodded. "Sarajevo, the man said."

"Where is that?" said Rosalind.

"Bosnia-Herzegovina," said Victoria.

"It won't affect us," said the waitress, "it's too far away." She departed.

Victoria stared out the window.

"A penny for them, Victoria." Rosalind picked up her glass, and took a sip of water.

Victoria lifted her patterned cup. "Just reflecting." She sipped her tea.

A short time later, both women finished their liquid refreshment, then went to the counter. Rosalind took a small purse out of her leather bag, and paid the waitress. After leaving the tearoom, Victoria looked at Rosalind. "Thanks for that."

"My pleasure, Victoria."

"Is the police station far from here?"

Rosalind shook her head. "I will walk with you part of the way." She pointed. "It's in that direction."

Crossing a street, Victoria spotted a cyclist rubbing one of his eyes and heading straight for her and Rosalind. As Victoria tugged Rosalind's dress, she stopped, and the cyclist whizzed by.

"Phew!" said Rosalind.

"Did you not see him?"

"He was on my blind side." Rosalind pointed. "The police station is round that corner."

Victoria faced Rosalind. "Thank you."

"You and the boy have the same eyes." Rosalind smiled. "Goodbye."

"Bye."

Whilst Victoria walked to the police station, a passing trio of young men gave her a second look. She entered the building, walked up to a reception desk, and knocked twice. A constable appeared from a rear room, and gave a warm smile. "Can I help you, miss?"

"I have come to collect my young cousin."

The constable laid a pencil on the desk.

"I was told he was here."

"What is his name, miss?"

"James Carsell-Brown."

"Can you describe him?"

"Blond hair, eight years old, and when I last saw him, wearing a white top with a ladybird logo on the sleeve."

"Logo?"

"An emblem, a badge?"

The constable nodded. "Got you, miss." He lifted his pencil. "What is your name, miss?"

"Victoria." She hesitated. "Carsell-Brown."

The constable wrote on a sheet of paper. "Can you verify that, miss?"

"I have no documents on me." Victoria smiled. "Do you not believe me?"

The constable hesitated.

"We look alike do we not?"

"James is staying at the 'Korongo' guest house."

"Korongo?"

"The name of the guest house, Gaelic for a coastal part of the country."

"Where is it located?"

"Walk back to the main street, and it's third left." The constable laid down his pencil. "Ask for Alice Lawson."

"Thanks."

"James's mother and father must have been concerned?"

"I'll soon return James to his parent's time."

Victoria walked back to Ardrishaig's main street, and followed the directions given to her. Finding the guest house, she rang a brass doorbell, and waited. A middle-aged lady answered, and looked curiously at Victoria.

"I have come to collect James."

"I know you have," the lady smiled, "a constable from the police station just telephoned."

Victoria smiled.

"Come in." The lady opened the door. "I am Alice Lawson."

"I'm Victoria."

Stepping into a compact alcove, Victoria spotted a blond-haired boy in the hallway with a comic in his hand.

Alice Lawson glanced at James. "He loves reading my nephew's comics."

Victoria stared.

"I can see the family resemblance." Alice Lawson glanced at James, as he entered a room. "During his stay, he wore my nephew's spare clothes."

As they chatted, the telephone rang, and Alice Lawson excused herself. When she answered it, Victoria went into the room, and James put down his comic.

She whispered. "James, my name is Victoria, I will take you back to your parents."

James stared.

Victoria smiled. "Would you like to go now?"

James nodded.

"Come with me."

After James stood up, and took Victoria's hand, Alice Lawson came into the room. She smiled at James. "He has been well-behaved."

"Thank you for looking after him."

"It was no problem."

"Thank you," said James, "and Alan."

"Next time he visits, I will tell him."

Alice led both guests to the front door, and Victoria, once more, thanked her. As James walked with Victoria along the main street, he tugged her arm. "How are we getting back to Edinburgh?"

"First of all, we must return to your great-aunt's

property." And, my feet are killing me!

James pointed. "Victoria, a coach with two horses."

She looked. "Maybe it's for hire."

When they approached the stationary coach, its white-bearded driver looked at them from his elevated position.

"Are you by any chance for hire?" said Victoria.

"Where do you want to go, miss?"

"Dochar, and, a property called Docharnea."

James gazed at the driver's colourful green and black uniform. He came down from his seat, then opened the nearest coach door. Victoria and James stepped inside, and sat on a long black seat. The driver closed the door, returned to his perched position, and released a handbrake. As he threw the horses reigns forward, the coach moved off.

Twenty-five minutes later, the coach arrived at Docharnea and then entered its driveway. Outside the coach house, the driver applied the handbrake, and came down from his seat. After opening a door, his passengers got out.

"I believe the family are on holiday, miss."

"I'm looking after the property until they return."

James looked at the two black and white horses.

"How much do I owe you?"

The driver smiled. "Enough for a few beers, miss."

Taking two silver coins out of her trouser pocket, Victoria handed them to the driver. "Will that cover the fare?"

The driver laughed. "One half-crown will suffice for two nights of beer, miss."

Half-crown?

Meanwhile, James had approached the two horses, and both of them moved their long necks up and down. The driver looked at James, then Victoria. "They appear to like the young lad."

"Is this your full-time job?"

"Yes, miss, I bought the coach, plus both horses from a previous owner of this property. Some of the properties around here now have automobiles, but people still enjoy a traditional coach ride."

"You may become a tourist attraction."

The driver frowned. "Tourist attraction, miss?"

"For visitors to the area."

"I'll keep that in mind, the coach will now be parked every day in the main street."

"Thanks for the lift, what is your name?"

"Walter, miss."

As the coach departed, Victoria approached James, bent down and then smiled. "Ready to go home?"

"Where is your car, Victoria?"

"We are using a different way of getting home." Victoria glanced at the coach house. "The same way that brought you to this time."

James stared at Victoria. "But how?"

"First, we have to go into the coach house."

James looked at the coach house.

Victoria led him into the building, and as she closed the door, James looked at her. She smiled. "Don't worry."

As they went upstairs to the coachman's quarters, Victoria held James's hand. After entering the room, she placed James in front of a Gothic mirror. Again, he stared at Victoria.

"Don't be afraid, James." Victoria placed her palm on his head. "When you return to your great-aunt, and parents, it will be as if nothing had happened."

"Why?"

"It's for your own good." Victoria smiled. "Do you trust me?"

"Are you an angel?"

"No, but I've been given the power by someone to help you."

"Who?"

"It's a secret."

"Will we see each other again?"

"One day."

Victoria bent down, hugged James, and stood. "Look into the mirror, James, don't be afraid." She held his hand.

James gripped it.

Heading back to Ardrishaig, the coach driver dipped into his jacket pocket, and took out both silver coins. After examining them, he raised his white eyebrows. His perceived two half-crowns were £2 coins, dated 2014.

Victoria opened her eyes, blinked, and steadied herself. She shivered, and looked around the coachman's quarters. Daylight did not shine through the window, therefore, she presumed an early winter morning or late afternoon. Victoria reached for her coat, put it on, and looked at her watch. Whilst tapping it, she began to ponder about her important task ahead. To prevent James's death, she would have to arrive in Edinburgh before mid-day on the 3 November. Walking carefully cautiously down the staircase, and upon departing the coach house, a brighter sky greeted her. She entered the villa, collected her case, and locked the door. Whilst heading to the coach stop, a man walking his dog approached Victoria and tipped his cap.

"Excuse me," said Victoria, "what's the time?" She pointed to her watch. "The damn thing has stopped again."

The man looked at his wrist. "Almost 7.30, miss."

"Is this Monday, 3 November?"

The man stared.

Victoria sighed. "It has been one hell of a weekend."

He grinned. "Yes, it's Monday, and you also have the correct date."

"Is there a coach due?"

"Should be one due any minute."

At that moment, the sound of an approaching heavy vehicle could be heard and Victoria turned her head. As a single decker came around the bend, she held out her hand, and the coach slowed down. When it came to a halt, the entrance door opened, and Victoria boarded. After finding a seat close to a radiator, she reflected on recent events, and started to feel drowsy.

"Excuse me miss, miss!"

Victoria opened her eyes, gazed upwards, and yawned, whilst putting a hand over her mouth.

The coach driver grinned. "You're in Glasgow."

Victoria stood up. "I'll have to stop burning the candle at both ends."

The driver laughed.

"What time is it?"

The driver glanced at his watch. "9.47."

"Thanks."

Lifting her case, Victoria, got off, and departed Buchanan Bus Station. Whilst walking towards Queen Street railway station, it started to rain, and her steps became quicker.

Slightly damp, Victoria purchased a ticket, made haste for the platform, and watched as a train moved off. "Damn!"

"Don't worry, the next one is in fifteen minutes."

Victoria turned around.

A uniformed male railway employee grinned.

"Thanks."

After a train pulled in and passengers got off, eastbound travellers quickly boarded. Following a guard's signal, the Edinburgh-bound service left for its forty-five minute journey.

Victoria left the train at Haymarket Station, walked up a staircase to an exit, and emerged into the noise of heavy traffic. She looked at her watch - it had started to tick. Observing a large circular clock on a building, Victoria set her watch to the correct time, and pondered. It's 10.57, the incident will occur in just over an hour. Victoria spotted a coffee shop opposite and used the pedestrian crossing to get there. Upon reaching the other side, she stopped, and looked back to view where the incident happened. Victoria entered the coffee shop, and an assistant clearing a table looked her way. "Can I help you, miss?"

"Just a white coffee, please."

"Find yourself a table, and I'll bring it over." The assistant smiled.

"Thanks."

Victoria sat down at a table looking onto Haymarket Station. Outside, all types of vehicles passed in both directions heading and leaving the city centre. When the assistant came over with a coffee, Victoria looked up. "Thanks."

"Would you like something to eat?"

Victoria shook her head.

After the assistant departed, Victoria lifted her cup, and took a sip. She gazed out of the window, set her cup on the saucer and looked at her watch. Victoria finished her coffee, and once more, looked at her watch. A short time later, the assistant returned and lifted the empty cup and saucer. "Same again, miss?"

Victoria nodded. "Please."

Several minutes later, the assistant brought another coffee, and departed. Victoria lifted the cup, and whilst sipping, gazed at people passing. Moments later, the assistant returned with a newspaper. "It's today's edition, should you want something to read." The assistant laid it on the table.

Victoria looked up and smiled.

Finishing her coffee, she picked up the newspaper, and browsed through it. Twenty minutes later, Victoria looked at her watch, and put the newspaper aside. She picked up her small case from the tiled floor, and went to the counter. "Excuse me, where is the toilet?"

The assistant pointed. "Downstairs, and first left."

Victoria walked down a narrow bright staircase, and several minutes later, returned with her long blonde hair in a ponytail. "How much do I owe you?"

"£1.50, please, miss."

She handed a £2 coin to the assistant, who took it and

then gave Victoria change.

"That's okay."

"Thanks."

Victoria stared at a clock behind the counter. "Is that clock fast?"

The assistant nodded. "About five minutes."

Victoria sighed.

"Do you have an appointment?"

Victoria nodded. "An important one."

"Hope it goes well, good luck."

"Me too."

Victoria exited the shop, and took out a pair of dark glasses from her coat pocket. After putting them on, she surveyed the vicinity. Minutes later, a teenage boy approached the nearby pedestrian crossing. Whilst he waited for a signal to cross, Victoria approached him. "Excuse me."

The teenager looked at her.

"Can you tell me where the Afton Hotel is located?"

"In Eglinton Crescent." The teenager pointed. "Two streets back."

As the signal changed, a man with a small suitcase standing behind spoke. "The Afton Hotel is in Grosvenor Crescent, one street back."

The teenage boy looked at him.

Victoria stared at the man.

A speeding motorbike roared past the three pedestrians, followed by a chasing police vehicle. The man looked at his two younger fellow pedestrians, and relieved that neither had crossed at the green signal. As Victoria left the scene, the coffee shop assistant stared out the window, and a colleague approached her. "I heard a police siren."

"A police vehicle was chasing a motorbike." The assistant turned to her colleague. "The young woman sitting at the window."

"Long blonde hair?"

The assistant nodded. "If she and two other pedestrians had crossed at the green signal, they would have been hit by the motorbike."

"Why didn't they cross?"

"They appeared to be having a discussion."

"A well-timed one!"

"Wasn't it just."

Standing near the loch, James admired a scenic view of lush green hills and a clear blue sky. If this had to be his final place of residency, then it was an idyllic one. He spotted Abbie walking across the field, and as she approached, put her hand on his arm.

"What's wrong, Abbie?"

"It would appear your time has not yet come."

James frowned. "Not yet come?"

Abbie smiled. "Intervention from a special source."

"I don't understand." James gazed around the vicinity, then at Abbie. "What about the higher plain?"

"You still have much living to do, James." Abbie hugged him. "Stop complaining, you'll arrive here eventually." She smiled, and stood back.

"At least I know what to expect."

"You won't remember this experience."

"When will we meet again?"

"Goodbye, James."

"Your image is fading."

As Abbie continued to fade, so did the setting all around James. He started to feel dizzy, then lost consciousness.

James crossed the road, entered Haymarket railway station, and bought a ticket to Glasgow. Before going down a staircase to the departure platform, he checked the time on his watch. At the platform, James put down his suitcase, took off his watch, and examined it. After tapping it several times, he shook his head, and put the timepiece into his jacket pocket.

A short while later, the Glasgow-bound commuter service emerged from a tunnel, and stopped. James boarded, found an empty double-seat, and put his suitcase on the overhead luggage rack. After sitting down, a tall elegant young woman wearing joined him. "I didn't expect to meet you again," she said.

James stared. "Your change of hair colour threw me."

"I decided to become brunette."

"And a shorter style."

She nodded.

"Still in demand?"

"Yes, very busy."

I'll bet.

"I'm on my way to meet someone for a lunch appointment."

"An invitation?"

"Myself, and several men."

James raised his eyebrows.

"My appointment is accompanying a businessman to meet with former colleagues."

"A reunion?"

"He wants to impress them." The young woman smiled. "I'm half his age."

"Lucky guy."

She laughed, then looked at James. "Are you returning to Ardrishaig?"

James nodded.

"Pity there's no station in that part of Argyll."

Don't I know it.

"Are you married, or have a partner?"

"I did have a partner, she passed away."

The young woman touched James's arm. "I'm sorry."

A pause ensued, and a uniformed rail employee came into sight inspecting passengers' tickets.

"Where are you headed?"

"Linlithgow." The young woman glanced at her trim gold watch. "The train should arrive in about ten minutes." She brought a ticket out of her handbag.

When the rail employee approached, she presented a ticket, and he moved onto another passenger.

"Either you are invisible, or have an honest face."

"It's the second one."

The young woman laughed.

As Linlithgow Station came into view, James's companion looked at her watch, then him. "Bang on time!" She stood up. "Nice to see you again."

"Have a good day."

"And hopefully, my client will too."

James grinned.

The young woman left the train, made her way to the station exit, and got into a shiny black BMW. After the train departed, James fell asleep.

"Wake up pal, you're at Queen Street."

James opened his eyes.

"Last stop."

James looked upwards at a man standing over him with black rimmed spectacles and dark wavy hair.

"Thanks."

"No problem, pal." The man walked towards the open exit doors.

Following a yawn, James stood up, lifted his suitcase off the luggage rack, and left the train. After inserting his ticket into a mechanised barrier, he could not walk through. After another attempt failed, an observant rail employee came forward, and opened a nearby gate.

"Much obliged." James showed him his ticket.

"Fine, sir."

Leaving the station, James headed for Buchanan Street Bus Station and when rain started to fall, walked faster. At the bus station, he studied a timetable display, and noticed a bus for Ardrishaig was about to depart. James hurried to the stance, and joined a queue. After paying his fare, he took a welcome seat, and placed the suitcase on an overhead rack. After the coach moved off, James laid his head on the rest, and reflected on experiences in Edinburgh and Jersey. He glanced at his watch, which had started ticking. A woman sitting behind him moved forward on her seat. "Excuse me, young man."

James turned around.

"Your watch is slow."

"Can you give me the correct time, please?"

The woman showed James the face of her watch.

James set his watch to the correct time, turned round again, and thanked the observant woman.

"Are you visiting someone?" she enquired.

"Returning home, how about yourself?"

"I'm visiting my sister." The woman coughed. "I've travelled down from Aberdeen."

"Aberdeen?"

"It's a trek to Inveraray."

James nodded.

"I left Inveraray for the Granite City fifty years ago."

"Before the oil boom."

The woman nodded. "In those days, Aberdeen was known primarily for fishing."

"And a football team."

The woman raised her white eyebrows. "Eventually."

"Also an abundance of pubs and hotels."

"My family owned a hotel."

"In Aberdeen?"

The woman shook her head. "Inveraray, however, that was many years ago."

"What was the name of the hotel?"

"My memory isn't good." The woman paused. "Mother inherited it from my grandmother."

"What is your mother's name?"

"Julia Banks, she passed a long time ago."

"Then, your grandmother was Nora Banks?"

"Yes! How do you know?"

James recollected when in 1930, the rumours which surrounded Nora Banks, and her attempts to obtain a competitor's hotel in the town. When Nora Banks failed, the owner of the hotel was subjected to a character assassination, and later died of a stress-related illness.

"A relative who mentioned her name."

"It must have been an elderly relative."

"Or a time traveller!"

The woman laughed.

"Is the hotel still owned by your family?"

"No, my mother sold it to the person who owned the town's Burgess Hotel. A rivalry existed between the two owners, and our mother lost."

"To her main competitor."

"It broke my grandmother's heart, and soon after, her health started to deteriorate."

"A sad end."

The woman nodded.

James looked out the window.

"Where are you headed?"

He looked at the woman. "Ardrishaig."

"I detect an Edinburgh accent."

James nodded. My neck's getting sore.

"My sister's grand-daughter now works and lives in Edinburgh."

"What does she do?"

"According to my sister, she has a marketing position."

"Marketing covers a wide range of roles."

"My sister thought her granddaughter was destined for a career in modelling."

"Oh?"

"She's tall, slim and blonde."

"Ideal for agency work."

"Sorry, I didn't hear you."

"She is ideal for marketing agency work."
The woman nodded. "Definitely."

CHAPTER 16

JOURNEY'S END

James opened his eyes, lay for several moments, then looked at the bedside clock. Since returning from Jersey, waking up during the night had become a regular occurrence, reminding him of when he was a boy. Not long after visiting his great-aunt in 1967, James suffered visions of being without his parents and amongst strangers in a remote Scottish village. Although, this image of sharing a warm sunny day beside a loch with past family was not unpleasant, it did appear real. Once more, James looked at the bedside clock, and closed his eyes.

Later that morning, as James drew open the lounge curtains, late December sunshine filled the room. Entering the hall, he picked up a handset to call Julie at the guest house in Jersey. His dream, which included April, disturbed him, therefore, speaking to Julie would dismiss his concern. A few seconds later, James heard her voice.

"Hello, Julie, it's James." He gripped the handset.

"Hello, James, how are you?"

"Fine, yourself?"

"I'm okay, how is April?"

"Since your last call, there has been no change."

"Then she's still in a stable condition?"

"Yes."

James paused.

"What are your plans for New Year?"

"A neighbour has invited the residents of Dochar to a celebration."

"It must be a large property."

"It is, and just as well."

Julie laughed.

"What are your plans?"

"A family gathering at my aunt's house on the outskirts of St Helier."

"Have a terrific time, and I'll call again soon."

"Almost forgot!"

"Yes?"

"Victoria will be in Glasgow next month."

"Oh?"

"She is attending a company seminar, and would like to meet up with you."

"I'll look forward to it."

"Can I give her your number, and she can call?"

"Yes, that's okay."

"Speak to you later, James, take care."

"You too, bye."

James replaced the handset into the cradle, and sighed. Also, he could now meet Victoria. Julie set the handset on the kitchen table. She felt it advisable not to tell James that April recently suffered a relapse.

Five days into 2015, James travelled to Glasgow having arranged to meet Victoria at a popular bar in the city centre. After a two and a half-hour journey, he arrived at GiGis bar, just before two o'clock. James ordered a drink from the tall slim bar person with bobbed black hair. He sat down at a table with two chairs and unbuttoned his dark overcoat. After checking his watch, James gazed out a window facing the street. He took a sip of his drink, set it on the table, and looked around the subdued bar. It could be that following Glasgow's New Year celebrations, customers were still recuperating. James glanced at a large circular brass clock behind the long bar - 2.19. As his watch showed 2.09, maybe an astute member of staff had put the clock forward to ensure customers finish their drinks in good time. Then, a young woman with shoulder-length blonde hair entered the bar. Since she matched Julie's description, James got up, and the young woman spotted him.

James approached her. "Victoria?"

She nodded.

"Was the bar easy to find?"

"Yes, it's only a short walk from George Square."

"What would you like to drink?"

"A Perrier water, please."

"With ice?"

"No, thanks."

When James went to the bar, Victoria sat down, then unbuttoned her black coat. She observed James speaking to the bar person and pondered why he would leave his property to a stranger? It couldn't be because he knew Victoria's grandmother.

A few moments later, James returned with an empty glass, plus a bottle of Perrier water. Victoria poured the Perrier water into her glass and took a sip.

"Is it okay?"

She nodded, set her glass on the table, and looked at James. "You've a puzzled expression."

"You look familiar."

"In what way?"

"Hair, height and build."

Victoria lifted her glass and took another sip.

James lifted his glass. She was in my dream.

Victoria looked around the bar. "Gothic."

"It's a popular place in the evening."

She smiled. "But not during the day."

James grinned. "How was your meeting?"

"Fine."

"You work as an Account Manager?"

"For an advertising agency, just off Princes Street."

"Sounds interesting." This is surreal, it's definitely her.

"The work can be demanding, but I prefer it that way."

James took a sip. I have to pinch myself that this is also my granddaughter. He set his glass on the table.

Victoria looked at James. "A penny for them."

"How is your mother?"

"A slight improvement."

"That's good to hear."

As James lifted his glass, Victoria followed, and seconds later, looked at her watch.

"Do you have a train to catch?"

Victoria nodded. "There's one which leaves Queen Street in fifteen minutes." This is nerve-wracking.

"I will walk you to the station."

"It's no problem."

"I'm heading that way."

"To the bus station?"

James nodded.

He finished his drink, set the glass down, and glanced at Victoria's half-empty glass.

"I should have had it with ice."

Whilst leaving the bar, both customers received a friendly goodbye from the lone bar person.

Following a brisk walk to reach Queen Street railway station, Victoria gave James a relieved smile. "A pleasure to have spoken with you."

"If you're coming through to Glasgow, let me know."

"It's a long two and a half hours."

"You become used to it."

Victoria glanced at her watch.

"Safe journey home."

"Thanks, you also."

"Hopefully, after the recent strong winds, my roof will still be intact."

"It's a lovely property."

"Better not miss your train."

Victoria entered the station and as she walked towards the main platform area, looked behind and waved. James acknowledged, and whilst walking towards the bus station, pondered. How would Victoria know I have a lovely property? Also, she is spot on with the time it takes to

Dochar.

James reached the bus station, and headed for his departure stance. Stepping onto the stationary coach, he produced his return ticket, then sat down. As he waited for the coach to depart, James reflected on his day.

Victoria boarded the delayed Edinburgh-bound service and managed to get a window seat. As the train left Glasgow, she looked out. If James was eight years old in 1967, he would now be fifty-six, but appears early-forties. Nature has been kind to him.

Complete with winter attire, James departed Docharnea and made for Ardrishaig. Although freezing February had arrived, winter snow and ice did not fill the landscape, therefore, a safe casual walk ensued.

Twenty-five minutes later, James reached the main street, and entered a colourful pleasant-smelling shop. A petite woman preparing a display looked round then went behind the counter. James approached it, glanced at various arrangements of flowers and then looked at the shop assistant.

"Yes, sir."

"What would you recommend laying at a grave?"

"Any preference of flowers, sir?"

"Something fitting for a great-aunt."

The woman pointed. "Those white carnations, they represent remembrance."

James nodded. "Perfect."

The shop assistant came from behind the counter and put together a bouquet. She wrapped them in white paper, then handed them to James. After he paid, she smiled. "A lady was here just five minutes ago and bought light red carnations for a relative."

"Light red?"

"They represent admiration."

"I'll keep that in mind."

"I can tell you more, then again, I won't keep you."
"Thanks, anyway."
"Goodbye."
"Bye."

James left the shop and walked towards Ardrishaig's cemetery. On the way, he recalled previous visits, and two spirits that showed themselves to him, and no one else.

Upon entering the cemetery, he noticed a lady with shoulder-length raven hair, wearing a long black coat laying flowers beside a grave. When James got closer, she glanced his way. As she resembles Ann Anderson, James stared. The lady looked away, and James continued to his great-aunt's place of rest. He bent down, laid white carnations at the grey headstone, and stood. A gust of wind appeared, however, the carnations remained still. James reflected for sever moments, then left. Observing that the lady had also left, James walked over to where she had been standing. The writing on the headstone read, Ann Anderson 1894-1917.

After leaving the cemetery, James walked to the main street and once there, went into its popular coffee shop. An assistant wearing a red woollen top greeted him at the counter. "It is busy today, sir?"

James smiled. "To escape the cold."

"I'm well wrapped up!"

James looked around the shop.

The woman pointed. "Is that one in the corner okay?"

"Yes."

"What would you like?"

"Just a white coffee, please."

"I'll bring it over."

James sat down and looked around the popular outlet. Since moving to nearby Dochar, fifteen years had passed, but as a consequence of time travel, those years had been condensed into months! A woman with a brown walking stick entered and sought a chair for relief. Spotting James's table, she came across. He stood and presented a chair to her.

"Thank you." The woman sat down. "Ah, that's better!"

James smiled.

"I'm Agnes."

"James."

"Do you stay in Ardrishaig?"

"Just outside, at Dochar."

"In one of the Victorian properties?"

James nodded.

"Which one?"

"Docharnea."

"How long have you stayed there?"

"Almost fifteen years."

"I haven't seen you in the village." She placed the walking stick against her chair. "Fifteen years you say?"

"I've travelled a lot, therefore, my time here has been scarce."

"Where did you travel to?"

"Europe."

"Were the places interesting?"

"Yes, I witnessed extraordinary sights."

The woman smiled. "Oh well, that is good." She looked towards the counter, then at James. "Are you married?"

"Not yet." This feels like an interview.

"You're not one of those fussy types?"

James shook his head.

"There is no Miss Perfect in this world!"

James remained silent.

Once more, the lady looked towards the counter, raised her arm and looked at James. "We'll get served soon."

A few moments later, the assistant brought James his coffee, took the woman's order, and departed.

"I like to keep the staff on their toes."

James lifted his cup and then took a sip.

"Is it warm?"

He nodded and set the cup on its saucer.

"Last time I visited this place the coffee was cold and I told them!"

"Quite right."

"At least the shop disposed of that damn doorbell." The woman coughed. "When someone entered, or left, elderly people would jump out of their chair."

"It was loud."

The assistant returned with another cup of coffee, set it in front of the woman, and quickly left. She took a sip, then set her cup on the saucer. "They've learned from my last visit."

"Have you stayed in Ardrishaig long?"

"All my life, I worked in a nearby establishment for many years."

"What was it called?"

"The Grey Gull Inn."

"A long-standing establishment."

"I started as a bar waitress way back in 1950 and became manager in 1961." The woman coughed. "I stopped working thirty-six years later, and now live off my pension."

"Did you work at The Grey Gull until you retired?"

The woman shook her head. "I left in 1972, to work for the supermarket."

"Better working conditions?"

She nodded. "Less hours, and more pay."

"In 1967, a relative once stayed there."

"A male relative?"

James nodded. "He was complimentary about the staff."

"He must have met Abigail." The woman paused. "I hope your relative wasn't the rogue who left her in the lurch!" The woman shook her white hair. "Poor Abigail, having to bring up a child on her own."

James remained silent.

"You appear far away."

"Reminiscing about the past."

Following moments of silence, a well-groomed lady entered, looked around, and approached James's table. The woman looked up and acknowledged her.

"Apologies for being late, Agnes."

"Have a seat, Annabelle."

As the lady sat down, Agnes glanced at James, then Annabelle. "Do you know this gentleman?"

"This morning, our paths crossed at the cemetery." James looked at Agnes.

"Annabelle, this gentleman has recently returned to the area, and is unattached."

Annabelle stared at James, then at Agnes.

Agnes looked at James. "Are you rich?"

James shook his head.

"Nonsense, you own one of the properties in affluent Dochar."

"Which one?"

"Docharnea."

When a ping came from Annabelle's coat pocket, she brought out a small pink-coloured device, looked at the screen, and smiled at Agnes. "I have to go, catch up with you tomorrow."

"I'll look forward to a longer chat."

Annabelle glanced at James. "Bye."

"Bye."

After she left, Agnes and James lifted their cups, took a sip, and set them down. Agnes looked at James. "Is Docharnea haunted? There have been rumours and sightings going back a hundred years."

James shook his head.

"Annabelle's attractive, isn't she?"

James nodded.

"She's thirty-nine, how old are you?"

"Forty-three." Now that I've got rid of the beard, I'll look my age.

"You don't look it."

James smiled. "Are you related to Annabelle?"

"I'm a friend of the family." The woman coughed.

"Annabelle has recently arrived from France, where she spent most of her married life."

"Where in France?"

"Nice."

That's a coincidence.

Agnes lifted her cup, took a sip. "Annabelle's family are from Ardrishaig." She set the cup down. "There's a likeness to her and a distant relative."

"What was the relative's name?"

"Ann Anderson."

A lady rose from her chair, came across to the table, and sat next to Agnes.

"Daisy!"

"Hello, Agnes."

"I didn't notice you." Agnes touched Daisy's arm. "My eyesight is not as it once was."

Daisy laughed.

James stood up. "You will have to excuse me, ladies."

"Leaving already?" said Agnes."

James glanced at his watch. "Time for my trim at the hairdressers."

"Bye," said Agnes.

After paying for his coffee, James departed, and Agnes looked away from the entrance. "I tried to pair him with Annabelle."

"You're being optimistic!"

"Why do you say that?"

"Annabelle will no doubt be on her travels again." Daisy shook her short curly white hair. "She isn't the type to stay in one place."

"That gentleman is also a traveller, he has recently returned to the village."

"Where from?"

"He didn't say, keeps cards close to his chest."

Daisy grinned.

"What's funny?"

"Then he and Annabelle are suited."

Agnes laughed.

A worried Victoria prepared to catch the flight from Edinburgh Airport to Jersey. Two days earlier, Julie had made an urgent call concerning April's condition, and Victoria would visit on Valentine's weekend.

On the flight, she thought about her mother, then a certain James Carsell-Brown and the nagging question, why would he leave his property to her? She put her head on the seat rest, tried to relax, and heard a fellow passenger sneeze. Victoria opened her eyes and looked sideways.

"My apologies, I didn't mean to startle you."

"It's okay."

"I've had this bloody cold for two weeks." The lady sniffed. "I just can't get rid of it." She produced a paper tissue from her coat pocket.

"This damp weather doesn't help."

The lady dabbed her nose. "Too many glasses of wine last night didn't help."

"Do you stay in Jersey?"

"Yes, I was in Edinburgh on business."

"What is it you do."

"I work for a chain of exclusive hotels based in Jersey."

"A sales position?"

The lady nodded, and held out her hand. "Diana."

"Victoria." She shook the lady's hand.

"Are you visiting friends?"

"My mother, she isn't well."

"Last year, I sat beside a gentleman who was also visiting a sick relative." The lady stared at Victor. There's a likeness. She leaned forward and removed a magazine from the seat pocket in front and started to read it.

Victoria looked at the lady. "What was the gentleman's name?"

"Carlisle-Brown, James Carlisle-Brown."

"Carsell-Brown?"

"Yes, that was it." The lady sniffed.

Victoria pondered.

Seconds later, the flight went through strong turbulence, accompanied by gasps and groans from its passengers. The lady stared at Victoria. "Glad I declined a coffee." She looked at her watch. "Thankfully, not long to go."

Twenty minutes later, passengers sighed as they got off the aircraft. Colour returned to their faces whilst entering the airport terminal building. After collecting her suitcase, Victoria walked to the taxi rank, and joined a queue. When several taxi cabs appeared at once, she was soon en route to her mother's guest house.

As the taxi approached St Helier, Victoria looked at her watch, and asked the driver to make a detour.

"Where to, miss?"

"The hospital."

Not long after, the taxi drove into St Helier Hospital car park. Victoria paid the driver, got out, and went to reception. As nobody was in attendance, she pressed a buzzer, and a woman appeared from a back office. "My apologies, I had an urgent personal matter."

"Can I visit my mother, April Anderson?" Victoria glanced at a wall clock. "I realise visiting time isn't for another two hours."

"Yes, go ahead."

"Thanks."

When Victoria arrived at the ward, a nurse in attendance led her into the corridor. "Your mother has just woke-up from a long sleep."

"I wasn't due to visit until later, but wanted to see her." Victoria glanced towards the ward.

"Her condition is unchanged, she is in a stable condition."

"Can I see her?"

The nurse paused. "Okay, she is drowsy."

Victoria slowly entered, sat on a chair next to her mother's bed, and unbuttoned her coat. April blinked, then moved her head sideways on the pillow.

"Victoria!"

She smiled.

After April sat up, Victoria stood, and hugged her mother.

"I wasn't expecting you until tomorrow."

Victoria sat down. "How do you feel?"

"Just the same, what about yourself?"

"I'm fine."

"You look tired, how was the flight?"

"Okay, apart from sitting next to someone with a cold."

"Still enjoying your job?"

"Yes, I was on a business course in Glasgow, and met up with James."

"Is James your boyfriend?"

"The gentleman who visited you."

April paused. "Oh, yes, I remember."

"He lives in Dochar."

"Dochar?"

"Where you were born and raised."

April yawned, and put a hand over her mouth.

When her mother's eyes started to flicker and then close, Victoria paused for several seconds. Then got up. "I'll see you tomorrow, mother."

April nodded.

Victoria hugged her.

"Bye."

April closed her eyes, and Victoria slipped quietly away. Further down the corridor, she met the same nurse.

"My mother is feeling tired, I'll return tomorrow."

"See you then."

Rather than take a taxi to the guest house, Victoria elected to walk, and as she did so, a provoking thought re-entered her head. Why would James say he was visiting a relative? It could explain why he left Docharnea to a family member, but what was the connection?

With her aunt having an afternoon church social engagement, Annabelle sat in the living room with a laptop for companionship. She browsed through a variety of professional gentleman profiles wishing to meet a sophisticated lady. Returning from Europe, Annabelle found village life slow and mundane, thus a solution had to be found. Since a friend had met a charming gentleman through such means, this modern way of dating may provide the answer. Although, prior to meeting a knight in shining armour, fabricated profiles bemused and amused Annabelle's friend. Recalling what she had emphasised, Annabelle smiled. "It's just part of the emotional rigorous online dating process." Annabelle continued to browse, and after a frustrating forty minutes, shook her head, then muttered. "It would appear I'll have to withstand an uneventful village existence." She put the laptop aside, rose from an uncomfortable couch, and went into the kitchen to make a cup of coffee. As she returned, a buzzing sound came from the laptop. Fearing a malfunction, Annabelle set her cup on the side table, and sat down. The screen displayed a gentleman's profile not previously seen, therefore, Annabelle moved closer, raising her dark eyebrows. With the gentleman's photograph appearing familiar, Annabelle read personal details with interest. Several minutes later, she sat poised at the keyboard. "Let's find out if it is whom I suspect." After composing a short message, Annabelle pressed the SEND button. She lifted her cup of coffee, took a sip, and waited. Ten minutes later, she laid her empty cup on the table. "Perhaps he's offline." As Annabelle returned to the kitchen, her smartphone started to ring. She hurried into the living room and picked it up. "Damn!" A look at the screen revealed a withheld number.

A short while later, bored Annabelle went for a stroll in

the late February sunshine. As she walked along Ardrishaig's main street, a gentleman approached. "Lovely day."

"Yes, wonderful."

"Are you enjoying your stay in the quaint remote village?"

Annabelle hesitated.

"You should take a trip to Glasgow, it's a vibrant city."

"I've given that idea much thought."

"There are many good hill walks nearby, May is the best time."

"I'll be gone by then."

"Back to Italy?" She has an uncanny resemblance to Ann Anderson.

"I'm not sure."

"Where are you headed?"

"Nowhere in particular."

"Then, let's have a coffee in the main street's popular outlet."

"You mean the only one!"

James laughed. "There is the Grey Gull Inn, they serve coffee in the lounge."

Annabelle looked in the coffee shop's direction and smiled. "It'll do."

James and Annabelle entered, and sat in a discreet corner. A shop assistant came across to the table and took their order. Annabelle removed her scarf, laid it on an empty chair, and unbuttoned her coat. Whilst James unbuttoned his, Annabelle looked at him.

"At least, it's warm in here."

Annabelle nodded. Strange, that his profile appeared on my laptop, and meeting him soon after. Has he received my message? "Do you believe in fate?"

"You can call me, James."

Annabelle smiled. "Do you feel people have a destiny?"

"Yes."

"Do you have personal experience?"

"I feel, in certain cases, a person's path is predetermined."

"You didn't answer my question."

"During my recent travels, I had several experiences."

"In what way?"

The shop assistant returned with two cups of coffee, laid them on the table, smiled, and departed. James lifted his cup and took a sip.

Annabelle lifted her cup.

"How have you been spending your time in Ardrishaig?"

Annabelle sipped her coffee and looked at James. "Visiting relatives." He did receive my message, it's evident by his smug expression!

"In the evenings?"

"I read and listen to music."

"There is a hotel, not far from here that overlooks Loch Fyne."

Annabelle set her cup on the saucer. "I haven't been to it."

"It's an idyllic setting."

"For dinner?"

"Is tonight, suitable?"

Annabelle smiled. "Yes, tonight is fine."

Since Annabelle and James forged a relationship, five days had passed. They met each afternoon and evening, however, tomorrow, Annabelle was due to leave. The lure of a warm sunny vibrant European city swept aside Ardrishaig's rain and quaint environment. A ray of sunshine came in the form of cultured and charming James, but would he leave his beloved Docharnea? On their first evening, it became clear to Annabelle the affection James held for his family's place of residence. Sitting in her bedroom, she stared into the mirror of an antiquated dressing table, then at an empty suitcase. Then came a knock on the door, and her aunt entered. "Is everything okay, Annabelle, you've been in here all evening." She glanced at the suitcase.

Annabelle sighed.

"Having second thoughts?"

Annabelle turned round and looked at her aunt.

"What was your impression of Docharnea?"

"A lovely property, full of character and charm."

"Similar to its owner?"

Annabelle smiled. "The coach house is an intriguing building, James told me it has not been in use for over a century."

"Locals maintain it is haunted by a former coachman."

"I didn't bump into him."

Her aunt grinned. "Before going to bed, would you like a cup of tea?"

Annabelle nodded. "Yes, thank you."

After her aunt left, Annabelle gazed into the mirror, recalling her conversation with James. Suddenly, she screamed, and turned round. Her aunt rushed into the room, and Annabelle pointed. "I saw myself!" She took a deep breath. "Standing over there."

Her aunt looked towards a wall opposite the dressing table. "It would be your reflection, Annabelle."

She shook her head. "The person resembled me, but wore different clothes." Annabelle stared at her aunt.

"Let us have that cup of tea in the living room."

Annabelle rose from her chair, looked around the room, and followed her aunt.

As Annabelle sipped a cup of tea, her aunt set a half-empty cup onto a small oak table. "Discussing a ghost must have played on your mind."

"The reflection wasn't a coachman." Annabelle set her cup and saucer down. "Have you ever experienced a strange occurrence in the house?"

Her aunt shook her head.
"It was eerie."
"It would have been."
"Strange, I didn't feel afraid."
"Just the shock of seeing your reflection?"
Annabelle nodded.
"What was she wearing?"
"A pink gown."
"The colour of love."

Annabelle entered the hall with her suitcase, and laid it on the hall carpet. As she did so, her aunt came out of the kitchen.

"Thanks for putting me up."
"My pleasure, Annabelle."
Annabelle lifted her suitcase.
"Is it not heavy?"
"It's not far to the coach stop." She looked at her watch.
"What time is your flight from Glasgow?"
"Two o'clock, I'll be there in good time."
"What about James."
"We've said our goodbyes."

Annabelle's aunt went to the front door, opened it, and her niece stepped out. Due to an overnight low temperature, the pavement and road had a white blanket of frost.

"Take care, Annabelle, it's icy."
"I will, goodbye, Auntie."

Following a hug, Annabelle walked down the narrow garden path, opened a small wooden gate, and stepped onto the pavement. Her aunt waved, received a warm acknowledgement and then closed the door. As Annabelle walked to the stop, a van came around the corner and skidded. Hearing the sound of screeching tyres, Annabelle turned around.

Whilst in the kitchen, her aunt heard a loud knock on the door and went to answer it. A man stood with an expression of horror. "Janet, your niece, there's been an accident." He took a deep breath.

"What's happened, Sandy?"

"A van skidded." He took another deep breath.

Janet put a hand to her mouth.

"An ambulance is on its way."

"I must go to her."

The man shook his head. "Please, don't, Janet."

"Why not?"

"It's a horrible sight."

An ambulance's siren could be heard and as it arrived, an eerie lull ensued. Janet walked down the garden path, followed by the man. A small crowd had gathered around the ambulance, and murmurs began. When it moved off, Janet wiped a tear from her eye.

After composing herself, she called James, and as he answered, Janet dabbed her nose. "James, I have terrible news." Janet hesitated. "Annabelle has been involved in an accident."

"An accident!"

"Yes." Janet sniffed. "She was getting the 8.30 to Glasgow."

"What happened, Janet?"

"A driver lost control of his van near the stop, and it hit Annabelle."

James hesitated. "How is she?"

Janet's voice grew raspy. "I'm not sure, she's been taken to Lochgilphead General."

"I will go there, now."

"Poor, Annabelle." Janet sobbed.

"After visiting the hospital, I'll come around to your house."

"I hope she's okay."

James left Docharnea, and with his heart racing, arrived at the hospital. At reception, and after taking a deep breath, he pressed a buzzer, and a woman appeared.

"Annabelle Drake, how is she?"

"Annabelle Drake, sir?"

"She was admitted earlier this morning." James stared at the receptionist.

A second receptionist came forward. "Are you a relative, sir?"

"A good friend, I'm also here on behalf of her aunt."

"Your name, sir?"

"James Carsell-Brown."

"The lady has been taken to surgery."

"How is she?"

"It's a serious injury."

James glanced at a row of empty chairs. "Can I wait here for news?"

"If you wish, sir."

"There's a coffee shop along the corridor," said the other receptionist.

"Thanks." I need one.

After James departed, both receptionists looked at each other, with solemn expressions.

James returned to reception and waited for news. To alleviate his concern, he sat and browsed through a selection of magazines, although, not taking in their content. As footsteps on the polished vinyl flooring became louder, James looked up, and observed a middle-aged man in a long white coat. Standing up, James faced him.

"Are you the next of kin, Mr Carsell-Brown?"

"No, Ms Drake's aunt in Ardrishaig, but she is unwell. How is Annabelle?"

"I am afraid we couldn't save her."

James stared.

"Her internal injuries were too severe, I am sorry."

James sighed.

The doctor departed, and James sat down. After a few minutes, he rose and then left the hospital. Whilst walking to Ardrishaig, thoughts ran through his mind. A person's life was preserved in 1916, why not now? Also, as Annabelle is related to Ann Anderson, perhaps there is a spiritual connection.

Instead of going to Ardrishaig, James headed for Docharnea. He entered the coach house, walked up its wooden staircase, and into the coachman's quarters. Approaching the Gothic mirror, James stared into it, and waited. Experiencing no sensation, he spoke. "Grant me this favour, you owe me." Beginning to feel light-headed, James held onto a nearby chair. After composing himself, observed no mirror hanging on the wall, instead, it had fallen onto the wooden floor and lay in pieces. James walked with care back down the staircase, and when outside, looked around. "It's morning!" Those birds in the tree woke me up at 6.30 and chirped for three hours. James looked at his watch and entered the villa to check the correct time. A kitchen wall clock stated 7.59, therefore, he had thirty minutes to save Annabelle. He walked quickly, although, carefully along the frosty pavement towards Ardrishaig.

Upon reaching the main street, James observed a clock above the village hall. It showed the time was 8.23. Two minutes later, he spotted Annabelle leaving her aunt's house, and caught up with her. "Annabelle."

She turned around. "James!' Annabelle paused. "We've said our goodbyes."

"Yes, however, I'm about to save your life."

She frowned. "Save my life!"

"Stand here for a few moments."

Annabelle glanced at her watch.

"You'll still catch the bus."

She sighed, and laid her suitcase on the frosty pavement.

Seconds later, a van came around the corner, skidded, and careered onto the pavement hitting a wall. After its driver got out to check the damage, Annabelle stared at James. "How, how did you know?"

"To explain, will take a long time."

Annabelle smiled and then hugged her knight.

Janet walked up to James and Annabelle, looked at the van, then her niece. "Annabelle, it could have hit you!"

At that moment, the coach to Glasgow appeared and went past the stop. Janet looked at Annabelle. "What about your flight?"

Annabelle looked at James. "I want to hear this story."

That evening, James and Annabelle had a candlelit dinner at Docharnea, and after leaving the dining room, took their drinks into the lounge. Soon, James lifted Annabelle's empty glass, and went through to the kitchen. He opened a second bottle of wine, and filled Annabelle's glass. Whilst walking through the hall, James saw a young woman's reflection in the wall mirror. With long raven hair and wearing a pink gown, he stood transfixed, then recognised her.

She whispered. "Farewell, James, thank you."

James gripped the glass.

After Ann Anderson's image vanished, James returned to the lounge. He sat down and handed Annabelle a glass of Chardonnay. A few moments later, she looked at James. "Are you okay?"

He nodded, lifted his glass of red wine, and took a sip.

"Now, I want to hear this story that you promised."

James took another sip and set his glass on the table. "It begins sixteen years ago, just after the Millennium."

Annabelle sipped her wine.

James revealed that a mysterious force within Docharnea's coach house had sent him back to various timelines, and as a consequence, he prevented past members of his family from suffering serious injury, if not death. The first timeline he was sent back to was 1896...

Annabelle set her empty glass on the table and sat upright. "Do you expect me to believe that story?"

James smiled.

"Mind you, it is compelling."

He considered. Perhaps, I will write that book after all.

ABOUT THE AUTHOR

David Munro was born in Edinburgh and lived there until the age of 27. He was employed by a major brewery within the capital and relocated to Aberdeen, then Glasgow. David attended university and college to attain chartered status in an arts discipline. As an arts professional and with experience of different cultures, this lends itself to creative literature.

David's love of history allows him the opportunity to delve into past cultures and pinnacle events. His book, Awakening, has a First World War theme, telling the story of romance and heartache. However, as well as being set in 1914, it follows a time traveller's journey to 2014, where he also experiences contrasting emotions.

As a writer, David's ambition is to give his readers enjoyment through interesting stories with compelling characters. Awakening has one male and two female characters that readers will embrace. To achieve recognition for his novel in the form of a best-seller is a goal.

Printed in Dunstable, United Kingdom

66694006R00173